AMPHIBIANS AND REPTILES OF DELMARVA

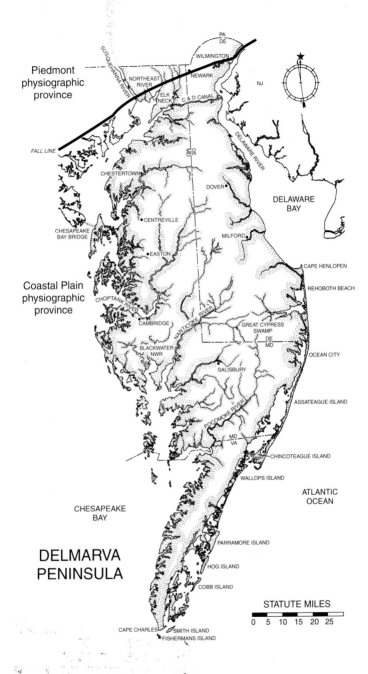

Piedmont physiographic province

SUSQUEHANNA RIVER

PA
DE
WILMINGTON

NORTHEAST
RIVER

NEWARK

NJ

ELK
NECK

C & D CANAL

DELAWARE RIVER

FALL LINE

DE
MD

CHESTERTOWN

DOVER

DELAWARE
BAY

CENTREVILLE

MILFORD

CHESAPEAKE
BAY BRIDGE

CAPE HENLOPEN

EASTON

REHOBOTH BEACH

Coastal Plain physiographic province

CHOPTANK RIVER

NANTICOKE RIVER

CAMBRIDGE

GREAT CYPRESS
SWAMP
DE
MD

BLACKWATER
NWR

OCEAN CITY

SALISBURY

POCOMOKE RIVER

ASSATEAGUE ISLAND

MD
VA

CHINCOTEAGUE ISLAND

WALLOPS ISLAND

ATLANTIC
OCEAN

CHESAPEAKE
BAY

PARRAMORE ISLAND

DELMARVA
PENINSULA

HOG ISLAND

COBB ISLAND

STATUTE MILES

0 5 10 15 20 25

CAPE CHARLES

SMITH ISLAND
FISHERMANS ISLAND

Amphibians and Reptiles of Delmarva

James F. White, Jr.
Amy Wendt White

Photography by James F. White, Jr.

Published in association with
the Delaware Nature Society, Inc., by

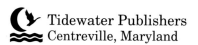 Tidewater Publishers
Centreville, Maryland

Library of Congress Cataloging-in-Publication Data

White, James F. (James Francis)
    Amphibians and reptiles of Delmarva / James F. White, Jr., Amy Wendt
White ; photography by James F. White, Jr.— 1st ed.
        p. cm.
Includes bibliographical references and index.
    ISBN 0-87033-543-X (pbk.)
    1. Amphibians—Delmarva Peninsula. 2. Reptiles—Delmarva Peninsula.
I. White, Amy Wendt, 1962- II. Title.
    QL653.D46 W55 2002
    597.9'09752'1—dc21

                                                    2002011950

Photographs by James F. White, Jr., unless otherwise noted.

Printed in China
First edition

To our sons James and Gregory
and to all other children who love the natural world

Ellen Wood

CONTENTS

PREFACE

This book is the first field guide to the amphibians and reptiles of the Delmarva Peninsula. We hope it will prove useful to a wide variety of people interested in these fascinating animals—from the curious child who brings home a salamander for identification to students, experienced naturalists, and professionals in need of life history, behavioral, and distributional information on Delmarva's amphibian and reptile species.

It is not an overstatement to say that Delmarva's amphibians and reptiles are overlooked by the vast majority of people living in this area. Many people have told us that they never have heard a Northern Spring Peeper call or never have seen a salamander, even though it's hard to go outside in the spring without being within earshot of a chorus of breeding "Peepers," and salamanders (specifically the Eastern Red-backed Salamander) are very common in most woodlands on the peninsula.

Misconceptions also abound. For example, people often tell us that they have seen Cottonmouths (or "water moccasins") on Delmarva, even though this venomous species is known to occur along the East Coast only as far north as Richmond, Virginia. Although it is found in Virginia Beach and Norfolk, Virginia, at the mouth of the Chesapeake Bay, it does not occur on Delmarva. Other common misconceptions include the beliefs that snakes are slimy or that handling a toad can give a person warts.

This book was written, therefore, to increase people's knowledge, enjoyment, and appreciation of Delmarva's amphibian and reptile species and to instill in the area's citizens a stronger conservation ethic that will lead to better protection of these animals and the habitats in which they live.

ACKNOWLEDGMENTS

We would like to thank the many people who helped make this book possible.

We express our sincere thanks to the many volunteers and staff of the Delaware Nature Society for their assistance with this project. Lorraine Fleming, former Associate Director, Advocacy, played a key role by guiding this project from its inception, through years of research and writing, to publication. Her energy and persistence were instrumental in moving this project to completion. Michael E. Riska, Executive Director, also supported the project from beginning to end, and Gregory Inskip, Esq., provided vital legal assistance. In addition, the following members of the Publications Committee reviewed draft sections of the entire manuscript as it evolved, providing helpful comments and advice: Nancy Frederick, Chair; Howard Brokaw, Richard Lighty, Anne Murray, Mary Richards, and Roland Roth. We are grateful to them all.

We also gratefully acknowledge the following Delaware Nature Society members for their financial support of the publication: Howard Brokaw, Margaretta and Tom Brokaw, Lorraine and Richard Fleming, Peter and Karen Flint, Nancy Frederick, Mary Fey Jenkins, Crawford MacKeand, Esther and Arthur Martin, Anne Murray, Edna and Bud Pierce, Michael Riska and Angie Dunson, Tom and Mary Shea, and Bob and Trudy Wendt.

We extend special thanks to the following professional and amateur herpetologists or naturalists who supplied us with information invaluable to this book: Joseph M. "Mick" McLaughlin, for sharing his vast knowledge of the herpetofauna of Delaware, for reviewing all of the species accounts, and for acting as a mentor to Jim White for the last twenty years; Bill Grogan, for his willingness to help throughout the project—sharing his knowledge of the herpetofauna of the Maryland Eastern Shore, providing numerous records and references, and reviewing the manuscript; Arnold "Butch" Norden, for enthusiastically responding to our many questions and for reviewing the manuscript; Rudy Arndt, for sharing his knowledge of the herpetofauna of Delaware and for reviewing the manuscript; Nate Nazdrowicz, for his vital assistance in locating relevant papers and for reviewing the box turtle account; Jake Bowman, Mac Given, Kitt Heckscher, Pam Plotkin, and Edna Stetzar, for reviewing species accounts in the areas of their expertise; and Irvin Ailes, Bob Chance, Brian Crother, James Eggers, Herb Harris, Rick Herbert, John Iverson, Dave Lee, Steve Carter-Lovejoy, Katherine Mansfield, Peter Meylan, Joe Mitchell, Jack Musick, Erin Seney, Scott Smith, Lee Spence, Glenn Therres, Ed Thompson, and Barry Truitt, for answering numerous questions and providing valuable distributional, natural history, and other information in the areas of their expertise.

We are indebted to the countless other scientists and naturalists whose contributions, on Delmarva and elsewhere, have brought the understanding of amphibians and reptiles to its present level.

We also thank Tony Amos and Herb Harris for supplying several much-needed photographs on very short notice, and Ellen Wood for granting permission to use her illustration on the dedication page.

In addition, we thank Roger Conant for reviewing the book prior to publication.

Finally, we wish to extend our sincere thanks to our parents, Trudy and Bob Wendt and Beverly and James White, Sr., whose extended babysitting services and moral support helped make this project possible.

AMPHIBIANS AND REPTILES OF DELMARVA

I. INTRODUCTION

The Delmarva Peninsula, or Delmarva, is centrally located along the mid-Atlantic coast and includes the entire state of Delaware and portions of the states of Maryland and Virginia. As referenced in this book the peninsula is bounded on the north by the Pennsylvania state line, on the west by the Susquehanna River and the Chesapeake Bay, and on the east by the Delaware River, Delaware Bay, and the Atlantic Ocean (see frontispiece).

This book describes all of the amphibians and reptiles known to occur on Delmarva. Amphibians and reptiles customarily have been grouped together, and their study is termed *herpetology*. In keeping with traditional classification, the amphibians found on Delmarva consist of two groups: salamanders and frogs. The term *frogs* as used in this book refers to all frog species, including those that are commonly called *toads*. The reptiles consist of three groups: turtles, lizards, and snakes. It is worth noting that many scientists now believe birds are actually a type of reptile (Pough et al. 2001); however, only the traditional reptile groups are included in this book.

This book contains 73 species of amphibians and reptiles. Of these, 70 species are *known* to occur on Delmarva (i.e., they have been scientifically documented by a museum specimen or their observation has been confirmed by knowledgeable herpetologists, and they are believed to have at least one viable population on Delmarva). These range from very common species to extremely rare species that are known on Delmarva by only a few records. The remaining 3 species are included because we believe either they possibly occur here or they previously occurred here and have become locally extinct (extirpated). Because a relatively small number of people study amphibians and reptiles on Delmarva, it is also possible that some species, not included in this book, will yet be discovered here.

Standardized English Names

The text shows the English (common) names for genus, species, and subspecies as listed in *Scientific and Standard English Names of Amphibians and Reptiles of North America, North of Mexico, With Comments Regarding Confidence in Our Understanding* (Crother et al. 2000). This list was selected because it is the current standardized list endorsed by the three major professional herpetological societies in the United States (i.e., the Society for the Study of Amphibians and Reptiles, the American Society of Ichthyologists and Herpetologists, and the Herpetologists' League). Although many readers may find some of the names unfamiliar or possibly objectionable (e.g., the use of single-word terms for Seaturtle, Cornsnake, etc.), they are used in the book because the authors strongly support standardization of names.

Additional information on the use of both English and scientific names is provided in section IV, "Species Accounts."

Using This Field Guide

To familiarize the reader with Delmarva, section II provides a brief introduction to its physiography and habitats. Photographs of key habitats are included in color plates. Section III describes how to find, observe, and photograph amphibians and reptiles and how to record observations as field notes. Also included in section III is information on how to report uncommon or rare species and how to confirm an observation.

Section IV, "Species Accounts," describes the species of amphibians and reptiles on Delmarva. To identify an amphibian or a reptile, it is probably easiest for the observer to first check the color photographs and note those species that most closely match the specimen, then turn to the species accounts (page references are underneath each photograph) and read the description for each of the noted species to find the one that it best matches. It will also be helpful to read the "Similar Species" subentry to differentiate among species. Individuals vary and may not look exactly like the ones in the photographs. In addition, individuals of some species change coloration at different body temperatures or levels of activity and/or as they age; this is usually noted in the description. The habitat description and range maps will also help in making an identification.

Because of the importance of preserving the area's natural heritage, a separate section on conservation is included (section V). A table lists Delmarva's amphibian and reptile species of special conservation concern.

At the back of the book are several other sections to assist the reader. The appendix is a checklist of Delmarva's amphibian and reptile species. A glossary is included to define some of the technical terms used in the book. The index includes all species arranged alphabetically including both English name and scientific name. In addition, species are listed under the appropriate order or suborder. The index includes the page number(s) of the text entries and the plate number for the photographs in boldface.

History of Delmarva Herpetology

Amphibian and reptile study and collection records from Delmarva prior to the twentieth century are relatively few and geographically spotty, in part because of the relative isolation of the peninsula and its then primitive transportation systems. Amphibian and reptile specimens that were deposited in museums were often collected by naturalists as a sideline to their investigation of mammals, birds, or flora on the peninsula.

The beginning of the twentieth century saw more extensive exploration of the peninsula's herpetofauna and an increase in the publication of results. The first naturalists to focus on the herpetofauna of Delmarva and to publish findings were *Henry W. Fowler* and *Roger Conant.* In the early part of the twentieth century Fowler made numerous field trips to Delmarva where he collected and/or noted many amphibian and reptile species. He published his findings in *Copeia,* giving locality listings for species in all three states (Fowler 1915, 1925a,b). In 1936 Roger Conant, then Curator of Reptiles, Philadelphia Zoological Gardens, began a truly systematic and comprehensive Delmarva herpetofauna investigation. Between 1936 and 1948 Conant made countless excursions to the peninsula to survey amphibians and reptiles. In 1945 the Society for Natural History of Delaware published Conant's *An Annotated Check List of the Amphibians and Reptiles of the Del-Mar-Va Peninsula.* Other notes and papers on individual species appeared in various journals through the 1940s and 1950s. However, a complete compilation of Conant's work on Delmarva has not been published. In 1948 Conant's focus shifted to other responsibilities, including preparation of his *Field Guide to Reptiles and Amphibians of the United States and Canada East of the 100th Meridian* (1958a). In the 1980s and 1990s Conant's work on Delmarva has been on the herpetofauna of Virginia's barrier islands (1981; et al. 1990). In addition to his distributional contributions, Conant was the first to develop a zoogeographic description of Delmarva and explain its relationship to the surrounding mid-Atlantic region. Certainly Conant is the "father" of modern herpetology of the Delmarva Peninsula; his initial studies spawned much collaborative work and inspired independent investigators in each of the three states.

   In the 1950s *Clyde F. Reed* began large-scale collecting on Delmarva, particularly in counties that had previously received little attention, such as Caroline and Somerset in Maryland and Accomack in Virginia. He published his findings in 1956, 1957, and 1958 in a series of articles (some of them privately published) under the heading "Contributions to the Herpetology of Maryland and Delmarva." One of these papers, "An Annotated Herpetofauna of the Del-Mar-Va Peninsula, Including Many New or Additional Localities" (1956d), listed all of the amphibian and reptile species known on Delmarva at that time and brought together many of the records of Fowler, Conant, and others.

Many other contributors have focused on the herpetofauna in one of the three states, on the barrier islands, in the Chesapeake or Delaware Bays, or in the Atlantic coastal waters. Following is a brief summary of their herpetological contributions.

Delaware

Apart from the fieldwork of Fowler and Conant, exploration of Delaware's herpetofauna in the first half of the twentieth century was very limited. *Witmer Stone* published some of the earliest records of Delaware's herpetofauna in 1906 based on several visits to Delaware as well as on examination of specimens collected by others. *Charles E. Mohr* contributed information on Delaware's salamanders and certain amphibian and reptile rarities.

A number of naturalists and herpetologists have contributed to contemporary understanding of Delaware's herpetofauna. *Joseph M. "Mick" McLaughlin* began looking at the distribution of amphibians and reptiles on Delmarva, primarily in Delaware, in the mid 1960s and continues to be an avid field investigator, contributing much to the knowledge of the state's herpetofauna. *Rudolf G. Arndt* conducted extensive fieldwork in Delaware during the 1970s and 1980s, adding greatly to the knowledge of the herpetofauna, particularly of the endangered Bog Turtle and Eastern Tiger Salamander, through both scientific papers and popular articles. *James F. White, Jr.,* has conducted distributional surveys on the peninsula since the early 1980s and has published several popular articles on Delaware's amphibians and reptiles. With the other principal investigators, Rudolf G. Arndt and Joseph M. "Mick" McLaughlin, White conducted a five-year statewide herpetological survey of Delaware, which began in 1986 and was supported by the Delaware Nongame and Endangered Species Program and coordinated by the Delaware Nature Society.

Mac F. Given has studied vocalizations, reproductive behavior, and distribution of Carpenter Frog and Pickerel Frog on Delmarva. *Roland R. Roth, Jake Bowman,* and *Nathan Nazdrowicz* have collectively monitored populations of Eastern Box Turtle in Delaware since 1965. *Christopher M. "Kitt" Heckscher* has published on the Eastern Mud Salamander and the potential occurrence of the Northern Pinesnake.

Maryland

A number of contributors have written publications covering the amphibians and/or reptiles of the entire state of Maryland which include the nine counties on Delmarva. *Howard A. Kelly, Audrey W. Davis,* and *Harry C. Robertson* published *Snakes of Maryland* (1936), the first book on Maryland reptiles. *Robert H. McCauley, Jr.,* collected reptile specimens from all counties on the Maryland Eastern Shore in the late 1930s and self-published *The Reptiles of Maryland and the District of Columbia* (1945), a two-hundred-page book that included description, distribution, habitat, and behavior information as well as spot distribution maps for each species. The first distributional survey of all amphibians and reptiles of Maryland (and the District of Columbia) was compiled by *John E. Cooper* (1960) and was reprinted and revised by *Herbert S. Harris, Jr.,* in 1965 (Cooper 1965). Harris later published more extensive distributional surveys that included a distributional map for each species and a comprehensive reference list.

In addition, the Natural History Society of Maryland (MNHS), founded in 1929, and one of its associates, the Maryland Herpetological Society (MdHS), founded by Herbert S. Harris, Jr., and *Richard Hahn* in 1965, have contributed greatly to the understanding of amphibians and reptiles throughout Maryland and the Eastern Shore. Members of these societies have conducted extensive fieldwork and collected specimens that have become the basis for much of the herpetological literature of Maryland, including the distributional surveys of John E. Cooper and Herbert S. Harris, Jr. Those who have published distributional records or studied the herpetofauna of the Maryland Eastern Shore (besides Cooper and Harris) include, but are not limited to, *Rick Czarnowsky, James A. Fowler, L. Richard Franz, William L. Grogan, Jr., Frank Groves, John Groves, Jerry D. Hardy, Jr., David S. Lee, Brooke Meanley, Robert W. Miller, Kenneth T. Nemuras, Arnold W. "Butch" Norden, Robert S. Simmons, William Sipple, Scott Smith, Charles J. Stine,* and *Peter Wemple.* Space does not permit further description of the valuable work of these individuals, but many of their papers are listed in the reference section.

The primary publications issued by MNHS and MdHS—*The Maryland Naturalist* and *The Bulletin of the Herpetological Society of Maryland,* respectively—contain a wealth of Delmarva herpetological information.

Virginia

In the early part of the twentieth century, *Emmett Reid Dunn* published papers on various reptiles in Virginia. He maintained a checklist of Virginia amphibians and reptiles which included the two counties on the peninsula, although apparently he never visited Delmarva. He published a preliminary checklist in 1918 and distributed mimeographed copies of updates until at least 1936. *William Leslie Burger* updated Dunn's list and published a revised checklist of Virginia's amphibians and reptiles in 1958.

The Virginia Herpetological Society (VHS), organized in 1958, initiated a project that ultimately produced the first comprehensive atlas of the state's herpetofauna based mainly on existing records, *Virginia's Amphibians and Reptiles: A Distributional Survey (Franklin J. Tobey* 1985). The VHS publishes a herpetological bulletin, *Catesbeiana,* twice a year.

Joseph C. Mitchell has played a key role in the understanding of the amphibians and reptiles of Virginia. He is the author of the comprehensive 352-page book *The Reptiles of Virginia* (1994), a coauthor with *Christopher A. Pague* of a review of reptiles of special concern in Virginia (1987), and a coauthor with *Karen K. Reay* of *Atlas of Amphibians and*

Reptiles in Virginia (1999), an update and expansion of the VHS work.

The Barrier Islands

Several herpetologists have published specifically on the herpetofauna of one or more of the peninsula's barrier islands. *Maurice K. Brady* reported species found on Hog Island (1925), and David S. Lee published on the amphibians and reptiles of Assateague Island (1972, 1973a). Roger Conant published the first list of the amphibians and reptiles of the Virginia barrier islands (1981) and, along with Joseph C. Mitchell and Christopher A. Pague, produced a more in-depth paper on this subject (1990). Joseph C. Mitchell and *John M. Anderson* published a 120-page book, *Amphibians and Reptiles of Assateague and Chincoteague Islands* (1994), which includes color plates of the species represented.

Chesapeake and Delaware Bays and Atlantic Coastal Waters

The seaturtles in the Chesapeake Bay and along Delmarva's Atlantic coast have been studied since the 1970s by *John A. Musick* and numerous other researchers at the Virginia Institute of Marine Science (VIMS), including *Debra E. Barnard, Barbara A. Bell, Sarah A. Bellmund, Richard A. Byles, John A. Keinath, Ruth Ellen C. Klinger, Molly Lutcavage, Katherine L. Mansfield, Roy A. Pemberton,* and *Erin E. Seney.*

Seaturtle strandings in Maryland waters have been a focus of workers from the Maryland Department of Natural Resources and the Maryland Sea Turtle Stranding Network. These workers include *T. David Schofield, Joyce J. Evans, Frances Cresswell, Kim Insley,* and *Susan Knowles.*

Seaturtles in the Delaware Bay have been studied by *James R. Spotila, Pamela T. Plotkin, Edna Stetzar,* and *Lee Spence.* Information regarding seaturtles incidentally captured at Public Service Electric and Gas Company's (PSE&G) Salem Generating Plant along the Delaware Bay has been reported by *James M. Eggers, Michael W. Haberland,* and *Jennifer C. Griffin.*

Authors' note: The "History of Delmarva Herpetology" section was intended to include the names of those who made major contributions to current knowledge of Delmarva's herpetofauna. The authors apologize if the names of any contributors have been omitted.

II. PHYSIOGRAPHY AND HABITATS OF DELMARVA

Physiography

The Delmarva Peninsula contains two distinct physiographic provinces: the Appalachian Piedmont province, which covers roughly the northernmost 5 percent of the peninsula; and the Atlantic Coastal Plain province, which covers the remaining 95 percent (see frontispiece).

The Piedmont represents the foothills of the Appalachian Mountains and is underlain by igneous and metamorphic rocks formed during ancient mountain-building episodes. This area is characterized by rolling hills, steeply sloped valleys, deciduous woodlands, and fast-flowing rocky streams. Located in northwestern Cecil County, the highest point on the Piedmont is approximately 540 feet above sea level.

In contrast, the Coastal Plain is underlain by geologically younger, unconsolidated or semiconsolidated sediments (gravels, sands, silts, and clays) deposited by the sea or eroded off the Appalachian Mountains by streams to the north and west. This area consists of relatively flat, sandy terrain, with deciduous and coniferous woodlands, wooded swamps, salt marshes, and slow-moving streams and rivers, many of which are tidally influenced. An exception to the relatively flat terrain on the Coastal Plain occurs in the vicinity of Elk Neck, Cecil County, Maryland, where wooded bluffs rise more than 100 feet above the Chesapeake Bay. In general, the land becomes increasingly flat as one moves south on the Coastal

Plain, with some of the southernmost counties averaging less than 10 feet above sea level. Along the Atlantic coast of the peninsula lies a series of barrier islands separated from the mainland by back bays.

The boundary between the Piedmont and the Coastal Plain is termed the Fall Line or Fall Zone. This boundary extends from near the mouth of the Susquehanna River through the city of Wilmington to the Delaware River. Along the Fall Line is a narrow zone where rapids and waterfalls are common and where many early settlements, including Wilmington, were built. The Fall Line acts as a range boundary for many of Delmarva's amphibian and reptile species—some occurring only on the Piedmont and others occurring only on the Coastal Plain.

The geographic position of the Delmarva Peninsula midway along the Atlantic coast also contributes to the peninsula's role as a transition zone between northern and southern species. Many northern floral and faunal species reach their southernmost range limits on Delmarva and, conversely, many southern species reach their northern range limits on Delmarva. This north-south transition effect results in a high diversity of species, including amphibians and reptiles, for the small size of the peninsula.

Amphibian and Reptile Habitats

Since the first European settlers arrived on Delmarva in the 1600s, the natural landscape of the peninsula has been drastically altered. Virtually all of the existing woodlands have been cut at least once, and most of the original forests have been lost to agriculture or commercial, industrial, or residential development. In addition, streams have been dammed or channelized, ponds constructed, swamps drained, and marshes diked or filled. Most of these alterations have been detrimental to amphibian and reptile populations, although some species have probably benefited from the creation of certain altered habitats (e.g., pond-dwelling frogs and turtles may be more abundant now, because of the construction of millponds). Fortunately, a variety of natural habitats supportive of amphibians and reptiles remain in public and private land holdings, although their total acreage on Delmarva continues to be drastically reduced.

A total of 17 amphibian and reptile habitats are described, categorized broadly as terrestrial, freshwater, or brackish-saline. More detailed descriptions are provided for key amphibian and reptile habitats. Selected habitats are illustrated by color plates 1 through 12.

Terrestrial Habitats

Woodlands (Inland): A variety of woodlands, all of which have been logged at some time, are found on Delmarva. In general, the woodlands of the Piedmont and northern Coastal Plain are dominated by deciduous species, whereas the proportion of coniferous species (particularly pines) gradually increases southward on the peninsula. In the southern part of the peninsula (i.e., south of Milford, Delaware) pines often dominate. Many species of amphibians and reptiles are found in the deciduous and mixed deciduous-coniferous woodlands. Pine woods, on the other hand, are not favored by most amphibians but do provide excellent habitat for some reptiles.

Woodlands (Maritime): Maritime woodlands, found adjacent to the Atlantic coast, are treated as a separate woodland category in this book because of the unique effects of salt-laden oceanic winds on their natural processes. These woodlands are typically coniferous or mixed deciduous-coniferous woodlands, and they support a handful of amphibian and reptile species, particularly snakes.

Old Fields and Hedgerows: Old fields and hedgerows generally contain a combination of small trees, shrubs, vines, and nonwoody plants, including numerous alien species. These areas are used by many lizards and snakes. Woods that have been selectively logged also fall within this category.

Open Fields: Open fields lack any sizable woody vegetation and include cultivated lands, fallow fields, pastureland, and meadows. Like the old fields and hedgerows, open fields are used primarily by lizards and snakes and a few frogs.

Areas Around Buildings: The vicinity of buildings, especially farm and other rural buildings, is a man-made habitat that is frequented by a number of lizard and snake species. In addition, some frog species are frequently found around houses, particularly at porches and other lighted areas, where they can feast on the many insects attracted to the lights.

Debris Piles: Debris piles include piles of wood, sawdust, compost, trash, cement slabs, rocks, and other natural or man-made materials. These man-made piles are often found around abandoned home sites and illegal roadside dumps. They provide excellent habitat for many lizard and snake species because of the abundance of cover objects under which the animals can hide and the presence of various types of prey (rodents, insects, worms, and so forth).

Coastal Dunes and Beaches: Delmarva's coastal dunes and beaches are very harsh environments that are utilized by only a few amphibian and reptile species.

Freshwater Habitats

Rocky Piedmont Streams and Rivers: Rocky streams and rivers occur on the Piedmont portion of the peninsula. They are fast-flowing and the overall gradient is relatively steep. This habitat is used by a variety of salamanders, frogs, turtles, and snakes.

Coastal Plain Streams and Rivers: Coastal plain streams and rivers are underlain by mud, sand, pebbles, and/or cobbles, and because the gradient is relatively flat they are generally slow-moving, although powerful currents occur in tidal sections. They are used by a few salamanders and a variety of frogs, turtles, and snakes.

Permanent Ponds, Lakes, and Impoundments: These man-made habitats include millponds, farm ponds, backyard ponds, golf course ponds, man-made lakes, reservoirs, waterfowl management impoundments, and large borrow pits. These are used by frogs, turtles, and a few snake species.

Wooded Swamps: Wooded swamps on Delmarva may contain bald cypress or Atlantic white cedar trees or a variety of deciduous trees, particularly red maple, green ash, black gum, and sweet gum. The swamps often occur along watercourses above the limits of brackish water influence. This habitat is particularly important to frogs, some turtles, and a few snakes.

Freshwater Marshes: Freshwater marshes are wetlands dominated by grasses, sedges, rushes, or various other herbaceous wetland plants (e.g., cattail, spatterdock, arrow-arum, pickerelweed, and wild rice). Occurring in both tidal and nontidal areas, the marshes range from small wetland pockets of less than an acre to extensive riverine marshes that contain thousands of acres, as along the Pocomoke, Nanticoke, Choptank, and Christina Rivers. This habitat is utilized by many of Delmarva's frog and turtle species.

Vernal Pools: Vernal pools are depressions that contain water only part of the year and include Delmarva Bays, floodplain ponds, flooded agricultural fields, ditches, and small borrow pits. Vernal pools are very important for Delmarva's amphibian species. One habitat in particular, Delmarva Bays, deserves special mention. Also called Coastal Plain ponds, Delmarva Bays are oval to circular depressions, generally 0.2 to 3.0 acres, that typically contain standing water during winter, spring, and early summer and dry up in late summer or early fall. With no inflow or outflow streams, the water level in these ponds is generally determined by the height of the local water table, which in turn is influenced by both the geology and the amount of rainfall in the area (Phillips and Shedlock 1993). The highest concentration of Delmarva Bays on the peninsula forms a band that trends northeast to southwest, from southwestern New Castle County and western Kent County, Delaware, into Caroline and Queen Anne's Counties, Maryland. Of more than one thousand Delmarva Bays on the peninsula, only a few are currently being protected from the prospect of development, and many have already been lost to ditching and draining. The vernal nature of Delmarva Bays creates ideal amphibian breeding habitat: fishless or nearly fishless bodies of water with ample herbaceous vegetation and macroinvertebrate food resources to support larval amphibians. In fact, Delmarva Bays maintain by far the largest diversity of amphibians of any Delmarva habitat. All but 2 of the 17 species of frogs and 5 of the 13 species of salamanders that occur on Delmarva have been found to breed in Delmarva Bays.

Spring Seeps: Spring seeps occur at the start of many streams where groundwater reaches the ground surface. They are especially common on the Piedmont. This habitat is very important to several salamander species on Delmarva.

Wet Meadows and Bogs: Wet meadows and bogs occur on poorly drained soil, often on the floodplains of streams and rivers. A number of salamanders, frogs, turtles, and snakes use these areas.

Brackish-Saline Habitats

Brackish-saline habitats include the coastal waters of the Atlantic Ocean, the back bays behind barrier islands, the Chesapeake Bay, the Delaware Estuary (i.e., the Delaware Bay and that portion of the Delaware River affected by tides), and portions of their tributaries and adjacent wetlands. For purposes of this book, this category of habitat is divided into brackish water and saltwater habitats, depending on the salinity (i.e., the amount of dissolved salts in the water). Salinity ranges from approximately 0 to 32 parts per thousand (ppt) in the Chesapeake Bay and the Delaware Estuary. Depending on rainfall and the influx of freshwater, it is near 0 ppt at the mouth of the Susquehanna River and in the Delaware River at the Delaware-Pennsylvania state line, and it approaches the salinity of seawater at the mouths of the Chesapeake and Delaware Bays. The average salinity in the open ocean is 35 ppt.

Brackish Water Habitats: Brackish water occurs in the broad zone where saltwater mixes with freshwater. The term *brackish* is used in this book for areas that have an average salinity between approximately 1 and 10 ppt. This includes the upper portions of the Chesapeake Bay and the Delaware Estuary, and parts of their tributaries and adjacent brackish water marshes. Relatively few amphibian and reptile species live in brackish water habitats.

Saltwater Habitats: Saltwater habitats are defined in this book as areas where the average salinity is between approximately 10 and 35 ppt. This includes the coastal waters of the Atlantic Ocean, the back bays behind Delmarva's barrier beaches, the lower portions of the Chesapeake Bay and the Delaware Estuary, and parts of their tributaries and adjacent salt marshes. Among Delmarva's herpetofauna only the Northern Diamond-backed Terrapin and the 5 species of seaturtles can tolerate the high salt content in these habitats.

III. HERPING: FINDING, OBSERVING, AND DOCUMENTING AMPHIBIANS AND REPTILES

The challenge of finding and observing an amphibian or a reptile in the field can be a rewarding experience. Although not as popular as birding, the pursuit of amphibians and reptiles, *herping,* is a growing interest among nature enthusiasts. In addition, information obtained from field observations made by amateur *herpers* can add greatly to the knowledge of Delmarva's native amphibians and reptiles. This section provides information on how to find and observe amphibians and reptiles; how to catch and release amphibians and reptiles; precautions regarding collection; how to document findings with photographs, sketches, and field notes; and how to report findings to the proper authorities.

How to Find and Observe Amphibians and Reptiles

Most amphibians and reptiles spend the majority of their lives under cover or in other ways out of sight of humans. However, by knowing the preferred habitats and the behavior of amphibians and reptiles (see section IV, "Species Accounts"), a patient herper can locate many species occurring on Delmarva with relative ease. Suggestions shown with each amphibian and reptile group will aid the searcher. Attention to these important guidelines will help to conserve amphibians and reptiles.

General Guidelines

- Minimize disturbance to the habitats of amphibians and reptiles and other animals while searching.
- If you turn over a log, rock, board, or other debris, make sure to return it to its original position; underneath most objects is a fragile, small ecosystem that may have taken many years to develop.
- Avoid destroying any logs or stumps.
- Be careful not to disturb mating pairs or eggs.

Salamanders

- To find terrestrial or semiaquatic salamanders, look under logs, rocks, or debris in woodlands and in or near small wooded streams, spring seeps, freshwater marshes, wet meadows, or bogs.
- To find aquatic salamanders or larval salamanders, use a dip net to explore freshwater habitats (especially ponds and vernal pools).
- Searching for salamanders on rainy nights with a headlamp or bright flashlight can be productive.

Frogs

- Look for terrestrial species on the ground while walking through woodlands or other terrestrial habitats.
- Look for semiaquatic species along the shoreline or on the surface of freshwater habitats.
- To find breeding frogs of most species, visit freshwater habitats (especially vernal pools and marshes) on a warm night in late winter, spring, or early summer, particularly during or just after rains. Listen for frogs calling, and search with a headlamp or bright flashlight.
- Use triangulation to locate an elusive, calling frog (two or more searchers stand 5 to 20 feet apart and point

toward the calling frog with their flashlights; look for the frog where the light beams intersect).

Turtles

- To find aquatic or semiaquatic turtles, visit a freshwater habitat on a warm morning or early afternoon. Look for turtles basking on logs, rocks, or stumps in the water or on the shoreline.
- Look for terrestrial turtles (e.g., Eastern Box Turtles) while walking through woodlands, old fields, or wet meadows in spring to early summer, especially after rains.
- Look for seaturtle tracks in the sand on Atlantic Ocean beaches.

Lizards and Snakes

- Search for basking lizards and snakes on warm, sunny mornings along edges of streams and ponds, on debris piles, and on rocks and fallen trees. Abandoned house sites and roadside dumps are often good places to search.
- Look for terrestrial snakes and lizards by walking quietly through woodlands or fields, watching and listening for movement along the trail. Turn over logs, rocks, boards, and other debris. Roadside debris piles can be especially productive.
- Look for semiaquatic snakes basking at the edges of freshwater habitats.

"Road Cruising"

Another way to search for amphibians and reptiles is to use your car. When "road cruising," consider the following:
- Choose a seldom-traveled road and drive slowly.

- Pick a warm night to observe snakes warming on the roadway.
- Pick a rainy night to see many frogs or salamanders (and sometimes snakes) moving across the wet road.
- Search in pairs, if possible—the driver can watch the road and an observer with a flashlight can jump out to check sightings.

Helpful Equipment

- *Binoculars* can be useful in identifying distant amphibians and reptiles, especially basking turtles, snakes, or lizards. Close-focusing binoculars are especially useful in allowing the observer to approach an amphibian or a reptile within 6 to 8 feet and get excellent close-up views of the animal without disturbing it.
- A *headlamp* or *bright flashlight* is essential for nighttime herping. Invest in a high-quality, bright flashlight; small, AA-powered flashlights are nearly useless for herping. A headlamp is good because it keeps the hands free.
- *Hip boots* or *chest waders* are helpful for exploring many aquatic and wetland habitats; *knee-high rubber boots* are adequate for exploring shallow-water habitats and are also useful in drier habitats for protection against chiggers and ticks.
- A *canoe* or *small boat* can be helpful for observing aquatic and semiaquatic amphibians and reptiles, especially turtles.

How to Catch and Release Amphibians and Reptiles

It is usually not necessary to catch an amphibian or a reptile in order to identify it. The descriptions provided for each species in section IV, "Species Accounts," focus on distinctive, readily observable features or field marks that can generally be seen from some distance. In addition, an observer can gain much enjoyment by watching the undisturbed animal from a distance. However, capturing is sometimes necessary to make a positive identification (particularly for beginners) and to measure or examine an animal more closely. Adherence to the important general guidelines below and the suggestions under each amphibian and reptile group will help keep the animal, its habitat, and you safe.

General Guidelines

- Never disturb mating or nesting animals.
- Take care not to harm the animal during or after capture.
- Never handle amphibians or reptiles with hands sprayed with insect repellent.
- Minimize the length of time an amphibian or a reptile is handled.
- Always return an animal to the exact place of capture.
- After handling an amphibian or a reptile found under an object (e.g., log or rock), always replace the object first and then release the animal next to the object.
- Always wash your hands thoroughly after handling any amphibian or reptile.

Salamanders and Frogs

- Wet your hands before handling any amphibian to minimize damage to the animal's protective layer of slime.
- Never grab a salamander by the tail; it may break off.
- Terrestrial salamanders can be captured by hand.
- Aquatic salamanders, salamander larvae, and tadpoles can be captured with a small plastic container or dip net.
- Most adult frogs can be caught by hand, although a long-handled net may be helpful.

Turtles

- Most turtles can and will bite in self-defense. Keep your fingers away from the turtle's mouth.
- Never grab a turtle by the tail (except Snapping Turtles, see below), because this can injure the turtle.
- The Eastern Box Turtle, Delmarva's only entirely terrestrial turtle, can be easily captured by grasping the carapace in one hand.
- Aquatic turtles are likely to quickly slip into and underneath the water surface when approached. A long-handled dip net and a great deal of patience are often required to catch one.
- When handled, the Eastern Snapping Turtle can be dangerous because of its powerful bite. Leave this turtle alone whenever possible. If you must move a Snapping Turtle, the safest method is usually to pick it up by the tail with a gloved hand, taking care to hold the turtle's body far away from your own. A large plastic garbage can or other container may be helpful in transporting the turtle to a safer location.

Lizards

- Lizards are highly mobile and are often difficult to catch.
- Capturing lizards is usually easiest in the morning, before the sun has warmed their bodies.
- Never grab a lizard by the tail as it will usually break off.
- A lizard noose can be a good way to capture lizards. Conant and Collins (1998) provide information on how to construct and use one.

Snakes

- Before capturing a snake, be sure that it is not venomous (the Copperhead is Delmarva's only

venomous snake; see section IV, "Species Accounts").
Never try to catch a venomous snake unless you have
received professional training.

- Wear gloves and long sleeves while capturing snakes.
  Many snakes will bite in self-defense, and this bite can
  be painful.
- Many snakes will remain motionless when approached,
  relying on camouflage and immobility to render them
  "invisible." In such circumstances an observer may be
  able to approach slowly and grab the snake with one
  hand just behind the head, keeping a firm hold but not
  squeezing. The other hand should be used to support
  the body of the snake.
- Special tools (e.g., snake sticks and snake tongs)
  are also helpful for capturing and handling snakes
  but should be used with care to avoid injuring the
  snake.
- If bitten by a nonvenomous snake, clean the wound
  with soap and water and apply an antiseptic.
- If bitten by a venomous snake, remain as calm as
  possible and seek medical attention immediately. Do
  not attempt to use the once recommended snakebite
  treatment of cutting at the wound site, attempting to
  suck out the venom, and then applying a tourniquet, as
  these actions can cause more harm than the actual
  snakebite. With proper medical treatment the
  possibility of fatality is extremely low.

What To Do If You Find a Turtle Crossing a Road

Do not endanger yourself or others to save the turtle! If safe
to do so, you can pull off the road and attempt a rescue. If the
habitat is adequate, place the turtle on the side of the road
toward which it was heading. If the habitat is highly
disturbed, note the location where the turtle was found and
take the turtle to a knowledgeable person (e.g., staff at a
state park or an environmental center) to decide where to
release the turtle.

What To Do If You Find a Snake in Your Yard or House

In the event that you find a snake in your yard or house and you wish to remove it, the first thing to do is make sure that the snake is not a Copperhead, the only venomous snake known to occur currently on Delmarva. (See section IV for a complete description, including information on its limited range on the peninsula.) Once assured that the snake is not venomous, consider the option of just leaving the snake alone. Besides being harmless and fascinating to watch, snakes are an important component of natural communities, and many snakes help to keep local rodent populations in check. However, if the option of sharing your yard or house with a free-roaming snake is intolerable to you, the best way to remove the snake is to catch it with a snake grab stick or with gloved hands (see the preceding guidelines on catching snakes). Animal control companies can also be hired to remove snakes, but be aware that many of these companies are inexperienced with snake removal, and a few may even try to exploit the unwary homeowner. Some products are available that claim to be snake repellents, but they usually do not produce satisfactory results.

Precautions Regarding Collection

Before collecting any amphibian or reptile, become familiar with applicable local, state, and federal regulations on the collection, transportation, and possession of these animals. This information is available through government agencies such as state fish, game, and wildlife departments. Some regulations are available through the state Web sites listed later in this section under "How to Report a Rare Species or an Extension of Geographic Range."

There are also ethical issues related to the collection, transportation, and maintenance of captive amphibians and reptiles. Some of the key points to remember are listed below.

Regulatory Guidelines

- It is illegal to collect or possess any of Delmarva's state-designated endangered or threatened amphibians or reptiles without appropriate state, and in some cases local, permits. If the species is federally listed, a federal permit is required. Refer to section V, "Conservation of Delmarva's Herpetofauna," for a list of protected species.
- While regulations vary from state to state, a permit is sometimes required to collect, transport, or possess even "common" native amphibians or reptiles.
- The sale of most native amphibians and reptiles collected from the wild is prohibited in Delaware, Maryland, and Virginia, with specific exceptions in each state's laws.

Ethical Guidelines

- Collection of amphibians and reptiles for sale in the pet trade, even when legal, should not be practiced; collection of common species should be for scientific, classroom, or home study purposes only, according to specific provisions in each state's laws.
- Proper containers should be used for transporting these animals; plastic containers with adequate ventilation are ideal for most amphibians and reptiles. Because snakes are escape artists, containers used to hold them must be secure. Plastic containers with screw-on lids and pillowcases that can be tied at the top work well.
- Captured animals must not be subjected to high temperatures or dry conditions; they can easily die in a hot car.
- Amphibians and reptiles brought into the classroom or into the home for study should be returned to the site of collection as soon as possible.
- If you are going to keep an amphibian or a reptile, know how to take care of it. Many excellent Web sites

with animal care information are available on the Internet.

- Consider purchasing a captive-raised animal instead of collecting one. It will usually do better in captivity than an animal born in the wild, and you will not be depleting the natural populations.

How to Document Observations

Whenever possible, observations of amphibians and reptiles, particularly rare or uncommon species, should be documented. Such documentation is absolutely necessary for an observation to provide valuable scientific data. The best way to document an observation is to take a good photograph. Tips on how to do this are provided in the paragraphs following. Sketches are also useful, particularly if a photograph cannot be taken. Measurements of amphibians and reptiles can also provide useful scientific information and add to the knowledge of Delmarva's herpetofauna. The correct way to take measurements is illustrated in the introduction of each order or suborder. Measurements can be made with a measuring tape, ruler, or caliper. In addition, an observer should take detailed field notes that include the following: (1) date and time of observation; (2) location; (3) habitat description; (4) local weather conditions; (5) detailed description of the animal, including size and coloration; and (6) behavior of the animal.

How to Photograph Amphibians and Reptiles

Photographs for documentation or identification purposes can be taken with any camera as long as the resulting image of the amphibian or reptile provides an adequate rendering of the animal. Of course the quality of the photograph will increase with the skill of the photographer and the quality of the photographic equipment, but basic point-and-shoot cameras, including digital varieties, are generally adequate for documenting all but the smallest amphibians and reptiles. It is important to take a number of photographs at different angles and distances so that positive identification can be made.

The amateur nature photographer who desires higher-quality photographs should use a single-lens reflex camera with a good flash or reflectors. A macro lens or extension tubes will be needed to photograph smaller animals. Helpful information on wildlife photography is available on numerous Web sites and at camera shops and bookstores.

How to Report a Rare Species or an Extension of Geographic Range

If you find an amphibian or a reptile that is listed in this book as rare, very rare, or extremely rare, or if you find one that represents an extension of the geographic range for that species, please report your findings to the appropriate Natural Heritage Program. Your report should include the following: name of observer(s), date of observation, precise location, brief description of habitat, and photograph(s), sketch(es), and/or detailed description of the specimen. Optional information to report includes weather conditions and comments on behavior.

Delaware Natural Heritage Program
Division of Fish & Wildlife
Department of Natural Resources & Environmental Control
4876 Hay Point Landing Road
Smyrna, DE 19977
302-653-2880
www.dnrec.state.de.us

Maryland Natural Heritage Program
Wildlife & Heritage Division
Department of Natural Resources
Tawes State Office Building
580 Taylor Avenue
Annapolis, MD 21401
410-260-8540
www.dnr.state.md.us

Virginia Natural Heritage Program
Department of Conservation and Recreation
217 Governor Street
Richmond, VA 23219
804-786-7951
www.dcr.state.va.us

The authors are also interested in information on
uncommon or rare species and possible range extensions and
can be contacted through the Delaware Nature Society, P.O.
Box 700, Hockessin, Delaware 19707. Phone: 302-239-2334.

How to Confirm an Identification

If you find an amphibian or a reptile for which you would like
an identification confirmed, you may contact author Jim White
at the Delaware Nature Society, P.O. Box 700, Hockessin,
Delaware 19707. Phone 302-239-2334. Be prepared to provide
the information shown in the "How to Document Observations"
section.

IV. SPECIES ACCOUNTS

Explanation of Species Accounts

The 5 orders and suborders and 18 families of amphibians and reptiles known to occur on Delmarva are arranged in phylogenetic (evolutionary) sequence in this book, beginning with the salamanders. At the beginning of each new order or suborder is a description of the order or suborder, including its unique characteristics, and illustrations depicting key morphological features that are useful in understanding the individual species accounts. Each new family (and subfamily, as appropriate) is introduced with a brief description. Within each family (or subfamily) the entries are arranged alphabetically by genus and species.

The following pages explain the information that is included in the individual species accounts.

English and Scientific Names: As with other organisms, amphibians and reptiles are classified scientifically using binominal nomenclature, a system that was largely developed by the eighteenth-century biologist Carolus Linnaeus. Under the Linnaean system each organism is given a two-part (or three-part) scientific name, always written in italics. For example, the Green Frog has the scientific name *Rana clamitans.* The first name, *Rana,* is the genus, or generic, name and is always capitalized. The second name, *clamitans,* is the species, or specific, name and is not capitalized. The specific name is unique within its genus. A species is defined as a population, or group of populations, of organisms that can produce fertile offspring but are reproductively isolated from other similar (related) species. Some species are subdivided further into subspecies to designate several races that are geographically distinct but that can still interbreed if their ranges overlap. For example, the Northern Green Frog, *Rana clamitans melanota,* is the name of the subspecies of Green Frog occurring on Delmarva. The subspecific name, *melanota,* is not capitalized.

The name of the individual who first described the species or subspecies follows the scientific name, along with the year the species or subspecies was first described. If the species has been divided into subspecies, then the subspecies present on Delmarva is the one that is included.

The English and scientific names used in this book for genus, species, and subspecies are taken from *Scientific and Standard English Names of Amphibians and Reptiles of North America, North of Mexico, With Comments Regarding Confidence in Our Understanding* (Crother et al. 2000). This list was selected because it is the standardized list endorsed by the three major professional herpetological societies in the United States (i.e., the Society for the Study of Amphibians and Reptiles, the American Society of Ichthyologists and Herpetologists, and the Herpetologists' League).

Because Crother et al. (2000) did not include names for families, subfamilies, orders, or suborders, other references were needed for these names. The scientific nomenclature for families and subfamilies follows that presented in *Herpetology* (Pough et al. 2001), and the English names, with a few exceptions, follow those presented in *A Field Guide to Reptiles and Amphibians: Eastern and Central North America* (Conant and Collins 1998). Both English and scientific names for orders and suborders follow those presented in Conant and Collins (1998).

Other Names (included when appropriate): English and scientific names for amphibians and reptiles are sometimes changed as new information is obtained. Another English name is listed if any of the following apply: (1) the entry is listed in Conant and Collins (1998) under a different English name; (2) a different English name is frequently used on Delmarva (e.g., Spadefoot Toad); or (3) if there is a very old

English name that persists, despite elimination through standardization of names (e.g., DeKay's Snake). Former scientific names are listed if the animal was classified in a different genus in Conant (1975), Conant and Collins (1991), or Conant and Collins (1998).

Description: The first item under every description is the adult size, given in both metric and English units. Sizes in English units are as provided in Conant and Collins (1998) except that fractions are converted to decimals in this book. The English units (in decimals) were then converted to metric units. For all salamander, frog, and snake entries, the size range of average adults is listed first, followed (when available) by the longest recorded length of unusually large individuals. Most turtle entries are also listed in this manner. With some turtles, the males and females reach such different sizes at maturity that separate measurements are provided. For the lizards, which so frequently lose their tails and then grow new but shorter ones, two size ranges are listed: the first refers to the total adult length including tail, and the second refers to the snout-vent length. These measurements are illustrated at the introduction of each order or suborder.

Each entry also includes a description of coloration and pattern, including common variations observed between the sexes or at different ages. The descriptions focus on distinctive, readily observable features, or field marks, that can help distinguish a specimen from all other species. Most of these field marks can be seen without capture. This descriptive information is generally based on the authors' knowledge of Delmarva's herpetofauna supplemented with information published by other authors, including Conant and Collins (1998), Ernst et al. (1994), Mitchell (1994), and Petranka (1998).

For most species a description of juvenile and/or larval forms follows that of the adult forms. Tadpole measurements represent an approximate average maximum size. Tadpole measurements and descriptions, with a few exceptions, are as provided in Hulse et al. (2001).

Similar Species: Other species occurring on the Delmarva Peninsula that might be confused with the species under

---

discussion are listed in this section, with the most readily identifiable differences explained. In a few cases, species that occur near, but not on, Delmarva are included here (e.g., Northern Leopard Frog).

Overall Range: Overall ranges are based on those provided in Conant and Collins (1998); they have been simplified, however, to give only a general outline of the overall range. The North American range of each species (or subspecies, where applicable) is provided except for the seaturtles, for which the worldwide distribution is listed.

Range and Status on Delmarva: A range map is included for each species known to occur on Delmarva (with the exception of the seaturtles) and is designed to show at a glance the known distribution of the species. In general, county lines are used as the boundaries for shading (i.e., an entire county is shaded if there is at least one confirmed record in that county). Exceptions to this format occur in New Castle and Cecil Counties, where the Fall Line is also used as a shading boundary for species that occur on the Piedmont but not on the Coastal Plain, or vice versa. Another exception occurs in Cecil County—the Susquehanna River watershed divide is used as a shading boundary for the 11 species that occur in the Susquehanna River watershed but not elsewhere on the Piedmont. In addition, a handful of species are shown by irregularly shaded boundaries that cut across county lines (e.g., maps for the Green Treefrog and the Northern Diamond-backed Terrapin are shaded only near the coastlines to more accurately reflect their ranges). Figure 1, a reference for the range maps, illustrates the county names and boundaries as well as the Fall Line.

The range is also described in the narrative. Distributional information provided here is a combination of the authors' knowledge of the herpetofauna of the peninsula; personal communications with other knowledgeable naturalists and herpetologists on the peninsula; records from the Delaware, Maryland, and Virginia Natural Heritage Programs; and records from various published sources, including *An Annotated Check List of the Amphibians and Reptiles of the Del-Mar-Va Peninsula* (Conant 1945), the

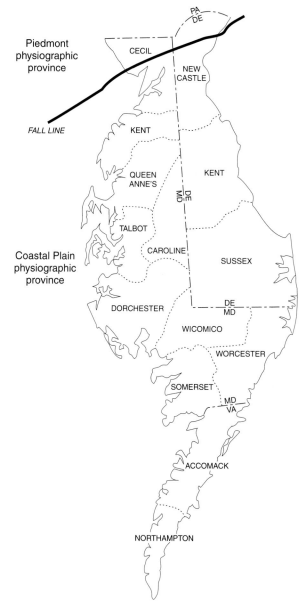

Piedmont
physiographic
province

FALL LINE

Coastal Plain
physiographic
province

PA
DE

CECIL

NEW
CASTLE

KENT

QUEEN
ANNE'S

KENT

DE
MD

TALBOT

CAROLINE

SUSSEX

DORCHESTER

DE
MD

WICOMICO

WORCESTER

SOMERSET

MD
VA

ACCOMACK

NORTHAMPTON

Figure 1. Counties of the Delmarva Peninsula

Distributional Survey (Amphibia / Reptilia): Maryland and the District of Columbia (Harris 1975), the *Atlas of Amphibians and Reptiles in Virginia* (Mitchell and Reay 1999), and numerous scientific journal articles. Because the range maps are too small to readily designate the presence or absence of species on the barrier islands, occurrence on these islands is included in the narrative where appropriate. The barrier island information was obtained from the following sources: Brady (1925), Conant (1981), Conant et al. (1990), Lee (1972, 1973a), Mitchell and Anderson (1994), and Scott (1986).

   The status of the species refers to its general abundance on Delmarva, ranging from very common to extremely rare. Additional fieldwork will undoubtedly improve knowledge of both the range and status of Delmarva's amphibians and reptiles.

Habitat: Habitat preferences discussed for each species or subspecies can be supplemented with the habitat descriptions and color photographs shown in section II. Habitat information provided here is based on the authors' knowledge of Delmarva's herpetofauna supplemented with other published information, particularly Ernst et al. (1994), Mitchell (1994), and Petranka (1998).

Voice: Voices are only listed for the Order Anura (frogs) because this is the only group among Delmarva's herpetofauna that makes significant vocalizations. An explanation of frog calls is provided in the introduction to the Order Anura. Voice information is based on the authors' field experience with Delmarva's frogs, unless otherwise noted.

Reproduction and Development: This section gives, when available, information on courtship, mating, deposition of eggs, incubation, hatching, care of the young, and development to maturity. Where possible, the information provided is from the authors' experience on Delmarva, but for many of the species the work of others has been drawn upon for the information presented. In the interest of readability, rather than add a citation at the end of every sentence, collective citations which refer to all the material following the previous citation are placed at the end of a paragraph and are enclosed in parentheses. When information on Delmarva populations is not available, data from studies conducted in nearby states are included, and references are provided.

Remarks: This section includes additional interesting information on natural history, conservation, or other topics that do not readily fall into one of the other categories.

Photographs: The color plates illustrate all 73 species and subspecies either known to occur on, believed to possibly occur on, or believed to have been extirpated from Delmarva. These photographs are of animals found on the Delmarva Peninsula, unless otherwise indicated. In addition, all photographs were taken by author Jim White, unless otherwise noted.

Amphibians (Class Amphibia)

Amphibians first appeared on earth in the Devonian period about 350 million years ago, evolving from fishlike vertebrates. The word *amphibian* is derived from the Greek words *amphi-* (double, both) and *bios* (life), referring to the fact that most amphibians live a "double life": first as an aquatic larva with gills and then, following metamorphosis, as a terrestrial or semiaquatic adult with lungs or other respiratory structures to permit gas exchange with the atmosphere.

However, even terrestrial adult amphibians have not completely left an aquatic existence. The skin of most species is highly permeable and unable to prevent desiccation, necessitating a life in wet or moist habitats. In addition, the vast majority of species must return to the water or other wet habitats to reproduce because the amphibian egg is covered by a gelatinous envelope instead of a shell and will desiccate if deposited on dry land.

Amphibians are ectothermic vertebrates—they are unable to produce enough body heat through internal processes to maintain optimal body function and instead obtain their body heat either directly or indirectly from the sun or another external heat source. On Delmarva many amphibians become inactive (hibernate) during the coldest months, burrowing underneath leaves, logs, rocks, or other debris or into the substrate in freshwater habitats. In addition, many amphibians become inactive (estivate) during the hot, dry periods of summer, retreating to cool, moist microhabitats.

Amphibians have soft, glandular skin that contains mucus and poison glands but lacks scales. Their limbs lack nails or claws. The amphibian heart has three chambers, and most species have lungs although they are secondarily lost in some salamanders.

Living amphibians are divided into three distinct groups or orders: (1) Order Caudata—the salamanders, (2) Order Anura—the frogs, and (3) Order Gymnophiona—the caecilians. There are more than 4,880 amphibian species worldwide: approximately 415 salamanders; more than 4,300 frogs; and

165 caecilians (Pough et al. 2001). Only salamanders and frogs are found in North America. Amphibians known to occur on the Delmarva Peninsula include 13 salamander and 17 frog species.

Salamanders (Order Caudata)

Salamanders are called the "tailed" amphibians, as implied by the name Caudata (Latin *cauda* means tail), because unlike frogs, adult salamanders retain their tails after metamorphosis.[1] Salamanders also differ in general appearance from frogs by having elongated bodies and usually 2 pairs of relatively equal-sized limbs. Vertical grooves on the sides of the body, termed *costal grooves,* vary in number according to species and can therefore be an aid in identification of some salamander species (fig. 2). Salamanders are similar in body shape to lizards, with which they are sometimes confused; lizards, however, have dry, scaly bodies and claws on their toes.

The majority of salamanders are aquatic as larvae and are terrestrial, semiaquatic, or aquatic as adults. On the Delmarva Peninsula, only the Eastern Red-backed Salamander and Northern Slimy Salamander lack an aquatic larval stage.

Salamanders must live in wet or moist environments to avoid desiccation. Many terrestrial species hide under rocks or logs or in burrows during the day and emerge at night to feed. Others are fossorial and spend both day and night underground, where they feed. All salamanders are carnivorous, feeding primarily on insects, spiders, worms, millipedes, and other invertebrates. Some species, particularly larger ones, also feed on small fish and other amphibians and their eggs.

With the exception of the Eastern Hellbender, which employs external fertilization, Delmarva salamanders reproduce by internal fertilization of the eggs without copulation. Courtship and mating may occur on the land or in the water, depending on the species. Elaborate rituals of "dancing," nudging, rubbing, grasping, and/or biting are often

---

1. The term Urodela is also often used for this order. Pough et al. (2001) explains that Urodela may best be used to include only the extant (i.e., living) species, whereas Caudata includes both extant and extinct species. This book uses Caudata because it is the term used by Conant and Collins (1998).

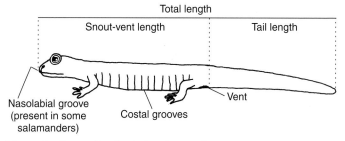

Figure 2. Generalized adult salamander

involved. If the female is receptive, the male deposits one or more spermatophores either directly on the substrate or on a fallen leaf, stick, rock, or other debris in the breeding habitat. The spermatophores are pyramid-shaped structures that are capped with sperm cells (termed the *sperm capsule*). Fertilization occurs when a female inserts the sperm capsule into her cloaca, bringing the sperm in contact with her eggs internally. The eggs are deposited in aquatic habitats or moist microhabitats and may be laid singly or in gelatinous masses or strands, depending on the species. Female salamanders of many species brood the eggs until hatching.

The aquatic larvae are typically dull in coloration, without the adult markings, and therefore can be difficult to identify. They can be divided into two general morphological groups: (1) those that live in standing water and have *pond-type morphology,* characterized by bushy external gills and a long, prominent dorsal fin that extends from behind the head to the tip of the tail; and (2) those that live in moving water and have *stream-type morphology,* characterized by shorter, reduced gills and a shorter lower dorsal fin that extends from near the hind limbs to the tip of the tail (fig. 3). Depending on the species, the duration of the larval period ranges from a few months to several years. Following metamorphosis, the *subadults* are generally similar to the adults in appearance and behavior but are not sexually mature. It takes up to six additional years for the subadults to reach sexual maturity, depending on the species (Petranka 1998).

Salamanders   41

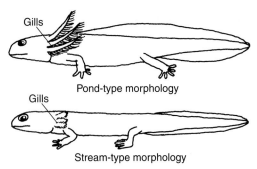

Figure 3. Two morphological types of larval salamanders

Worldwide there are 10 living families of salamanders, encompassing approximately 415 species (Pough et al. 2001). North America contains by far the greatest number and diversity of salamander species, with representatives from 9 of the 10 living families. On the Delmarva Peninsula there are 13 species representing 4 families: the Hellbenders and Giant Salamanders (Family Cryptobranchidae: 1 species), the Mole Salamanders (Family Ambystomatidae: 3 species), the Newts (Family Salamandridae: 1 species), and the Lungless Salamanders (Family Plethodontidae: 8 species).

Hellbenders and Giant Salamanders (Family Cryptobranchidae)

The Family Cryptobranchidae contains the largest salamanders in the world, reaching up to 1.8 meters (5.9 feet) in length. The two largest species live in Japan and China, and the single other species, the Hellbender, is found in eastern North America. Members of this family are completely aquatic as both larvae and adults. They undergo incomplete metamorphosis—the adults retain one pair of gill slits and lack eyelids. The bodies are dorsoventrally flattened, and the heads are extremely flattened. Unlike most other salamanders, members of the Family Cryptobranchidae fertilize their eggs externally.

Eastern Hellbender   **Plate 13**
Cryptobranchus alleganiensis alleganiensis (Daudin, 1803)

Description: 29.2 to 50.8 cm (11.5 to 20.0 in.); record 73.9 cm (29.1 in.).

A very large, entirely aquatic salamander. The back is generally gray or brownish (rarely yellowish or greenish) with numerous irregular dark spots. The belly is also brownish but may be a slightly lighter shade. The dorsoventrally flattened head is rounded when viewed from above. Small, beady, lidless eyes are located on top of the head. The body, also dorsoventrally flattened, has wrinkled folds of skin extending down the sides between the front and back limbs. The tail is laterally compressed with a well-developed dorsal fin. The adults lack gills but retain large, conspicuous gill slits. The larvae are brownish with dorsal spotting and have conspicuous external gills.

Similar Species: This bizarre salamander is not apt to be confused with any other species on Delmarva because of its large size and distinctive body shape.

Overall Range: Found from southern New York to northern Georgia and west to southern Illinois and northeastern Mississippi but not on the Coastal Plain.

Range and Status on Delmarva: Extremely rare to absent; found historically in the lower Susquehanna River and its larger tributaries in Cecil County, Maryland. Formerly well established in the Susquehanna watershed (H. W. Fowler 1915; J. A. Fowler 1947), this salamander is believed by some herpetologists to be extirpated from Delmarva, possibly as a result of degradation of its stream habitat. However, relatively recent unconfirmed sightings from the lower Susquehanna River watershed suggest that at least one population may still exist on the Delmarva Peninsula (S. Smith personal communication). More thorough field surveys are required to establish its true status on Delmarva. The Eastern Hellbender is listed as endangered in Maryland.

Habitat: Found in clear, fast-flowing rivers and large streams with shelter in the form of large flat rocks, snags, and other

---

debris. Most are found in areas with sandy or gravelly bottoms where the water is 20 to 50 cm (8 to 20 in.) deep (Hulse et al. 2001).

Reproduction and Development: Courtship and mating take place in late summer and early fall. The male typically prepares a nest by digging an underwater depression under a large rock slab, forming a cavity that he defends from other males. Males may also nest in cracks in rocks or under overhanging bank rocks. The male waits at the entrance of the cavity for a gravid female to approach and then guides or forces her into the nest cavity, where he may guard her and prevent her from escaping until her eggs are laid. Unlike other Delmarva salamanders, the Eastern Hellbender fertilizes its eggs externally. The female deposits her eggs in strands resembling strings of beads that settle in a clump on the bottom of the cavity. The male emits a milky solution containing sperm that fertilizes the eggs as they are deposited. Soon after the eggs are deposited, the male drives away the female and begins to brood the eggs. The male guards the eggs from other males and females that might eat them. Males have been seen fanning the eggs with their bodies, apparently supplying fresh, oxygenated water to the eggs. The eggs hatch in two to three months. The larvae undergo incomplete metamorphosis at about two years of age, at which time the gills are reabsorbed. They reach sexual maturity between five and eight years of age. (Bishop 1941; Hulse et al. 2001; Petranka 1998.)

Remarks: The Eastern Hellbender is by far the largest salamander on Delmarva. Although ferocious in appearance, it rarely bites, and contrary to popular belief, it is not poisonous. The slime-coated skin of this salamander, however, makes it difficult to handle. In other parts of its range where it is common, this species is sometimes accidentally caught on hook and line by fishermen.

The Eastern Hellbender is primarily nocturnal, foraging on the stream bottom at night and hiding during the day. During mating season it is active both day and night. This salamander was once thought to feed extensively on fish and fish eggs and was therefore blamed for reductions in gamefish stocks. However, research indicates that, although small fish are eaten regularly, crayfish are the mainstay of the Eastern Hellbender's diet (Hulse et al. 2001).

Mole Salamanders (Family Ambystomatidae)

Mole Salamanders are large and stout-bodied with relatively well-developed limbs and conspicuous costal grooves. There are approximately 32 species of Mole Salamanders in North America (Pough et al. 2001), 3 of which are found on the Delmarva Peninsula. The Delmarva species spend most of their lives underground or underneath logs or other debris, emerging during the breeding season to mate and lay eggs in dry or flooded vernal pools, depending on the species. The larvae develop in the vernal pools and have pond-type morphology, with conspicuous external gills and a long dorsal fin that extends from the tip of the tail to just behind the gills. The subadults and adults have well-developed lungs.

Spotted Salamander   Plate 14
Ambystoma maculatum (Shaw, 1802)

Description: 11.2 to 19.8 cm (4.4 to 7.8 in.); record 24.9 cm (9.8 in.).
    A large, stout-bodied, brightly spotted salamander. The body is black or steel gray (sometimes appearing bluish) with 2 rows of very distinct, bright yellow or orange spots on the back extending from the head to the tip of the tail. Additional spots are usually present on the legs. Unspotted individuals are found rarely. The belly is grayish. The larvae are grayish brown with no prominent markings and are light-colored on the belly. Subadults are similar in coloration to the adults, attaining the brightly colored spots soon after metamorphosis.
Similar Species: The adult Eastern Tiger Salamander has irregularly shaped dorsal spots that are often fused together to form large blotches or bands that extend down onto the sides.

The subadult Eastern Tiger Salamander is dark with yellowish spots scattered randomly over the entire body, including on the lower sides.

Overall Range: Found from Nova Scotia to Georgia and west to south central Ontario and eastern Texas.

Range and Status on Delmarva: Found only in the northern half of the peninsula, specifically in New Castle and Kent Counties, Delaware, and Cecil, Kent, Queen Anne's, and Talbot Counties, Maryland. Very uncommon on the Piedmont because of the loss of habitat, and uncommon to locally common on the Coastal Plain.

Habitat: Prefers moist, mature deciduous woodlands associated with vernal pools such as floodplain ponds or Delmarva Bays. The Spotted Salamander also inhabits younger deciduous and mixed deciduous-coniferous woodlands that have associated vernal pools.

Reproduction and Development: On warm, rainy nights in late February, March, or early April, adult male and female Spotted Salamanders emerge from their subterranean burrows and crawl downslope to the nearest vernal pool. Once in the water, males swim along searching for females. When a female is encountered, the male (or several males) attempts to gain her attention by performing an underwater courtship dance, circling and nudging her. If receptive, the female will return the nudging, enticing the male to deposit spermatophores on the pool bottom. The male may repeat his dance several times before the female is ready to search the bottom for spermatophores. Once the female encounters a spermatophore, she straddles it and picks up the sperm capsule with her cloacal lips, pulling it inside her body to allow internal fertilization of her eggs. The female often mounts between 15 and 20 spermatophores before ending courtship. (Arnold 1976; Petranka 1998.)

A few days after mating, the female lays her eggs in firm, gelatinous masses attached to submergent vegetation or debris. The egg masses are round to oval, variable in size (from 5 to 25 cm [2 to 10 in.] long), and may be either clear or milky in color. Females typically deposit 2 to 4 egg masses, each containing up to approximately 250 eggs. The eggs hatch in four to seven weeks, depending on the water temperature. The larvae grow rapidly on a diet of aquatic invertebrates and usually metamorphose into subadults two to three months after hatching. The relatively small (approximately 5 cm [2 in.] long) subadults disperse from the breeding pool and live underground for two to five years until they reach maturity. (Bishop 1941; Petranka 1998.)

Remarks: The Spotted Salamander is primarily a subterranean animal, spending most of its life in small mammal burrows, where it feeds on a variety of invertebrates. Spotted Salamanders have lived up to twenty-five years in captivity (Pope 1928, 1937).

The outer gelatinous membrane of the Spotted Salamander egg mass usually has imbedded in it unicellular green algae, *Oophila amblystomatis,* which give the egg mass a greenish appearance. The oxygen produced by the photosynthesizing algae is utilized by the developing embryos, thereby possibly increasing survival (Petranka 1998).

Marbled Salamander   Plate 15
Ambystoma opacum (Gravenhorst, 1807)

Description: 8.9 to 10.9 cm (3.5 to 4.3 in.); record 12.7 cm (5.0 in.).

A medium-sized, stout-bodied salamander with a short, thick tail. The body is black with gray to silvery white markings that vary from individual blotches to crossbands or stripes. The belly is uniformly black. The males are more striking in appearance than the females, having larger, brighter, silvery white markings compared to the smaller, dull gray markings of the females. Hatchling larvae are black with large external gills, whereas older larvae are generally brown with small, light spots along the sides. Recently transformed subadults are brownish with gray flecks and usually begin to develop adult coloration in one to two months.

Similar Species: Recently transformed Eastern Tiger Salamanders are mostly dark but lack the Marbled Salamander's gray to silvery white markings, and they are also longer.

Overall Range: Found from southern New Hampshire to northern Florida and west to southern Illinois and eastern Texas.

Range and Status on Delmarva: Common throughout most of the Coastal Plain, although records are lacking from Northampton County, Virginia. Absent from the barrier islands. Absent from the Piedmont except in the Susquehanna River watershed in Cecil County, Maryland (Harris 1975).

Habitat: Found in deciduous, coniferous, and mixed deciduous-coniferous woodlands that have adequate wetland areas for larval development (e.g., Delmarva Bays, borrow pits, or other vernal bodies of water).

Reproduction and Development: Marbled Salamanders breed on rainy nights in late summer and early fall. Courtship and mating apparently occur both en route to and in the dried vernal pools where the eggs are laid (Krenz and Scott 1994). A male initiates courtship by nudging and lifting other males and females, particularly in the tail and cloacal region. If a female responds by nudging a male in his cloacal region, the two may pair off and move away together in circular fashion, nudging each other as they crawl. The male eventually deposits a spermatophore on the substrate and attempts to lead the female to it. If receptive, the female will straddle and pick up the sperm capsule with her cloacal lips, pulling it inside her body to fertilize her eggs. (Petranka 1998.)

The female burrows out a shallow depression under leaf litter, bark, a log, or other debris, or in an animal burrow, in the bed of the dried vernal pool. She then lays approximately 50 to 150 eggs in the nest. The female typically broods her eggs, defending them against predators and reducing the possibility of desiccation. Females often remain with the eggs until the nest becomes flooded with rainwater, which may be several weeks or months later. The eggs hatch anywhere from several hours to several days after the nest becomes flooded. The larvae grow quickly, feeding on aquatic invertebrates and other amphibian larvae and metamorphose into subadults in May and June. (Petranka 1998.)

Remarks: The Marbled Salamander is the only Delmarva ambystomid species that does not mate and deposit its eggs in water. Adults are most often found by turning over logs or debris in moist woodlands or by searching roadways during spring and fall rains. Larvae can be seen in flooded vernal pools, even active under the ice in winter (A. Norden personal communication). In May and June if conditions are right, large numbers of recently transformed subadults may be observed crossing roads after leaving their breeding pools.

Eastern Tiger Salamander   Plates 16, 17
Ambystoma tigrinum tigrinum (Green, 1825)

Description: 17.8 to 21.1 cm (7.0 to 8.3 in.); record 33.0 cm (13.0 in.).

A large, stout, big-headed salamander. The back is very dark brown or black with a variable pattern of cream color to greenish yellow, irregular blotches or spots that often form bands that extend onto the sides. The belly is yellowish with dark marbling. During the breeding season adult males have a long, laterally compressed tail and a swollen cloaca. Hatchling larvae are grayish with dark bands across the back. Older larvae are olive green or brownish above and whitish underneath. Many have dark spots or marbling on the back and sides, and some have a light lateral stripe between 2 darker longitudinal bands. Recently metamorphosed subadults are mostly dark with remnants of external gills still evident. Older subadults usually have cream to greenish yellow spots over the entire body.

Similar Species: The Spotted Salamander usually has rounder, brighter yellow or orange spots forming 2 irregular rows on the dorsal surface, and the spots do not extend onto the sides.

Overall Range: Found on the Atlantic Coastal Plain from Long Island, New York, to northern Florida and southern Mississippi, and also throughout much of the Midwest. Disjunct populations occur in other areas.

Range and Status on Delmarva: Very rare; found only in isolated populations on the Coastal Plain in New Castle and

---

Salamanders   *49*

Sussex Counties, Delaware, and Kent, Queen Anne's, Caroline, Dorchester, Somerset, and Worcester Counties, Maryland. This salamander is absent from the barrier islands and from the Piedmont. Additional field investigations may identify populations in Kent County, Delaware, and Talbot and Wicomico Counties, Maryland. This salamander is listed as endangered in Delaware, Maryland, and Virginia.

Habitat: Prefers moist, often sandy, deciduous, coniferous, or mixed deciduous-coniferous woodlands that are associated with adequate breeding pools, such as Delmarva Bays, fishless artificial ponds, or borrow pits. This salamander is primarily fossorial, spending most of its life underground in small mammal burrows or in tunnels that it digs itself. It is very rarely encountered except during the breeding season and when recently transformed subadults are leaving their larval pools.

Reproduction and Development: On mild, rainy nights in December, January, and February (rarely in March), adult male and female Eastern Tiger Salamanders emerge from underground and crawl to the breeding pools. Once in the water, the male seeks out a female and, stimulated by a well-choreographed courtship dance that includes aggressive nudging and tail-wagging, attaches a spermatophore to a submerged twig, leaf, or other bottom debris. The female is then led over the spermatophore while participating in what has been called a *tail-nudging walk.* She then picks up the sperm capsule with her cloacal lips and inserts it into her cloaca, thus fertilizing her eggs. During courtship, another male may attempt to steal the female away from the attending male by shoving her away, or he may intercede between the male and female during their tail-nudging walk, taking the female's place while mimicking her movements and covering up the rival's spermatophore with his own. A male can deposit up to 37 spermatophores in a single night. (Arnold 1976; Petranka 1998.)

After mating, the females lay their eggs in soft, gelatinous egg masses attached to underwater twigs and vegetation. The incubation period for the eggs varies depending on the water temperature but averages approximately one month. The larvae grow quickly, feeding on aquatic invertebrates and other amphibian larvae. Metamorphosis to subadults may start as early as mid-June and continue to late August. The duration of the terrestrial subadult stage is highly variable, from less than one year to several years. (Arndt 1989; Lee and Franz 1974; Petranka 1998; Stine 1984; Stine, Fowler, and Simmons 1954.)

Remarks: The Eastern Tiger Salamander is one of the largest terrestrial salamanders in the world. It is also one of Delmarva's rarest amphibians. The loss and degradation of Delmarva Bays, other vernal wetlands, and quality upland woodlands is threatening the existence of this salamander on Delmarva. The preservation and proper management of these habitats throughout the peninsula will be necessary if this and other rare amphibians are to survive on Delmarva.

Eastern Tiger Salamanders are sometimes found trapped in window wells into which they accidentally fell while migrating to, or dispersing from, breeding pools.

Newts (Family Salamandridae)

Members of the Family Salamandridae are found primarily in Europe and Asia, with only 2 genera occurring in North America. The only newt found on the Delmarva Peninsula is the Red-spotted Newt, which belongs to the genus *Notophthalmus*. Most members of the Salamandridae are wholly or partially aquatic as adults and have skin that is rougher than members of other salamander families. The genus *Notophthalmus* is unique in that instead of the usual two postembryonic developmental stages found in most other amphibians (i.e., aquatic larva and terrestrial adult), there are often three distinct developmental stages: aquatic larva, terrestrial subadult, and aquatic adult.

Red-spotted Newt   **Plates 18, 19**
Notophthalmus viridescens viridescens (Rafinesque, 1820)

Description: 5.8 to 12.2 cm (2.3 to 4.8 in.); record 14.0 cm (5.5 in.).

A small salamander with distinctive black-bordered reddish spots. The aquatic or semiaquatic adults are usually olive to brownish green above and yellowish below. Black-bordered reddish spots occur on the back, and small black spots are scattered on the sides, tail, and legs. During the mating season, males have tails with enlarged fins above and below, a swollen cloacal vent, enlarged hind legs, and black horny growths on the toes and inner surfaces of the thighs. Breeding females tend to be lighter in overall color than males.

Mature Red-spotted Newt larvae have slender bodies, blunt noses, and conspicuous external gills and are tan to yellowish brown with a dark stripe running from the snout through each eye. Aquatic subadults resemble miniature aquatic adults, whereas the terrestrial subadults (efts) are typically bright reddish orange with black-bordered reddish dorsal spots and have coarse, granular skin. The bright reddish orange coloration of the eft is usually obtained in one to two weeks after metamorphosis and is thought to be an example of Mullerian mimicry, that is, warning predators that the salamander is toxic. Older efts that are nearing sexual maturity are often less brightly colored. (Petranka 1998.)

Similar Species: The adults and subadults are not easily confused with other salamanders because no other salamander has black-bordered reddish spots on the back. The larvae are similar in appearance to other pond-type salamander larvae (e.g., the Ambystomatidae) but can be differentiated by the dark stripe from the snout through the eye.

Overall Range: Found from the Canadian maritime provinces to central Georgia and west to Ontario and Alabama. It is one of the most widely distributed salamanders in North America.

Range and Status on Delmarva: Probably found in suitable habitat throughout the peninsula, although records are lacking from Kent County, Delaware; Somerset County, Maryland; and Accomack County, Virginia. Particularly common on the Piedmont. Absent from the barrier islands.

Habitat: The adults, aquatic subadults, and larvae are found in ponds, freshwater marshes, slow-moving sections of streams, and vernal pools that remain wet most of the year. The terrestrial subadults (efts) occur in moist, mature deciduous woodlands.

Reproduction and Development: The Red-spotted Newt has the most complex and variable life cycle of the Delmarva salamanders, having an aquatic larval stage with gills; a subadult stage with lungs that can be either terrestrial (termed the *red eft*) or aquatic; and a lunged adult stage that can be either aquatic, semiaquatic, or terrestrial, depending on the population and environmental circumstances.

Courtship and mating take place in the pond (or other aquatic habitat) primarily in the spring on Delmarva. The male initiates courtship, which apparently takes one of two forms, depending on the responsiveness of the female. If the male finds a female that is "immediately" responsive to him, he performs a brief courtship display called a *hula* (in which he undulates his body and tail), and then, once the female nudges his tail with her snout, he deposits one or more spermatophores on the pond substrate for her to pick up. The more typical type of courtship behavior occurs if a male encounters an unresponsive female, in which case the male swims above the female, grasps her with his enlarged hind legs just in front of her forelegs, and then whips his tail erratically and rubs his forelegs alternately on the pitlike genial glands on the side of his head and on the female's snout, presumably transferring chemicals that stimulate the female to mate. In this type of courtship the male may remain clasped to the female for several hours before he finally releases her, deposits 1 or more spermatophores, and then tries to guide her over the spermatophore so that she can pick up the sperm capsule with her cloacal lips. (Arnold 1977; Bishop 1941; Pope 1924; Verrell 1982.)

The females deposit their eggs in the spring, attaching them singly to submerged aquatic vegetation. They may take several weeks to complete egg deposition, scattering a few eggs per day throughout the breeding habitat. The incubation period depends on water temperature and ranges from twenty to thirty-five days. The larvae feed on aquatic invertebrates, metamorphosing into lunged subadults in approximately two to five months. (Bishop 1941; Petranka 1998; Pope 1924.)

Remarks: On the Delmarva Peninsula, red efts are found mainly on the Piedmont, and even there they are infrequently observed (compared to populations in more northern and mountainous regions in the United States). Only a few records of red efts exist from the Coastal Plain of Delmarva (Grogan 1985). It appears that on Delmarva (especially on the Coastal Plain) the terrestrial red eft stage is usually omitted and the larvae transform instead into aquatic subadults that then mature into aquatic adults. If the wetland habitat dries out (e.g., in late summer and fall on Delmarva), the aquatic subadults and adults may become temporarily terrestrial, living under logs or in animal burrows.

In addition to feeding on a wide variety of aquatic invertebrates and small fish, the adults are known to feed on the eggs of other pond-breeding salamanders and frogs (Petranka 1998).

Lungless Salamanders (Family Plethodontidae)

Plethodontidae is the largest family of salamanders in the world, containing approximately 266 species (all but 2 of which are New World species). As the common name for the family implies, adult plethodontids lack lungs, with oxygen exchange occurring instead through the skin and mouth lining. All members of this family on the Delmarva Peninsula have a small groove (the *nasolabial groove*) extending from each nostril to the upper edge of the jaw, although this is often difficult to see without magnification. For many plethodontids, elaborate courtship rituals culminate in a *tail-straddle walk,* in which the female straddles the male's tail and is led by the male over the top of his spermatophore. She then picks up the sperm capsule with her cloacal lips and inserts it into her cloaca, thus fertilizing her eggs. There are 8 species in the Family Plethodontidae found on the Delmarva Peninsula.

Northern Dusky Salamander   Plate 20
Desmognathus fuscus (Green, 1818)

Description: 6.4 to 11.4 cm (2.5 to 4.5 in.); record
14.2 cm (5.6 in.).

A small to medium-sized salamander with
highly variable coloration. Adults are usually gray to
dark brown with a broad, lighter stripe extending
down the back onto the tail. There is also usually a
distinct, light stripe that extends at an angle from the eyes to
the back of the jaw. The tail is keeled and is generally
triangular in cross section. The belly is variably colored, but
often gray to brown with mottling. There are 14 costal grooves.
The larvae and young subadults have 5 to 8 pairs of dark
blotches on the back between the front and hind limbs. As
these salamanders age, the dark blotches fuse to create dark
parallel lines that border the light stripe on the back. Older
adults usually become very dark, appearing dark brown to
black.

Similar Species: The Northern Dusky Salamander can be
difficult to identify because of the lack of easily observed field
marks. However, it is the only salamander in our area that has
a light stripe extending from the eye to the back of the jaw.
The Northern Two-lined Salamander is more slender, is
usually lighter in color, and lacks the stripe from eye to jaw.
The Eastern Red-backed Salamander is also more slender and
has a longer tail that is usually more than half the animal's
total body length.

Overall Range: Found from southern New Brunswick to
South Carolina and west to southern Quebec and Kentucky. It
is one of the most common salamander species in North
America.

Range and Status on Delmarva: Common on the Piedmont
and uncommon to rare on the Coastal Plain. Records are
lacking from Sussex County, Delaware; Dorchester, Somerset,
and Worcester Counties, Maryland; and Accomack and
Northampton Counties, Virginia, including the barrier
islands. All observations on the Coastal Plain should be
documented.

Habitat: Found in small streams and spring seeps, usually within or near deciduous woodlands.

Reproduction and Development: Courtship and mating take place in fall and/or spring on the Delmarva Peninsula. The male entices the female to mate by performing a series of exaggerated and aggressive body movements that include: (1) walking toward the female while moving his forelimbs in a synchronized manner that resembles the butterfly stroke of a swimmer, (2) erratically jerking his body and tail, and (3) rubbing his snout and chin on the female's body and biting and scraping her with his teeth in an attempt to inoculate her with glandular secretions that presumably encourage her to mate. Mating ensues when the male and female engage in tail-straddle walking behavior, in which the male leads the female over his spermatophore and the female inserts the sperm capsule into her cloaca. (Organ 1961; Uzendoski and Verrell 1993.)

In late spring or summer the females deposit clusters of 10 to 42 eggs, either in shallow depressions in the mud apparently created by the female or in natural cavities under rocks, logs, leaf clumps, or moss adjacent to woodland streams or spring seeps. The eggs are usually attended by the female until they hatch in late summer or early fall. The larvae wriggle to the water, metamorphosing to subadults in approximately one year. The males mature approximately two years after hatching, whereas the females mature in approximately three years. (Green and Pauley 1987; Krzysik 1980; Mohr 1935; Petranka 1998.)

Remarks: An observer can find the Northern Dusky Salamander with relative ease by turning over flat rocks and logs in or along the edges of small rocky streams or spring seeps in or near deciduous woodlands.

The adults are primarily nocturnal and during warm months spend much of the night foraging for terrestrial and semiterrestrial invertebrates on the ground surface near their freshwater habitat. This species is a significant predator in small streams and the adjacent streambanks, feeding on many types of aquatic and terrestrial invertebrates (Petranka 1998).

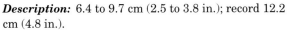

Northern Two-lined Salamander   Plate 21
Eurycea bislineata (Green, 1818)

Description: 6.4 to 9.7 cm (2.5 to 3.8 in.); record 12.2 cm (4.8 in.).

A small, slender, yellowish salamander with 2 usually conspicuous, dark brown or black stripes extending from behind each eye back onto the tail. The back is greenish yellow to orangish yellow and is often spattered with black spots. The belly is yellowish. The tail is laterally compressed and constitutes just over half the total body length. There are 15 to 16 costal grooves. The larvae have stream-type morphology and are dusky colored above with 6 to 9 pairs of light spots on the back and sides, and a squarish snout.

Similar Species: The Long-tailed Salamander is somewhat similar; however, it is longer, is usually brighter in color, lacks the dark, longitudinal stripes, and has 13 to 14 costal grooves. The Northern Dusky Salamander is heavier bodied and usually darker overall, and has a light stripe running at an angle from behind each eye down to the jaw. At first glance, the Northern Two-lined Salamander also resembles the Little Brown Skink, which is a lizard. The skink, however, has scales and claws.

Overall Range: Found from southern Quebec to northern Virginia and west to Ontario and central Ohio, with isolated populations in Labrador.

Range and Status on Delmarva: Common on the Piedmont but only rarely encountered on the Coastal Plain. Records are lacking from Sussex County, Delaware; Dorchester and Somerset Counties, Maryland; and Accomack County, Virginia. Absent from the barrier islands.

Habitat: On the Piedmont, commonly found under rocks, logs, or debris along the edges of shallow, rocky, swift-moving streams and in spring seeps. Coastal Plain populations are usually associated with swamps, river floodplains, and spring seeps. In moist forested areas, the adults may wander away from their aquatic or wetland habitat, especially during periods of wet weather.

Reproduction and Development: Courtship and mating
probably take place in fall or spring on the Delmarva
Peninsula. It is unknown whether courtship occurs primarily
on land or in the water, as there are no published accounts of
its observation in the wild. Observations of captive specimens
by Noble (1929) suggest that courtship is initiated by the male
as he nudges the female and typically bends his head around
her snout, sometimes remaining in this position for an hour or
more. The female eventually moves behind the male,
straddling his tail with her forelimbs and pressing her head
against the glands at the base of his tail. The pair then crawls
around together (i.e., the tail-straddle walk), with the male
erratically wagging his tail from side to side while the female
turns her head in the opposite direction. Although never
observed, the male presumably deposits a spermatophore and
leads the female over it so that she can pick up the sperm
capsule with her cloacal lips.

In the spring, females deposit up to 100 eggs, attaching
them in tight clusters to the undersides of rocks, usually in
fast-moving water. In Coastal Plain populations, females may
attach eggs to vegetation or debris, sometimes scattering
them about instead of placing them in tight clusters. Females
usually attend the eggs, probably defending them from
predation by invertebrates. The eggs hatch in four to ten
weeks, depending on the water temperature. The larvae feed
along the bottom on aquatic invertebrates and metamorphose
into subadults in the spring or summer in one to three years.
(Bishop 1941; Bruce 1985; Petranka 1998; Wilder 1924a,
1924b.)

Remarks: The Northern Two-lined Salamander and the
Northern Dusky Salamander are the most common
salamanders in the clear, rocky streams and spring seeps of
the Piedmont portion of the Delmarva Peninsula. An observer
can find the adults most readily by carefully lifting up flat
rocks or logs that lie along stream and seep margins. The
adults can also be seen crossing roads near suitable habitat on
rainy nights in late winter and early spring. The larvae hunt
underwater at night and can be observed by searching streams
and seeps with a flashlight.

Long-tailed Salamander   Plate 22
Eurycea longicauda longicauda (Green, 1818)

Other Names: Longtail Salamander.
Description: 10.2 to 16.0 cm (4.0 to 6.3 in.); record
19.8 cm (7.8 in.).
    A medium-sized, very slender, yellowish
orange salamander with small, black spots on the
sides and back. The tail is very long, comprising up
to 60 percent of a mature adult's total length. The sides of the
tail have diagnostic vertical black markings that often
resemble a herringbone pattern. There are 13 to 14 costal
grooves. The larvae have stream-type morphology. Recently
hatched larvae are whitish with black specks on the back,
whereas older larvae develop dark mottling all over the body.
Subadults attain adult coloration within a few months after
metamorphosis.
Similar Species: The Northern Two-lined Salamander is
somewhat similar, but it has 2 distinct lines running
longitudinally down its body and tail and has 15 to 16 costal
grooves.
Overall Range: Found in the Appalachian region from
southern New York to northern Georgia and west to
southeastern Missouri and northern Alabama.
Range and Status on Delmarva: Uncommon on the
Piedmont; apparently absent from the Coastal Plain.
Habitat: Usually found in cool, relatively high-quality
streams, springs, and spring seeps, and also in associated
nearby deciduous woodlands. Sometimes found in moist
microhabitats some distance from water.
Reproduction and Development: Courtship and mating of the
Long-tailed Salamander apparently occur primarily in the fall
and early winter (Cooper 1960b; Petranka 1998). Full
courtship behavior has not been described, but Cooper (1960b)
described partial courtship behavior in which the male chased
the female and rubbed his head against her cloacal region and
snout.
    From mid-October to March, the white eggs are laid
singly (often in a row) and are attached to submerged rocks or

---

Salamanders   59 stone walls in springs, small creeks, and springhouses. The incubation period may last as long as three months. The larvae grow to approximately 2 to 2.5 cm (0.8 to 1.0 in.) in length and typically metamorphose to subadults in less than one year. Sexual maturity is reached one to two years after metamorphosis. (Mohr 1943; Petranka 1998.)

Remarks: Because the Long-tailed Salamander is found almost exclusively in clean, cool water habitats, it is often considered an indicator of relatively good water quality. This salamander is found fairly commonly in old springhouses or spring encasements associated with old farmhouses. Congregations of twenty or more salamanders are not uncommon during the colder months.

Four-toed Salamander   Plate 23
Hemidactylium scutatum (Schlegel, 1838)

Description: 5.1 to 8.9 cm (2.0 to 3.5 in.); record 10.2 cm (4.0 in.).

A small, slender salamander with a rusty to yellowish brown head, back, and tail. The belly and underside of the tail are white with conspicuous black specks. A distinct constriction is present at the base of the tail. Each hind foot has 4 toes (instead of the usual 5). The rarely encountered larvae are slender with pond-type morphology and a mottled, yellowish brown appearance. Subadults resemble the adults in coloration but have proportionally shorter tails.

Similar Species: The Eastern Red-backed Salamander and Northern Dusky Salamander have 5 toes on each hind foot and lack both the constriction at the base of the tail and the white, black-speckled belly.

Overall Range: Found in disjunct locations from Nova Scotia to northern Florida and west to Wisconsin and Louisiana.

Range and Status on Delmarva: Uncommon; found in widely scattered, localized populations throughout most of the peninsula. It is considered uncommon largely because of the lack of suitable breeding habitat. Records are lacking from Somerset County, Maryland. Absent from the barrier islands.

Habitat: The adults are found in moss and under logs, rocks, and leaf litter in deciduous and mixed deciduous-coniferous woodlands that are associated with fishless freshwater wetlands (especially sphagnum bogs and spring seeps) suitable for larval development. Winters are apparently spent in subsurface cavities in the woodlands (Petranka 1998).

Reproduction and Development: Courtship and mating (including a tail-straddle walk to lead the female over the male's spermatophore) take place in the woodland habitat in the late summer and fall. On rainy nights between mid-February and April, gravid females move from the woodlands to freshwater wetlands for egg laying. Clumps of approximately 30 to 50 eggs are deposited under moss or other vegetation above the water line of the wetland. Clumps of eggs from several females are often clustered in communal nests, with one or more females attending the eggs until hatching (typically in six to nine weeks). The hatchling larvae wriggle into the water where they spend three to seven weeks before metamorphosing into terrestrial subadults. Sexual maturity is reached one to two years after hatching. (Berger-Bishop and Harris 1996; Bishop 1941; Blanchard 1923; Branin 1935; Martof et al. 1980; Mohr 1935; Petranka 1998.)

Remarks: The Four-toed Salamander is the only member of the genus *Hemidactylium*. Because of its subterranean habits, this species is rarely encountered except during the late winter and early spring breeding migrations, when the females can be found crossing roadways that bisect upland woodlands and freshwater wetlands.

The constriction at the base of the tail marks the point where the tail can break away if grasped by a predator, thus allowing the salamander to escape. The Four-toed Salamander is one of the few salamanders that can also voluntarily lose its tail without being grasped (autotomy), and the tail section still wiggles after being disconnected (Bishop 1941).

Eastern Red-backed Salamander   **Plates 24, 25**
Plethodon cinereus (Green, 1818)

Other Names: Redback Salamander.

Description: 5.8 to 10.2 cm (2.3 to 4.0 in.); record 12.7 cm (5.0 in.).

The Eastern Red-backed Salamander is a small, slender salamander with proportionally slim, short legs. Two general color morphs exist: (1) The red-backed morph has an orange to red, sometimes tannish, wide straight-edged stripe extending down the back and often onto the tail, and (2) the lead-backed morph lacks the stripe and is generally dark gray to black on the back. Both morphs have black and white mottling on the belly and usually have black and white flecking on the sides, the back of the head, and the tail. The tail is generally longer than half the animal's total length and is round in cross section. Subadults resemble the adults in coloration but have shorter tails relative to body size and proportionally broader heads (Bishop 1941; Petranka 1998).

Similar Species: The Northern Dusky Salamander has a stouter body with a shorter keeled tail that is usually less than half the animal's total length.

Overall Range: Found from the Canadian maritime provinces to North Carolina and west to Minnesota and Illinois.

Range and Status on Delmarva: Very common in suitable habitat throughout the peninsula. This is the only salamander found on the barrier islands; it has been recorded only from Chincoteague Island.

Habitat: The preferred habitats of this terrestrial salamander are well-drained, deciduous, coniferous, or mixed deciduous-coniferous woodlands with deep soil and an abundance of logs and rocks. However, Eastern Red-backed Salamanders also occur in wet or degraded woodlands, gardens, and other disturbed sites.

Reproduction and Development: Courtship and mating take place primarily in the fall and spring. Males appear to locate females by following scent (pheromone) trails. When a female is located, the male, through a series of courtship maneuvers (including nudging, rubbing, and tail-straddle walking), entices the female to collect and insert into her cloaca the spermatophore that the male deposits on the ground. The female may be stimulated to mate by a gland secretion delivered to her by the male when he bites and scrapes her skin. (Arnold 1977; Gergits and Jaeger 1990; Petranka 1998; Saylor 1966.)

In late spring or early summer (rarely in fall), the female lays up to 14 relatively large (3 to 5 mm diameter), pale yellow or whitish eggs. The eggs are deposited in hanging clusters in crevices within rotten logs, underneath rocks and logs, and in subsurface animal burrows. Females (and rarely males) brood the eggs, protecting them from predators and helping to prevent egg desiccation. Unlike all other Delmarva salamanders except the Northern Slimy Salamander, the Eastern Red-backed Salamander spends both the embryonic and the "larval" stage within the egg and does not have an aquatic life stage. When the eggs hatch after approximately six to eight weeks, the emerging subadults are prepared for a terrestrial life. The hatchling subadults are approximately 1.6 cm (0.6 in.) long and reach maturity in approximately two years. (Bishop 1941; Mohr 1935; Sayler 1966.)

Remarks: The Eastern Red-backed Salamander is the most commonly encountered salamander on the Delmarva Peninsula and is most easily found under logs, rocks, or other cover in woodlands. On damp nights it can be observed crawling around on the forest floor or even climbing small shrubs in search of prey. In high-quality woodland habitats this salamander can reach very high population levels and is often the dominant vertebrate predator of the forest floor, eating a wide variety of small invertebrates (Burton 1977). The Eastern Red-backed Salamander is also one of the few species among Delmarva's herpetofauna that can be observed in every month of the year, albeit much less frequently in the winter months and in times of drought.

Northern Slimy Salamander   Plate 26
Plethodon glutinosus (Green, 1818)

Description: 12.2 to 17.3 cm (4.8 to 6.8 in.); record 20.6 cm (8.1 in.).

The Northern Slimy Salamander is a long, moderately slender, black salamander typically with numerous small, silvery white or cream spots on the head, back, sides, limbs, and anterior portion of the tail. Brassy flecks sometimes occur in or between the spots. The throat and belly are slate gray. Secretions of the skin glands are very sticky, like glue. Mature males have a prominent circular mental gland under the chin and small, yellow or orange glands on the belly. Hatchlings may lack bright spots.

Similar Species: Other Delmarva salamanders of somewhat similar appearance, although not "sticky," include (1) the lead-backed morph of the Eastern Red-backed Salamander, which is also dark but is more slender and has only very tiny pinprick-sized white spots (or lacks spots altogether), and (2) the subadult Eastern Tiger Salamander, which is stouter with a shorter tail, has spots that are usually greenish yellow, and lacks a nasolabial groove; and (3) the Marbled Salamander, which is also stouter-bodied with a shorter tail, has larger white or silvery blotches or crossbands, is black on the lower sides and belly, and lacks a nasolabial groove. Although not on Delmarva, about 12 other species of slimy salamanders are found in the eastern United States. These other species are virtually indistinguishable in the field and can only be positively identified by range and genetic analysis.

Overall Range: Found from New York to Georgia and west to Illinois and Alabama.

Range and Status on Delmarva: Found only on the Piedmont in Cecil County, Maryland, where it appears to be uncommon.

Habitat: Prefers moist wooded ravines, hillsides, and floodplains. Found under rocks, logs, and other debris in deciduous woodlands, especially on moist slopes above streams.

Reproduction and Development: Courtship and mating usually take place in late summer and fall (Bishop 1941; Petranka 1998). Organ (1960) describes the elaborate courtship behavior that includes various forms of body contact (including the male rubbing his mental gland on the female's head, body, and tail) and a *foot dance,* in which the male repeatedly raises and lowers his limbs as if marking time. The courtship behavior culminates in tail-straddle walking, during which the male deposits a spermatophore on the ground surface and the female picks up the sperm capsule with her cloacal lips. Some males have been observed acting like females, tricking rival males into depositing, and thereby wasting, spermatophores (Arnold 1977).

In late spring or early summer, females deposit a globular cluster of white eggs, often suspended from the roof of a natural cavity (e.g., in or underneath a decaying log or in a rock crevice). Females guard the eggs for two to three months until they hatch. As with the Eastern Red-backed Salamander, the Northern Slimy Salamander spends both the embryonic and the "larval" stage within the egg and does not have an aquatic life stage. The hatchlings, which are completely terrestrial, apparently wait until the following spring to emerge on the ground surface. Most individuals breed at five years of age. (Petranka 1998.)

Remarks: This salamander forages for invertebrates on the ground surface on moist nights. The Northern Slimy Salamander is well named; when handled it can secrete an extremely sticky substance from its tail. The secretion is very difficult to remove from human skin and is probably a defense mechanism that deters predators (Brodie et al. 1979).

Eastern Mud Salamander   **Plate 27**
Pseudotriton montanus montanus (Baird, 1849)

Description: 7.6 to 16.5 cm (3.0 to 6.5 in.); record 20.6 cm (8.1 in.).

A medium-sized, moderately stout salamander with a relatively short tail. The back and sides are usually red, orange, or pink with well-spaced, rounded, small black spots; adults may become darker with age, however, and the spots become obscured. The belly is usually lighter than the back and often has small, brown spots. The eyes are brown and snout is short. The hatchling larvae are light brown above and white below with stream-type morphology. Subadults are similar in coloration to young adults (Petranka 1998).

Similar Species: The Northern Red Salamander is very similar, but has yellow eyes; more numerous and tightly spaced, irregular-shaped spots on the back; and a longer snout.

Overall Range: Found from southern New Jersey to South Carolina; west to central Maryland and northeastern Georgia.

Range and Status on Delmarva: Extremely rare. Most records come from the floodplains of the Nanticoke and Pocomoke watersheds in the central part of Delmarva, although this salamander may occur in scattered populations throughout the Coastal Plain. In the last forty-five years, the only confirmed specimens found have been from two areas in Sussex County, Delaware; there were unconfirmed reports from Worcester County, Maryland, in 1979 and 1981 (Heckscher 1995). Older, confirmed records exist for New Castle County, Delaware, and Queen Anne's, Wicomico, and Worcester Counties, Maryland. The species is absent from the barrier islands and from the Piedmont.

Habitat: Inhabits muddy areas in or adjacent to springs, wet floodplains, wooded swamps, bogs, and small streams. The larvae prefer sluggish water and spend much of their time under vegetation, rocks, and leaf litter (Petranka 1998).

Reproduction and Development: Courtship and mating have apparently not been observed or described. Limited field and laboratory observations indicate that this salamander breeds in late summer and fall in other parts of its range (Bruce 1975). On Maryland's western shore and in South Carolina, eggs have been found in the winter, suspended either singly or in clusters from gelatinous stalks in underground burrows or other well-hidden sites in or near aquatic habitats (Bruce 1975; Fowler 1946). The only report of probable Eastern Mud Salamander eggs on Delmarva describes eggs with well-developed yellow embryos found in a mossy seep in Worcester County, Maryland, in May 1994; but although they were definitely *Pseudotriton* eggs they could not be positively identified to species (Heckscher 1995; A. Norden personal communication).

The clutch size is large; up to 192 eggs in the ovaries of gravid female have been documented. The eggs hatch in winter, and the larvae usually metamorphose between one and two years after hatching. An additional one to two years is required to reach sexual maturity. (Bruce 1974, 1975, 1978.)

Remarks: Eastern Mud Salamanders are the most secretive of all the salamanders on Delmarva. Rarely found on the surface, they prefer to spend their lives underneath natural or man-made objects or burrowing in muddy wetlands far out of the sight of all but the most persistent naturalist. Many adults apparently excavate complex networks of burrows and water-filled tunnels that connect to adjacent waterways. Adults have been observed under leaves or other vegetation at the mouths of their burrows, into which they quickly retreat when disturbed (Bruce 1975).

Northern Red Salamander   Plate 28
Pseudotriton ruber ruber (Latreille, 1801)

Description: 10.2 to 15.2 cm (4.0 to 6.0 in.); record 18.0 cm (7.1 in.).
 A medium- to large-sized, stout-bodied salamander with relatively short, thick legs and tail. Younger adults are bright orange to coral red with many irregularly shaped, small, black spots on the back and sides. Older adults are dark orange to dark purplish brown with larger, less distinct spots that often fuse together. The irises of the eyes are yellowish. Larvae have stream-type morphology and are generally light brown, often becoming lightly mottled or streaked as they grow older. Subadults attain adult coloration several months after metamorphosis.
Similar Species: The Eastern Mud Salamander is very similar, but it has dark eyes and usually fewer spots, which are more widely scattered.
Overall Range: Found from New York to South Carolina and west to Ohio and Alabama; absent from most of the Coastal Plain.
Range and Status on Delmarva: Fairly common on the Piedmont but very uncommon to rare on the northern half of the Coastal Plain. Apparently absent from the lower half of the peninsula. Records are lacking from Kent County, Delaware; Dorchester, Wicomico, Somerset, and Worcester Counties, Maryland; and Northampton and Accomack Counties, Virginia.
Habitat: Usually found under rocks, moss, logs, or debris or in small animal burrows in or near clean small streams, springs, or boggy wetlands.

Salamanders

Reproduction and Development: Courtship and mating
probably take place in spring or fall on the land, although
these activities have apparently not been observed in the wild
(Petranka 1998). Laboratory observations by Organ and Organ
(1968) of closely related *Pseudotriton r. nitidus* from Virginia
suggest that courtship behavior in this species is less complex
than in other plethodontids, apparently consisting of a male
approaching a female and rubbing her with his head and body.
The pair then engages in tail-straddle walking, and the male
deposits a spermatophore on the ground. He leads the female over
the spermatophore, and she picks it up with her cloacal lips.

Females probably lay their eggs in fall or early winter on
Delmarva, depositing them under stones or debris in small
streams or springs. The females apparently brood the eggs until
they hatch in two to three months. The larval stage of this
species is one of the longest of Delmarva's salamanders, lasting
up to three and one-half years. Following metamorphosis, the
subadults take an additional one to two years to become
sexually mature. (Bell 1956; Bishop 1941; Petranka 1998.)

Remarks: The Northern Red Salamander is the jewel of small
streams and springs. The bright orange or red color of the
younger adults is more reminiscent of tropical animals than
the drab colors of most northern species. Although scientists
agree that the bright coloration of this salamander likely
serves as a warning to keep away predators, there is
disagreement regarding the full meaning of the warning.
Some feel that this coloration, as used by numerous other
animals, serves to warn predators that the Northern Red
Salamander is distasteful (i.e., an example of Mullerian
mimicry). Others believe that the salamander is not
distasteful enough to deter predators and instead the purpose
of the coloration is to fool predators by mimicking the highly
toxic red eft stage of the Red-spotted Newt (i.e., an example of
Batesian mimicry).

The adults often move away from their wetland habitat
on rainy spring nights and can sometimes be seen crossing
roads. They may stay away until early summer, when dryness
forces their return. At times, larvae can be seen active at night
in clear streams and spring seeps.

Frogs (Order Anura)

The Order Anura, and the term *frogs* as used in this book, refers to all frog species, including those species that are commonly referred to as "toads." Frogs are called the tail-less amphibians, because unlike the salamanders, all frogs lose their tails during metamorphosis to the adult stage. Frogs also differ in general appearance from salamanders by having a relatively short body, with a head that is not separated from the trunk by a discernible neck (fig. 4). The hind legs of frogs are longer than the front legs and have powerful muscles that give many frog species amazing jumping abilities.

All but a few species of frogs in North America are aquatic as larvae (tadpoles) and terrestrial or semiaquatic as adults. The majority of frogs live in moist or wet environments. Some live in or near wetlands and moist woodlands; others avoid desiccation by living under logs and debris or in underground burrows. Tadpoles are largely herbivorous, feeding primarily on algae and other aquatic vegetation (although fellow tadpoles are sometimes eaten). Adult frogs are carnivorous, feeding primarily on invertebrates such as earthworms, spiders, and insects. When they can, larger species such as the American Bullfrog also take larger prey,

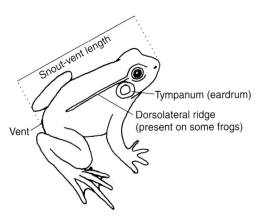

Figure 4. Generalized adult frog

including other amphibians and small reptiles, birds, and mammals.

All Delmarva frog species are capable of producing sound. Single or paired vocal sacs (fig. 5) connected to the throat are inflated during calling to modify and amplify the sound. A variety of vocalizations are made:

- *Advertisement call*—made by the males, it is the dominant sound heard during the breeding season and is usually quite loud. Distinctive for each species, this call presumably advertises the male's presence to other members of its species, defining calling sites and

Single external vocal sac

Paired external vocal sacs

Internal vocal sac(s);
throat and sides of body expand

Figure 5. Vocal sacs in male frogs

attracting females to the breeding area. The quality of an individual male's call probably influences his attractiveness to females.

- *Rain call*—usually a weak version of the advertisement call, emitted for unknown reasons outside the breeding period, typically in association with rain events
- *Release call*—often a chirplike sound, usually accompanied by body vibrations, emitted mostly by males to discourage other males that are mistakenly attempting to mount them or by females that are trying to thwart or terminate mating
- *Alarm call*—often a loud squeak emitted as a frog attempts to escape a predator
- *Aggressive call*—often a grunt, growl, or trill sounded by a male when he is defending a calling site.

Most frogs also have a well-developed sense of hearing, and many have a conspicuous tympanum (eardrum) on each side of the head.

Reproduction is accomplished in all Delmarva frogs by external fertilization of the eggs. The males generally migrate first to the breeding sites, which are often fishless, nonflowing freshwater habitats such as freshwater marshes, wooded swamps, vernal pools, ditches, or ponds, but may also include the slow-moving portions of creeks and rivers. The males use the advertisement call to attract females to the breeding sites and, in some species, to the male's breeding territory. Once a male encounters a female, he attempts to clasp her in a mating embrace, called *amplexus.* In Delmarva species, the male clasps the female just behind her front legs (*axillary,* or *pectoral,* amplexus), with the exception of the Eastern Spadefoot in which the male clasps the female just in front of her hind legs (*inguinal,* or *pelvic,* amplexus). The eggs are deposited in the water and are fertilized by the male as they are laid. Unlike some salamanders, Delmarva frogs do not brood their eggs. The eggs hatch in a few days to a few weeks, depending on the species and the water temperature.

The tadpoles are typically dull in coloration and difficult to identify in the field. A generalized tadpole is illustrated in figure 6. Tadpoles metamorphose from the aquatic form into

---

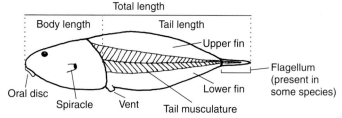

Figure 6. Generalized tadpole (frog larva)

tail-less, carnivorous, terrestrial to semiaquatic juveniles (froglets or toadlets), which generally require one to three years to reach sexual maturity.

Worldwide there are approximately 27 living families of frogs, encompassing more than 4,300 species, with many new species being discovered each year (Pough et al. 2001). On the Delmarva Peninsula there are 17 frog species representing 5 families: the Spadefoots (Family Pelobatidae: 1 species), the True Toads (Family Bufonidae: 2 species), the Treefrogs and their allies (Family Hylidae: 7 species), the Narrow-mouthed Toads (Family Microhylidae: 1 species), and the True Frogs (Family Ranidae: 6 species).

Spadefoots (Family Pelobatidae)

The Family Pelobatidae contains 11 species, found in North America, western Eurasia, and northwestern Africa. Spadefoots are similar in general body shape to the True Toads (Family Bufonidae), being broad-headed, short-legged, and stout. A broad, black spadelike tubercle is found on the inside of each hind foot and is the source of their common

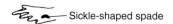 Sickle-shaped spade

Figure 7. Hind foot of Spadefoot

name (fig. 7). This "spade" is used to dig backwards into the ground. These toads are fossorial and typically spend most of their lives underground. Explosive breeders, they mate and deposit eggs in temporary pools on only a few very rainy days and nights each year. The egg and tadpole stages are aquatic and extremely short in duration. Only 1 species of Spadefoot, the Eastern Spadefoot, is found on the Delmarva Peninsula.

Eastern Spadefoot
Scaphiopus holbrookii (Harlan, 1835)

Plate 29

Other Names: Spadefoot Toad.
Description: 4.6 to 5.8 cm (1.8 to 2.3 in.); record 7.1 cm (2.8 in.).

A medium-sized, stout, short-legged frog with a rounded head and large, bulging eyes. The back is usually light to dark brown with two wavy, yellowish lines that start behind each eye and meet on the midline at the rump. These lines roughly form the shape of a lyre. There is sometimes an additional yellowish line on the side of the body. The skin is relatively smooth with numerous small tubercles, and the parotoid glands are inconspicuous. The throat and chest are white. The eyes have vertical pupils, unlike all other Delmarva frogs. A sickle-shaped, horny, black spade that is used for digging is found on each hind foot (best viewed from underneath). The tadpoles are small (up to about 3 cm [1.2 in.]), dark brown to bronze overall, with the eyes located close together on top of the head. The tail fins are translucent and unmarked.

Similar Species: The Eastern Spadefoot superficially resembles the true toads (i.e., the Eastern American Toad and the Fowler's Toad of the Family Bufonidae). However, the true toads have warty, dry skin; horizontal pupils; and prominent parotoid glands behind the eyes (see figure 8 with "True Toads" introduction). They lack the sickle-shaped spade on the hind feet.

Overall Range: Found from Cape Cod to the Florida Keys and west to eastern Missouri and Louisiana.

Range and Status on Delmarva: Uncommon to common on the Coastal Plain; absent from the Piedmont. Recorded in all counties except Cecil County, Maryland. Absent from the barrier islands.

Habitat: The Eastern Spadefoot is primarily a fossorial animal that lives in areas of loose, usually sandy soil relatively close to ephemeral wetlands or vernal pools. On Delmarva it seems to prefer poorly drained, often man-made depressions and degraded Delmarva Bays as breeding sites.

Voice: The advertisement call, produced through a single vocal sac, is a loud, abrupt, nasal snore or grunt that is repeated frequently. The head is thrust upward while calling.

Reproduction and Development: The Eastern Spadefoot is an unpredictable and explosive breeder. On mild afternoons and nights in spring, summer, or early fall, during or just after very heavy rains and low barometric pressure, male and female Eastern Spadefoots dig their way to the ground surface and migrate to recently flooded ephemeral pools or ditches. The males, usually arriving first, enter the pools and begin to emit their loud advertisement calls, creating a chorus that can be heard for a considerable distance. Shortly thereafter the females arrive and begin to swim around searching for mates. Mating ensues after a female brushes up against a stationary male. The male grasps the female from behind, around the waist and just above her hind legs. This form of breeding embrace is called inguinal amplexus and is thought to be a more primitive type of amplexus than that used by all other frogs in the area. (The males of the other frog species grasp the females just behind the front legs.) The female, carrying the male, then swims to the bottom of the pool and finds a suitable stem, twig, or blade of grass and moves along it, laying eggs as she goes. The eggs typically first appear as strands or bands attached to the vegetation, but later they swell into loose, irregular, elongated bunches along the plant or twig. The eggs hatch rapidly, often within two to three days. The tadpoles also develop very rapidly, with metamorphosis occurring in as little as two weeks. (Green and Pauley 1987; Tyning 1990; Wright 1932.)

Remarks: Eastern Spadefoots spend the daylight hours burrowed underground, emerging for a few hours at night to forage if humidity levels are favorable (Pearson 1955). On rainy nights the adults can be seen on roadways. During dry conditions this species secretes a fluid that hardens the surrounding soil in the walls of its temporary burrow, thus helping to maintain moisture in the burrow and prevent desiccation (Tyning 1990; Wright 1932).

True Toads (Family Bufonidae)

Members of this family are stout-bodied and usually have thick, dry, glandular skin with well-defined warts. Most species have relatively short limbs and digits and therefore have reduced jumping ability (i.e., they hop instead of leap). Breeding males are often much smaller than breeding females; the males also have dark throats and dark pads on their thumbs and inner fingers. Some species, including those on the Delmarva Peninsula, have prominent parotoid glands behind the eyes that produce defensive chemicals (fig. 8). Delmarva species also have cranial crests—raised, bony ridges between and/or behind the eyes—although these are not visible in young toads. The Family Bufonidae is distributed throughout most of the temperate and tropical regions of the world, with approximately 400 species worldwide (Pough et al. 2001). Only 1 genus, *Bufo,* is found in the United States. This genus is represented by 2 species on the Delmarva Peninsula: the Eastern American Toad and the Fowler's Toad.

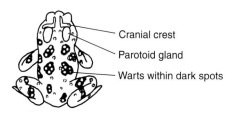

Figure 8. *Generalized True Toad*

Eastern American Toad   **Plate 30**
Bufo americanus americanus (Holbrook, 1836)

Description: 5.1 to 8.9 cm (2.0 to 3.5 in.); record 11.2 cm (4.4 in.).

A medium- to large-sized, stout, brown to reddish brown toad with dark brown dorsal spots that each contain 1 or 2 warts. A light, mid-dorsal stripe is often present. This toad has a large, oblong parotoid gland behind each eye that is either not connected to the cranial crests or is connected by a small spur (fig. 9). Large warts are present on the thighs. The chest and forward part of the belly are usually darkly mottled. Adult males are smaller than adult females and have black rather than tan or whitish throats. Netting (1929) suggests that the male's throat may be black only during mating season. The tadpoles are small (up to about 3 cm [1.2 in.]), dark brown to black overall, with translucent fins on the short, rounded tail.

Similar Species: The Fowler's Toad is very similar but has parotoid glands that touch the cranial crests, and it usually has 3 or more warts in the dark dorsal spots. The Eastern Spadefoot can be distinguished by its relatively smooth skin, bulging eyes, vertical pupils, lyre-shaped marking on the back, and horny black spade on each hind foot.

Overall Range: Found from the Canadian maritime provinces to North Carolina and west to Manitoba and Mississippi.

Range and Status on Delmarva: Very common on the Piedmont; rare to absent on the Coastal Plain. Except for a

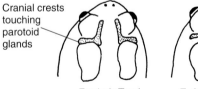

Cranial crests touching parotoid glands

Cranial crests not touching parotoid glands or connected by a short spur

Fowler's Toad   E. American Toad

Figure 9. Cranial crests and parotoid glands

narrow band immediately south of the Fall Line, records on the Coastal Plain are from southern Cecil, Wicomico, Somerset, and Worcester Counties, Maryland, and Accomack County, Virginia. Absent from the barrier islands.

Habitat: Prefers deciduous and mixed deciduous-coniferous woodlands but also commonly found in a variety of more disturbed areas, including open fields and residential yards that are near adequate breeding sites.

Voice: The male advertisement call is a long, musical, high-pitched trill, lasting approximately five to thirty seconds. This call is produced through a single vocal sac that is large and round when inflated. The males also give a chuckle-like chirp as a release call when grasped by another male or a predator.

Reproduction and Development: On mild, rainy nights from mid-March to early May, males and females, sometimes in very large numbers, make their way to breeding areas, which include vernal pools, freshwater marshes, roadside ditches, slow-moving streams, and river edges. Breeding occurs primarily at night but also during the day under optimal conditions. Some breeding congregations number in the hundreds, with males far outnumbering females. Males call loudly from the shallow water in hopes of attracting females. A successful male clasps a female just behind her front legs in the typical mating embrace (axillary amplexus). The male holds on tenaciously with his enlarged front legs, stimulating the female to lay thousands of eggs in long, gelatinous double strands. Under peak breeding conditions, the frenzied males compete aggressively for each female, sometimes forming large "toad balls" composed of numerous males clambering to embrace a single female.

The toad eggs generally hatch in less than a week unless unusually cold water temperatures delay the hatching. The small, black tadpoles stay near the eggs, sometimes creating a dense, black mass. Gradually, the tadpoles disperse, seeking algae to feed on. Metamorphosis into tiny toadlets takes place in about four to eight weeks, often in late May and early June. Sexual maturity is attained by the second spring following metamorphosis (Green and Pauley 1987; Hulse et al. 2001).

Remarks: American Toads, like other members of the genus *Bufo,* secrete a powerful toxin from their parotoid glands when disturbed. The toxin is distasteful to many predators, especially mammals. In humans, the toxin can cause extreme discomfort if it is ingested or comes in contact with the eyes. Contrary to popular belief, the toxin secreted by toads does not cause warts.

Hundreds of American Toads are killed on roadways on peak breeding nights.

Fowler's Toad   **Plate 31**
Bufo fowleri (Hinckley, 1882)

Description: 5.1 to 7.6 cm (2.0 to 3.0 in.); record 9.7 cm (3.8 in).

A medium-sized, stout toad that is variable in color with large, dark dorsal spots that generally contain 3 or more warts each. The overall body color is usually light to dark brown, but sometimes olive, gray, or reddish. A light, mid-dorsal stripe is usually present. This toad has a large, oblong parotoid gland behind each eye that is connected directly to the cranial crests (see fig. 9). The belly is usually white, often with a single dark breast spot. Adult males are smaller than adult females and have dark throats. The tadpoles are virtually indistinguishable in size and coloration from those of the Eastern American Toad (see previous species account).

Similar Species: The Eastern American Toad is very similar but usually has only 1 or 2 large warts in each of the large dorsal spots; its parotoid glands are either separate from the cranial crests or are connected to them by short spurs. In addition, the upper belly and chest of the Eastern American Toad is usually spotted. The Eastern Spadefoot can be distinguished by its relatively smooth skin, bulging eyes, vertical pupils, lyre-shaped marking on the back, and horny, black spade on each hind foot.

Overall Range: Found from New Hampshire to North Carolina and west to Michigan and Louisiana.

Range and Status on Delmarva: Very common on the Coastal Plain, including many barrier islands. Absent from the Piedmont except in the Susquehanna River watershed.

Habitat: Found in various Coastal Plain habitats, including deciduous, mixed deciduous-coniferous, and coniferous woodlands; fields; the borders of ponds and wetlands, including freshwater, brackish, and salt marshes; and wooded or shrub-covered dunes. This species appears to be especially common in areas with sandy soil. The Fowler's Toad can also be found in areas very close to relatively dense human habitation (e.g., within towns).

Voice: The advertisement call is a loud, nasal *w-a-a-a-h,* lasting one to four seconds. This call is produced through a single vocal sac.

Reproduction and Development: Breeding usually begins on warm nights in mid-April or May (typically after the Eastern American Toads have completed the majority of their breeding) and may continue through midsummer. In the southern part of the peninsula they are occasionally found breeding as early as mid-March (Grogan and Bystrak 1973b; J. White personal observation). Peak breeding occurs on warm, rainy nights from late April to early June, when the loud calls of males can be heard emanating from a wide variety of wetlands, including ditches and vernal pools, as well as shallow areas of permanent bodies of water. Courtship behavior appears to be similar to the Eastern American Toad.

Females deposit up to 8,000 black eggs in 2 long, gelatinous strands (Hulse et al. 2001). The eggs hatch in as little as one week, and the tadpoles metamorphose about one to two months later (Martof et al. 1980). It is not uncommon to find hundreds of tiny, newly transformed toadlets hopping underfoot near Coastal Plain wetlands between late May and late July.

Remarks: Like the Eastern American Toad, the Fowler's Toad has well-developed parotoid glands that secrete a powerful toxin when the animal is disturbed by a potential predator or handled by an inquisitive human. Although most responsible humans are not likely to ingest this toxin directly, hands should be washed thoroughly after handling a toad because toxin contact with human eyes can be very painful.

Treefrogs and Their Allies (Family Hylidae)

Hylidae is a large and diverse frog family containing approximately 760 species with representatives on all continents except Antarctica (Pough et al. 2001). The family is divided into 4 subfamilies, of which only the Subfamily Hylinae is found on the Delmarva Peninsula. Members of this subfamily are highly variable in size and external appearance. Most species are relatively smooth skinned and many are brightly colored. Most also have well-developed toe pads that enable them to be successful in an arboreal lifestyle. The exceptions are all the species of the genus *Acris* (Cricket Frogs), which have less-developed toe pads and live a terrestrial existence. There are 7 species of the Subfamily Hylinae on the Delmarva Peninsula.

Eastern Cricket Frog   **Plate 32**
Acris crepitans crepitans (Baird, 1854)

Other Names: Northern Cricket Frog.
Description: 1.5 to 3.6 cm (0.6 to 1.4 in.).

A small, rough-skinned, short-legged frog, the Eastern Cricket Frog is Delmarva's smallest frog. The coloration on the back is extremely variable, with combinations of bright green, yellow, red, brown, or gray common. A variably colored median stripe that sometimes forms a Y is also usually present. The most distinguishing traits include (1) rough skin with fine warts; (2) a dark triangle usually discernible between the eyes; (3) a dark, ragged stripe on the rear surface of each thigh; and (4) extensive webbing on the hind feet. The hind legs, when extended forward, usually do not extend past the snout. The belly is cream-colored, and the male usually has a yellowish vocal sac. The tadpoles are medium-sized (up to about 5 cm [2 in.]), with a body that is green above and lighter below. The tail musculature has black mottling, and the tail has a distinctive black tip.
Similar Species: The Northern Spring Peeper has smooth skin and dark markings on the back that typically form an X

shape. The New Jersey Chorus Frog has smooth skin, dark stripes on the back and sides, and a light line on the upper lip. Another very similar frog is the Coastal Plain Cricket Frog *(Acris gryllus gryllus),* formerly called Southern Cricket Frog, which occurs close to, but apparently not on, Delmarva. The Coastal Plain Cricket Frog has a clean-cut dark stripe on each thigh, less webbing on the toes, and proportionally longer hind legs which, when extended forward, usually reach past the snout.

Overall Range: Found from southern New York to the Florida panhandle and west to Arkansas and Texas. This frog is absent from most of the Atlantic Coastal Plain south of Delmarva.

Range and Status on Delmarva: Common throughout the Coastal Plain except for the barrier islands, where it is absent. Absent on the Piedmont except in the Susquehanna River watershed. Recorded in all counties.

Habitat: Found in moist, grassy or sedge-covered areas along the edges of permanent ponds, vernal pools, swamps, fresh and slightly brackish water marshes, and slow-moving streams. This frog is especially common in and around Delmarva Bays and other large vernal pools.

Voice: The advertisement call, produced through a single vocal sac, is a loud, sharp clicking, repeated in rapid succession. The call is reminiscent of the sound produced by hitting two stones or glass marbles together and can be heard for a considerable distance. Often heard in large choruses.

Reproduction and Development: Eastern Cricket Frogs begin breeding in late spring and continue well into the summer. Peak breeding occurs in May and June. Mating is accomplished through axillary amplexus, with the male clasping the female just behind the front legs as they float on the water. The females lay up to 250 eggs either singly attached to aquatic vegetation or in small clusters on the bottom (Hulse et al. 2001). Most tadpoles metamorphose into tiny froglets by mid-August (Martof et al. 1980).

Remarks: Unlike most other members of the Family Hylidae, Eastern Cricket Frogs do not climb. The adults search during the day for insect prey along grassy edges of wetlands or in drying vernal pools. Despite the relatively short hind legs, they are excellent jumpers. They are often encountered around freshwater wetlands outside their breeding period, and they appear not to have extended hibernation, as they are sometimes active on mild winter days.

Gray Treefrog/Cope's Gray Treefrog   **Plate 33**
Hyla versicolor (LeConte, 1825) and *Hyla chrysoscelis* (Cope, 1880)

These 2 species are treated together here because they are identical in appearance. They can be distinguished in the field only by their vocalizations (see "Voice"). Genetically these 2 species are very different: the Cope's Gray Treefrog is diploid, having two sets of chromosomes per cell, whereas the Gray Treefrog is tetraploid, having four sets of chromosomes per cell. The following information applies to both species.

Description: 3.3 to 5.1 cm (1.3 to 2.0 in.); record 6.1 cm (2.4 in.).

A medium-sized, stout, warty treefrog that can change colors depending on activity level, temperature, and humidity. The head, body, and legs are usually light to dark gray or grayish green above and are covered with numerous small warts. A darker, irregular blotch is located on the center of the back, and the legs usually have dark crossbars. A white spot is located below each eye. The hidden surfaces of the hind legs are bright orange or yellow with black mottling. Toe pads are well developed and the hind feet are entirely webbed. The belly is white, and males have a dark throat. The tadpoles are medium-sized (up to about 5 cm [2 in.]) and have a greenish brown body flecked with gold. The tail, which is often reddish and is heavily mottled with black, has a high upper fin and a well-developed flagellum. Recently transformed froglets are often lime green, turning grayish as they mature.

Similar Species: Adults are not easily confused with other frogs on Delmarva. Recently transformed Gray Treefrogs are similar in appearance to juvenile Green Treefrogs and Barking Treefrogs, but they are usually not as bright a green.

Overall Range: The combined overall range of these 2 species is from Maine to Florida and west to Manitoba and Texas. The individual range of each species is poorly understood.

Range and Status on Delmarva: The Gray Treefrog appears to be most common in the northern portion of the Coastal Plain, including along the Fall Line, and may not occur in the southern third of Delmarva. It is absent from the Piedmont except in the Susquehanna River watershed. The Cope's Gray Treefrog is fairly common from southern New Castle County, Delaware, and Kent County, Maryland, to places south. It is apparently absent from the Piedmont entirely. Neither species has been found on the barrier islands. More field study is required to better define the Delmarva ranges of these 2 species.

Habitat: Found in or near deciduous and mixed deciduous-coniferous woodlands that have vernal pools or nearby ditches for breeding. Both species are primarily arboreal and search for insects and other invertebrates in trees and shrubs.

Voice: The advertisement call of both species is produced through a single vocal sac and can be described as a loud, flutelike trill typically lasting for about one-half to two seconds. Under like conditions the trill of the Gray Treefrog is lower-pitched, shorter in duration, and slower than that of the Cope's Gray Treefrog. Therefore, it is relatively easy to differentiate the calls of these species when both are calling in the same area. However, positive identification is difficult when only one species is present because of the lack of a basis for comparison and because the trill rates and sound quality are affected by air temperature (the calls are slower at lower air temperatures). Researchers (Johnson 1966; Zweifel 1970) have found that trill rates of less than 25 pulses per second can be attributed to the Gray Treefrog, whereas trill rates greater than 36 pulses per second can be attributed to the Cope's Gray Treefrog. Intermediate trill rates (between about 25 and 35 pulses per second) can apparently be produced by either species (i.e., by the Gray Treefrog under warmer conditions and by Cope's Gray Treefrog under cooler conditions). Ideally, documentation of these species should be by sonogram analyses of advertisement calls in relation to air temperature.

Reproduction and Development: Both species breed in Delmarva Bays, ditches, and flooded agricultural fields. Males call from the middle of April through the summer, with peak breeding occurring from early May to late June. The following behavior is typical of the Gray Treefrog but is probably also valid for the Cope's Gray Treefrog. The males make their way to the breeding areas first and set up small territories, usually calling from a branch over the water. If rival males get close to each other, they may emit an aggressive call consisting of a short whooping sound repeated several times. Females are attracted to the calling males and move toward them. When a female approaches, the male may change his call slightly, lengthening it a bit to produce a courting call. If the female is responsive, she touches the male, sometimes aggressively jumping on him. The male then mounts her from behind, clasping her with his front legs. They may remain in amplexus at the calling perch for several hours. Eventually, with the male still holding on tightly, the female crawls down to the water and deposits up to 2,000 eggs, either singly or in many small masses attached to aquatic vegetation. The eggs develop quickly and usually hatch in two to five days. Tadpoles metamorphose in approximately two months. (Hunter et al. 1992; J. White personal observation.)

Remarks: On Delmarva the presence of strong breeding populations of either of these species is often an indicator of relatively high quality wetlands. Both of these species are sometimes referred to as "tree toads."

Green Treefrog   **Plate 34**
Hyla cinerea (Schneider, 1799)

Description: 3.3 to 5.8 cm (1.3 to 2.3 in.); record 6.4 cm (2.5 in.).

A medium-sized, slender, long-legged treefrog with relatively smooth skin. The overall color is usually vivid green, although inactive or cold individuals may be dark green to grayish. A white to cream-colored stripe typically extends from the upper jaw to the side of the belly, though this stripe is reduced in length or is lacking in many individuals. Sometimes small golden spots are on the back. The belly and throat are white. The tadpoles are small to medium-sized (up to about 4 cm [1.6 in.]), dark or greenish overall with a yellowish tinge. They are speckled on the throat and have pale lines from the eyes to the nostrils.

Similar Species: The Barking Treefrog is stouter and rougher skinned and usually has dark spots on the back. It also has a wider, more jagged lateral stripe.

Overall Range: Found from Delaware to the Florida Keys and west along the Gulf of Mexico Coastal Plain to Texas. This species reaches the northern limits of its range just north of the Chesapeake and Delaware Canal in New Castle County, Delaware, and Cecil County, Maryland.

Range and Status on Delmarva: Common on the Coastal Plain within a few miles of the Delaware River, Delaware Bay, Chesapeake Bay, and Atlantic Ocean, as well as inland along tidal portions of their tributaries. On the barrier islands, it has been found on Assateague and Chincoteague Islands. The frog has also been found within a few miles north and south of the Chesapeake and Delaware Canal. Records are lacking from Caroline County, Maryland. Absent from the Piedmont.

Habitat: On Delmarva this species appears to be most common in or near freshwater marshes and swamps along tidal rivers, in man-made impoundments, and along the perimeter of ponds, especially where cattails are present. It is particularly common in man-made freshwater impoundments in wildlife management areas along coastal Delmarva. Green Treefrogs can also be found near, and possibly in, slightly brackish water and will venture well into moist woodlands during the nonbreeding season.

Voice: The advertisement call is a loud *queenk, queenk, queenk* repeated as many as 75 times per minute (Conant 1975). This call has been likened to the sound of a cowbell when heard from a distance. The call is amplified through a single vocal sac connected to the throat. Green Treefrogs can also be heard calling from areas other than their breeding sites, often outside the breeding season. These vocalizations, called *rain calls,* are most often given on warm, rainy nights and sound similar to the advertisement call but are hoarser and weaker in volume.

Reproduction and Development: Male and female Green Treefrogs make their way to breeding areas primarily from early May through July. Males grasp the females just behind the front legs (axillary amplexus). Females lay about 400 eggs, depositing them in several small egg masses that may be free floating or attached to submerged vegetation (Martof et al. 1980). The eggs generally hatch in less than one week, and the tadpoles metamorphose in approximately seven to nine weeks (Wright 1932).

Remarks: The Green Treefrog is often found on or near porches, where it feeds on insects that are attracted to exterior lighting. This frog remains active well into autumn, when it can be encountered in coastal cattail marshes, resting vertically, pressed flat against cattail leaf blades, or jumping from plant to plant.

Barking Treefrog   Plate 35
Hyla gratiosa (LeConte, 1857)

Description: 5.1 to 6.6 cm (2.0 to 2.6 in.); record 7.1 cm (2.8 in.).

A large, stout treefrog that varies in color from light green to brown depending on the body temperature and the activity level of the frog. The dorsal surface has a rough appearance and usually has dark, circular spots. A creamy white stripe on the upper lip extends jaggedly down the sides of the body; this stripe may be bordered in part by a purplish brown stripe or blotch. There are sometimes small golden or white spots on the back. The males have a greenish throat, and the females a white throat. The belly is white or yellowish white. The tadpoles are large (up to about 7 cm [2.8 in.]) with a generally dark brown body and a light, unmarked throat. The tail has a well-developed flagellum, dark brown musculature, and translucent fins that may be amber in color with dark brown flecking.

Similar Species: The Green Treefrog is smaller and more slender; it is smooth-skinned and has white side stripes that are straight instead of jagged.

Overall Range: Found primarily on the Coastal Plain, from Virginia to Florida and west to Louisiana, with isolated populations in Tennessee, Kentucky, Maryland, and Delaware.

Range and Status on Delmarva: Very rare; small, isolated populations have been found on the Coastal Plain in southern New Castle and eastern Sussex Counties, Delaware, and eastern Kent, eastern Queen Anne's, and northern Caroline Counties, Maryland. This frog is listed as endangered in Delaware and Maryland and threatened in Virginia.

Habitat: Found only in moist Coastal Plain woodlands associated with medium to large, fishless or nearly fishless vernal pools (e.g., Delmarva Bays) or borrow pits. The warm months are spent in trees and shrubs. Winter months and dry weather are spent underground or in other moist, protected areas.

Voice: The advertisement call is a loud, houndlike bark, usually uttered from the surface of the breeding pool (rarely from vegetation just above the water). The call is produced through a single vocal sac. A rain call, sounding hoarser and somewhat weaker than the advertisement call, is sometimes produced on rainy nights as the frogs move from the trees toward the breeding pool.

Reproduction and Development: Barking Treefrogs breed in flooded vernal pools on warm humid nights from late April through July. Here the males, which greatly outnumber the females, attempt to attract mates by calling loudly while floating on the water's surface. If a female is receptive, amplexus ensues, with the male grasping the female just behind her front legs (axillary amplexus). The eggs can be laid either singly or in masses and, as with all other Delmarva frogs, are fertilized by the male as they are laid. The eggs hatch quickly into tiny tadpoles that metamorphose into froglets in six to nine weeks.

Remarks: The Barking Treefrog is the largest treefrog native to the United States and is primarily a frog of the southeastern part of the country. Until the 1980s the Barking Treefrog was thought to occur only as far north as Norfolk, Virginia (a population found in southern New Jersey in the 1950s was considered likely to have been introduced [Black and Gosner 1958]). However, in 1982 an adult female was found in Caroline County, Maryland (Anderson and Dowling 1982), and in 1984 a population of Barking Treefrogs was discovered in southern New Castle County, Delaware, by the authors (Arndt and White 1988; White 1987a). Populations have since been found by author Jim White and others in Kent, Queen Anne's, and Caroline Counties, Maryland, and Sussex County, Delaware. The Barking Treefrog populations currently on the Delmarva Peninsula, and formerly in southern New Jersey, are now believed to be remnants of a historically larger range of this species that once extended through much of the Middle Atlantic states.

Northern Spring Peeper   Plate 36
Pseudacris crucifer crucifer (Wied-Neuwied, 1838)

Other Names: Formerly classified as *Hyla crucifer crucifer*.
Description: 2.0 to 3.3 cm (0.8 to 1.3 in.); record 3.8 cm (1.5 in.).

     A small, smooth-skinned, relatively slender treefrog. The overall color is variable but is generally light tan to medium brown, sometimes almost pinkish. The most distinctive field mark is a large, brownish X on the back, although this pattern is often broken and not clearly evident. Darker lateral stripes are also present on the legs, and a dark V-shaped marking runs between the eyes on the top of the head. The belly is whitish. Males have a yellowish throat that turns dark, sometimes with yellow dots, during the breeding season. The tadpoles are small (up to about 3.5 cm [1.4 in.]), with a mostly greenish body that is sometimes flecked with gold and a whitish, iridescent belly. The tail fins are translucent and the upper fins are patterned with small, dark spots.
Similar Species: The New Jersey Chorus Frog is very similar, but it has 3 dark stripes extending down the back, a dark

lateral stripe running through the eye to the groin, and a light line on the upper lip. The Eastern Cricket Frog is slightly smaller and has shorter legs; rough, warty skin; and typically a dark triangular mark between the eyes.

Overall Range: Found from Nova Scotia to Georgia and west to Manitoba and eastern Texas.

Range and Status on Delmarva: Very common in all counties on the peninsula. Absent from the barrier islands.

Habitat: Largely a terrestrial frog, the Northern Spring Peeper is found in a variety of habitats, including deciduous, coniferous, and mixed deciduous-coniferous woodlands and old fields that are associated with shallow or vernal freshwater wetlands.

Voice: The advertisement call of the male is a very loud, high-pitched *peep,* ending in an upward slur. As many as 25 peeps per minute can be emitted by an individual male. The call is amplified through a single vocal sac that is round when inflated. The smaller the male, the higher the pitch of the call. Occasionally males give a short, high-pitched trill when another male approaches (i.e., an aggressive call) (Rosen and Lemon 1974).

Reproduction and Development: The Northern Spring Peeper is one of the first Delmarva frogs to begin calling each year, beginning in late February or March. Breeding choruses may continue to be heard through May. On mild rainy nights in late winter, the frogs migrate from their nonbreeding terrestrial sites to freshwater wetlands, where the males call from selected sites on the ground or on low vegetation. There is evidence that females tend to select males with loud, fast calls (Forester and Czarnowsky 1982). For those males successful in attracting a female, amplexus ensues, and the female then moves with the male to a suitable egg-laying site. The female lays some 200 to 1,200 eggs, depositing them singly on submerged vegetation (Hulse et al. 2001). The eggs hatch in one to two weeks, depending on water temperature. The tiny tadpoles metamorphose to froglets in two to three months and reach sexual maturity in one year (Delzell 1958).

Remarks: A chorus of Northern Spring Peepers is truly a harbinger of spring. Choruses can be heard on warm, rainy spring nights just about anywhere on the Delmarva Peninsula. Males can also be heard calling weakly from upland areas during late summer and fall and even on warm winter days.

Standing amid a large chorus of Northern Spring Peepers can be painful to the ears because of the loud, shrill quality of the calls. Despite their loud calls, however, individual frogs are sometimes difficult to see. Triangulation, as described in section III, is usually the best way to locate one.

New Jersey Chorus Frog
Plate 37

Pseudacris feriarum kalmi (Harper, 1955)

Description: 2.0 to 3.8 cm (0.8 to 1.5 in.).

A small, smooth-skinned, relatively slender treefrog with dark stripes. The background color is light brown to gray. Three dark, ragged, relatively thick stripes extend down the back from behind the eyes to the groin. These stripes are occasionally broken. A dark lateral stripe runs from the snout through the eye to the groin, and a light line is present on the upper lip. A dark, triangular mark is sometimes present between the eyes. The throat, chest, and belly are cream-colored, sometimes with a few dark markings. The tadpoles are small (up to about 3 cm [1.2 in.]), with a dark brown, bronze-flecked body, a bronze, iridescent belly, and translucent tail fins that have small, black spots.

Similar Species: The Northern Spring Peeper is very similar, but it lacks the light upper lip and has dark markings on the back that typically form an X shape. The Eastern Cricket Frog has shorter legs and rough, warty skin; it lacks the light upper lip and dark stripes. The Upland Chorus Frog *(Pseudacris feriarum feriarum),* which replaces the New Jersey Chorus Frog immediately to the north and west of Delmarva, is very similar; but the stripes on the back are thinner and are broken into dashes or spots.

Overall Range: Found on the Coastal Plain from Staten Island, New York, to the southern tip of the Delmarva Peninsula.

Range and Status on Delmarva: Common throughout the Coastal Plain, but absent from the Piedmont except in the Susquehanna River watershed. On the barrier islands, it has been recorded only from Assateague Island. Recorded in all counties.

Habitat: Found in a variety of moist habitats, including grassy floodplains and wet woodlands that have shallow, usually vernal, wetlands in which they breed.

Voice: The advertisement call is a ratchety trill that rises in pitch, sounding similar to but much louder than the sound produced by scraping a fingernail over a comb from the coarse to the fine teeth. The call is produced through a single vocal sac.

Reproduction and Development: The New Jersey Chorus Frog is one of the first Delmarva frogs to breed each year, often beginning in mid-February. Breeding usually reaches its peak in March but may continue into May. Males and females gather at breeding sites that include vernal pools, ditches, wooded swamps, and freshwater marshes. The males call loudly day and night from the water's surface or from floating vegetation and debris. Females deposit their eggs in delicate masses that are attached to submerged vegetation (Wright and Wright 1949). The tadpoles develop rapidly, metamorphosing in the late spring.

Remarks: Except during the breeding season, the New Jersey Chorus Frog is rarely encountered. Both the recently transformed froglets and the adults apparently move away from the breeding areas by late spring and are rarely seen or heard until the following year. Even during the breeding season, seeing a calling New Jersey Chorus Frog can be quite challenging for two reasons. First, the frog's ventriloquistic ability often makes determining the frog's exact location difficult. Second, this frog tends to stop calling when approached closely, except during ideal breeding conditions like warm, rainy nights. Triangulation, as described in section III, is the best method for locating a calling New Jersey Chorus Frog.

Some authorities consider the New Jersey Chorus Frog to be a distinct species, *Pseudacris kalmi* (Hulse et al. 2001).

Narrow-mouthed Toads (Family Microhylidae)

Members of the Family Microhylidae occur in many parts of the world (i.e., North, Central, and South America; Africa; Asia; and Australia), with 1 subfamily (Microhylinae) occurring in North America. Narrow-mouthed Toads of the Subfamily Microhylinae are small, stout-bodied frogs with pointed heads and a characteristic fold of skin across the back of the head. Most are semifossorial and are rarely encountered in the open except at breeding sites. They typically prey on ants or termites. This subfamily is represented on the Delmarva Peninsula by 1 species, the Eastern Narrow-mouthed Toad.

Eastern Narrow-mouthed Toad **Plate 38**
Gastrophryne carolinensis (Holbrook, 1836)

Other Names: Eastern Narrowmouth Toad.
Description: 2.3 to 3.3 cm (0.9 to 1.3 in.); record 3.8 cm (1.5 in.).

A small, stout, short-legged frog with a narrow, pointed head. The overall color is variable, with the top of the head and back usually gray, brown, or reddish. Some individuals have a broad, dark area on the back that is flanked by wide, lighter-colored stripes, but this is obscured by patches or mottling in other individuals. The belly is heavily mottled. Unique among Delmarva frogs is the presence of a fold of skin across the back of the head. The tadpoles are small (up to about 3 cm [1.2 in.]), dorsoventrally flattened, and unique in having a soft rather than horny oral disc and a single spiracle located at the middle rear of the body. There are large, pale blotches on the sides, belly, and parts of the tail, and the margins of the tail musculature are dark.
Similar Species: The Eastern American Toad and Fowler's Toad have very warty skin and prominent parotoid glands behind the eyes and lack the fold of skin behind the head. The Eastern Spadefoot has a much rounder snout, bulging eyes with vertical pupils, and a sickle-shaped spade on each hind foot and also lacks the fold of skin behind the head.

Overall Range: Found from the southern Delmarva Peninsula to the Florida Keys and west to Missouri and Texas.

Range and Status on Delmarva: Extremely rare; found only in the southern half of the peninsula, where it reaches the northern edge of its overall range. Records exist from Dorchester, Somerset, and Worcester Counties, Maryland, and Northampton County, Virginia. Absent from the barrier islands. Breeding activity has not been confirmed on Delmarva in more than twenty-five years. It is listed as endangered in Maryland.

Habitat: Little is known about the habitat requirements of this species on Delmarva. The only recent records were near a cypress swamp along a tributary of the Pocomoke River. In other parts of its range, the Eastern Narrow-mouthed Toad can be found in a variety of open and forested habitats associated with freshwater wetlands such as floodplains, marshes, bald cypress swamps, and vernal pools. This species is fossorial, spending most of its time in underground burrows or under logs, bark, or other debris.

Voice: The advertisement call is similar to the bleat of a lamb, lasting for approximately one-half to three seconds, and is produced through a single vocal sac.

Reproduction and Development: Eastern Narrow-mouthed Toads are explosive breeders, congregating in shallow wetlands on warm, very rainy nights in late spring or summer. In more southerly parts of its range it often congregates in large numbers (Martof et al. 1980; Wright 1932); however, on Delmarva choruses may be composed of only a few males due to low population levels. The males call loudly, usually from a vertical position in the water, holding onto vegetation with their front legs. Amplexus is similar to most other species of Delmarva frogs, with the male mounting the female from behind, usually grasping her just behind her front legs (axillary amplexus). Eggs are deposited in strands that float on the surface as a thin film, sometimes creating dense mats. Development is rapid, with eggs hatching within four days. The tadpoles metamorphose after four to six weeks and sexual maturity is reached at two years. (Anderson 1954; Wright 1932.)

Remarks: This species specializes in eating ants but also eats termites and other small insects. The fold of skin at the back of the head can be extended forward over the eyes, apparently to protect them from biting insects (Conant 1975). Surveying for the presence of this species is difficult because of its sporadic breeding episodes and fossorial nature.

True Frogs (Family Ranidae)

The Family Ranidae is the largest and most widespread frog family, with more than 700 species distributed on all continents except Antarctica (Pough et al. 2001). Frogs in this family are variable in size, but many are very large, including the largest frog in the world, the Goliath Frog *(Conraua goliath)* from Africa, which can reach a snout-vent length of about 30.5 cm (12 in.). Representatives of this family in the United States all belong to the Subfamily Raninae. The external appearance of these frogs is usually what people think of as a typical frog: a large head with a wide mouth; long, powerful hind legs with webbed feet; and a body color of some shade of green or brown. Many species have *dorsolateral ridges* (a glandular fold or ridge along each side of the back); also many have conspicuous tympanums (eardrums). Breeding males have enlarged thumbs and front legs. Many species are semiaquatic, spending much of their adult lives in or near water. There are 6 species on the Delmarva Peninsula, all in the genus *Rana.*

American Bullfrog   **Plate 39**
Rana catesbeiana (Shaw, 1802)

Other Names: Bullfrog.
Description: 8.9 to 15.2 cm (3.5 to 6.0 in.); record 20.3 cm (8.0 in.).
       A large to very large, robust frog, the American Bullfrog is Delmarva's largest frog. The back and upper sides can be various shades of green, brown, or almost black, sometimes with dark blotches or spots. The face

is usually bright green. Dorsolateral ridges are lacking, but a distinctive short fold of skin begins just behind the eye and curves down immediately behind the tympanum. The belly is whitish with dark mottling. Adult males have a yellowish throat and tympanums that are larger than their eyes; females have a whitish throat, and their tympanums are equal to their eyes in diameter. The tadpoles are very large (often more than 13 cm [5.1 in.]), greenish brown overall, with well-defined black spots on the back and the upper half of the tail and a yellowish belly.

Similar Species: The Green Frog is similar but has well-defined dorsolateral ridges.

Overall Range: Found from Nova Scotia to Florida and west to Wisconsin and New Mexico. Introduced westward to California and elsewhere, including Mexico, Cuba, and Jamaica.

Range and Status on Delmarva: Common throughout most of the peninsula; rare to absent on the barrier islands (recorded from only one location on Assateague Island). Recorded in all counties.

Habitat: Found in or near many types of permanent to semipermanent bodies of water, including streams, rivers, ponds, freshwater marshes, and swamps. This species is especially common in man-made ponds such as millponds, backyard ponds, and golf course ponds.

Voice: The advertisement call is the familiar, resounding, deep-throated "jug-o'-rum" call. The sound is produced by a single internal vocal sac that inflates to form a bulge under the chin. The alarm call is a loud, abrupt shriek.

Reproduction and Development: Breeding occurs over an extended period from midspring through the summer. Breeding males set up and defend territories in the water, where they call and attempt to attract females. The larger males usually hold the choice territories and will defend them by vigorously fighting off challenging males. When a female approaches, the male remains passive until she touches him, and then he swims behind her and clasps her just behind her front legs (axillary amplexus). The pair swims about in amplexus, searching for a place to deposit eggs. Up to 20,000 eggs are deposited by the female. The eggs form a thin, foamy sheet up to 2 feet or more in diameter on the water's surface. After the female completes egg deposition the male returns to his favorite calling spot and resumes defending his territory, attempting to attract another female. (Emlen 1968; Hulse et al. 2001; Ryan 1980; Walker 1946.)

The eggs often hatch in three to four days. The larval stage is long, with tadpoles reaching a length of up to 15 cm (6 in.) before transforming, usually late in the following summer but sometimes not until the third summer. It takes several more years for the froglets to reach sexual maturity. (Hulse et al 2001; Hunter et al. 1992.)

Remarks: American Bullfrogs have voracious appetites and will feed on just about any animal that they can capture and swallow, including other frogs, small snakes, turtles, mammals, birds, and various invertebrates. This frog is the only amphibian in the United States that is commonly hunted and eaten. The frog legs are considered a delicacy by many, and Delaware, Maryland, and Virginia each have hunting seasons for American Bullfrogs. For this culinary reason the American Bullfrog has been introduced to areas outside its natural range, establishing nonnative breeding populations in much of the western United States. Some scientists believe that these nonnative American Bullfrogs, because of their voracious appetites, have contributed to the decline of several western species of amphibians and small reptiles.

Northern Green Frog   **Plate 40**
Rana clamitans melanota (Rafinesque, 1820)

Other Names: Green Frog.
Description: 5.8 to 8.9 cm (2.3 to 3.5 in.); record 10.9 cm (4.3 in.).

A medium- to large-sized frog that, despite its name, is highly variable in color. The back is usually green, brown, or bronze, often with dark spots or blotches. A few metallic blue individuals have also been found on Delmarva (Arndt 1977a; J. White personal observation).

The side of the face below and in front of the eye is usually green. A pair of distinct dorsolateral ridges extends two-thirds of the way down the back. The belly is white. Adult males, unlike the females, have bright yellow throats and tympanums that are larger than the eyes. The tadpoles are large (up to about 10 cm [3.9 in.]) and are very similar in color to those of the American Bullfrog (see previous species account) except that the tail usually has more dark blotches.

Similar Species: The American Bullfrog has a wider head and lacks dorsolateral ridges. The Carpenter Frog also lacks dorsolateral ridges and has 4 light stripes on the back and sides. The Southern Leopard Frog and Pickerel Frog have dorsolateral ridges that extend to the groin and usually have distinct spotting. The Wood Frog has a dark facial mask.

Overall Range: Found from the Canadian maritime provinces to South Carolina and west to southwestern Ontario and Oklahoma.

Range and Status on Delmarva: Common throughout most of the peninsula; recorded in all counties. Rare to absent on the barrier islands; recorded only on Assateague Island.

Habitat: Found in and around a variety of shallow freshwater habitats, including freshwater marshes, swamps, spring seeps, vernal pools, ditches, permanent ponds, and streams.

Voice: The advertisement call is a single explosive note that sounds similar to the plucking of a loose banjo bass string. Sometimes the males give this note 2 or 3 times in rapid succession, each note getting progressively quieter. The call is produced through a pair of internal vocal pouches.

Reproduction and Development: Breeding begins in late April or May and extends well into the summer. The males set up, defend, and call from one or more territories that are maintained throughout the breeding season. These territories are usually some distance from other calling males. Females appear to seek out and select males according to the suitability of the male's territory for egg laying (possibly depending on the presence or absence of aquatic vegetation). The female initiates mating by approaching underwater and surfacing just in front of the male. She then slowly backs into him, stimulating the male to mount and clasp her just behind her front legs (axillary amplexus). The female then lays up to 5,000 eggs, which form a raftlike surface mass approximately 15 to 30 cm (6 to 12 in.) in diameter. The eggs hatch in less than one week. Tadpoles from eggs that are laid early in the season may metamorphose later in the summer, whereas tadpoles from later clutches usually overwinter as tadpoles and metamorphose during the second summer. (Hunter et al. 1992; Tyning 1990.)

Remarks: The Northern Green Frog is probably the most often encountered amphibian on the Delmarva Peninsula. It can be found in or near almost any freshwater habitat.

Pickerel Frog   Plate 41
Rana palustris (LeConte, 1825)

Description: 4.6 to 7.6 cm (1.8 to 3.0 in.); record 8.6 cm (3.4 in.).

A medium-sized frog with a light- to medium-brown ground color and dark brown, squarish blotches. A pair of distinct, light-colored dorsolateral ridges extend from behind the eyes to the groin. Between and parallel to these ridges are 2 rows of irregularly square, dark brown blotches. These blotches run together on some individuals. Additional squarish blotches are on the sides of the body, and dark brown bands cross the legs. The concealed surfaces of the hind legs are bright yellow to orange. The belly and throat can be plain whitish or mottled with dark pigment. Subadult frogs are often metallic in appearance. The tadpoles are large (up to about 8 cm [3.1 in.]), greenish with small, black dots above, and white underneath.

Similar Species: The Southern Leopard Frog is similar in general appearance, but the spots on the back are rounder and usually more randomly placed; it lacks the yellow orange coloration on the hind legs and has a distinctive light spot in the tympanum.

Overall Range: Found from the Canadian maritime provinces to South Carolina and west to Minnesota and eastern Texas.

Range and Status on Delmarva: Common throughout most of
the peninsula. Records are lacking from Northampton County,
Virginia. A single specimen has been documented from the
barrier islands from Wallops Island, Accomack County,
Virginia.

Habitat: Found in or near small streams, freshwater marshes,
bogs, and other freshwater habitats. After breeding,
individuals often disperse into floodplain meadows and other
moist, grassy areas. In winter this species is often found
hibernating in springhouses.

Voice: The advertisement call, produced through a pair of
lateral vocal sacs, is a slow, raspy, low-pitched snore lasting up
to two seconds. M. Given (personal communication) described
two aggressive calls emitted during territorial contests
between males: (1) a *snicker,* similar to the advertisement call
but extremely short in duration, and (2) a *growl,* which sounds
like a slow series of clicks. In addition, some calls are made
underwater although the purpose of this is not fully
understood.

Reproduction and Development: Pickerel Frogs migrate to
breeding areas between mid-March and early April. Most
males set up calling territories that they apparently use
throughout much of the breeding season, which may last
through May (M. Given personal communication). The male
clasps the female just behind her front legs (axillary
amplexus), apparently sometimes holding on for days after the
eggs are laid. Each female lays up to 3,000 eggs in a clear,
globular mass that is attached to a submerged stick or aquatic
vegetation. The eggs typically hatch in less than two weeks,
and the tadpoles take approximately three months to
transform. It is thought that sexual maturity is reached in the
third year. (Green and Pauley 1987; Wright 1914.)

Remarks: Pickerel Frogs are often encountered in the
summer, hopping mouselike along footpaths in moist meadows.
The skin secretions of this species are apparently toxic or
distasteful to many predators, including some snakes and
mammals. Because the toxins are also poisonous to other frogs,
Pickerel Frogs should never be kept in enclosures with other
species of frogs.

Southern Leopard Frog   **Plate 42**
Rana sphenocephala utricularia (Harlan, 1825)

Description: 5.1 to 8.9 cm (2.0 to 3.5 in.); record 12.7 cm (5.0 in.).

A medium- to large-sized, long-legged, relatively pointy-nosed frog with a dorsal ground color of green and/or brown and a white belly. Dark, round to oval spots form irregular rows on the dorsal surfaces of the body and legs. A pair of distinct, often yellowish dorsolateral ridges extend from behind the eyes to the groin. There is a distinctive light spot in the center of the tympanum. The tadpoles can be large (up to about 8.5 cm [3.3 in.]), green to brown above, iridescent white underneath, and marked with dark spots and lines on the tail.

Similar Species: The Pickerel Frog has less-rounded spots and bright yellow-orange coloration under the hind legs and lacks a spot in the tympanum. The Carpenter Frog also lacks the spot in the tympanum and has 4 distinct, yellowish brown stripes on the back and sides. The Northern Leopard Frog (not found on Delmarva) lacks the central spot in the tympanum and is larger overall with a wider head.

Overall Range: Found from Long Island to the Florida Keys and west to Kansas and Texas.

Range and Status on Delmarva: Common throughout the Coastal Plain, including some of the barrier islands such as Assateague and Chincoteague Islands. Absent from the Piedmont.

Habitat: Found in or near freshwater and brackish water habitats, including marshes, vernal pools, freshwater impoundments, and Atlantic white cedar and bald cypress swamps. In the summer this frog often frequents grassy meadows and fields that are sometimes a considerable distance from the water.

Voice: The calls of this frog can be confusing, partly because several different vocalizations are often made in a single chorus. The advertisement call is typically a series of 3 to 5 loud clucks or chuckles, produced through a pair of lateral vocal sacs. This call is sometimes followed by a low growl that is reminiscent of the sound made when two balloons are rubbed together. The chuckle-like call of this frog can sometimes be difficult to distinguish from the call of the Wood Frog, especially in colder water, where the Southern Leopard Frog may only produce 2 or 3 clucks. Some calls are also made underwater, although their purpose is not yet understood.

Reproduction and Development: Southern Leopard Frogs breed in both temporary and permanent wetlands, primarily in late February through April, but they can also be heard calling in late spring or summer and sometimes even in the fall. As in most other frog species, the male grasps the female behind her front legs (axillary amplexus), stimulating her to lay eggs. The females lay firm, round to oblong egg masses containing several hundred to more than 1,000 eggs attached to submerged vegetation. The females often gather in groups during egg laying, creating a large aggregation of egg masses. The eggs hatch in one or two weeks, depending on water temperature, and about two to three months later the tadpoles metamorphose into brightly colored (often metallic-looking) froglets. (Hulse et al. 2001; Martof et al. 1980.)

Remarks: In late winter and early spring, Southern Leopard Frogs often form large breeding aggregations in freshwater impoundments and wetlands near the Delaware and Chesapeake Bays. Frogs in these large, loud choruses usually emit only a 2-note chuckle call along with a growl call. Southern Leopard Frogs are also sometimes heard calling on unusually warm days in autumn.

Wood Frog   **Plate 43**
Rana sylvatica (LeConte, 1825)

Description: 3.6 to 7.1 cm (1.4 to 2.8 in.); record 8.4 cm (3.3 in.).

A small to medium-sized, brownish frog with a distinctive dark brown mask. The top of the head, back, and sides are variably brownish, ranging from tan, to pinkish or reddish brown, to very dark brown. A dark brown mask on the side of the head extends from in front of the eye, back over the tympanum, to the rear of the jaw. This mask is bordered on the bottom by a light-colored line along the upper lip. A pair of prominent dorsolateral ridges is present. The belly is light, and the throat sometimes has dark spotting. The upper surfaces of the legs usually have dark crossbars. Adult males are smaller than females and often darker in coloration, especially during breeding season. The tadpoles are medium-sized (up to about 5 cm [2 in.]); the upperside is dark greenish brown with fine gold flecks, and the underside is pale iridescent. The tail musculature is paler than the body, and the upper tail fin is relatively high and may have small, black spots.

Similar Species: Very dark Northern Green Frogs and Southern Leopard Frogs may resemble Wood Frogs at first glance, but neither has the dark mask.

Overall Range: Found from Labrador to Virginia and west to Alaska and the southern Appalachian Mountains.

Range and Status on Delmarva: Fairly common throughout most of the peninsula, on both the Piedmont and the Coastal Plain. Records are lacking from Northampton County, Virginia, and only one record exists from Accomack County, Virginia, where this species reaches the southern limit of its range along the Atlantic coast. Absent from the barrier islands.

Habitat: Found in moist deciduous or mixed deciduous-coniferous woodlands with associated vernal pools or freshwater marshes. Often found a considerable distance from the water.

Voice: The advertisement call is an abrupt *cluck* that is repeated 1 to 5 times, sounding somewhat like a quacking duck. This call is produced through paired, lateral vocal sacs. The Wood Frog call does not carry very far, but large choruses can be fairly loud on windless nights. The male's release call is a quiet *chirp*.

Reproduction and Development: Wood Frogs are relatively explosive breeders, typically limiting the majority of their breeding to a few days and nights in February or March, returning soon thereafter to the woodlands. On unusually warm (above 50°F), often rainy days and nights in late winter, males congregate in flooded vernal pools and freshwater marshes and call while floating on the water surface. Receptive females enter the wetland and are quickly approached by males. Sometimes a female is engulfed by several eager males at once, creating a frenzied "mating ball," which occasionally results in the drowning of the female. During the peak of these mating frenzies, males attempt to mate with anything that swims nearby, including other male Wood Frogs, and occasionally other types of frogs or salamanders. A lucky male will succeed in clasping a female just behind the front legs (axillary amplexus) and will hold on tightly as the female swims around looking for a place to deposit her eggs. Some 500 to 3,000 eggs are deposited in clear masses about 7 to 13 cm (3 to 5 in.) in diameter; these are usually attached to sticks or other vegetation just under the water's surface (Green and Pauley 1987; Hulse et al. 2001). Often many females deposit their eggs in the same general location within the pool, creating large conglomerations of egg masses.

The eggs hatch in two to three weeks, and the tadpoles metamorphose about one and a half to two months later. During dry years it is not uncommon for many tadpoles to perish before metamorphosis as their pools dry prematurely. Recently transformed froglets leave their pools and make their way to moist upland woodlands. Maturity is reached in two years for males and three for females (Green and Pauley 1987).

Remarks: The range of the Wood Frog extends further north than any other North American amphibian or reptile. This species can actually withstand the complete freezing of its body. Author Jim White has found individuals that were frozen solid—their bodies as hard as ice and displaying a bluish tint—and has seen them become active after a slow thawing. Its tolerance for cold temperatures enables the Wood Frog to be one of the earliest frog species to breed on the Delmarva Peninsula each year.

Anyone interested in natural history should witness a breeding congregation of Wood Frogs. It is truly one of the most spectacular experiences that a nature watcher can have.

Carpenter Frog
Rana virgatipes (Cope, 1891)

Plate 44

Description: 4.1 to 6.6 cm (1.6 to 2.6 in.).

A medium-sized frog with brown head, body, and legs and 4 distinct, yellowish brown stripes on the back and sides. No dorsolateral ridges are present. The belly and throat are usually light-colored with dark mottling. A light line is present along the upper lip. The tadpoles are large (up to about 9 cm [3.5 in.]), with a brownish body speckled underneath with white. The tail has a dark stripe through the middle of the musculature and translucent fins that are distinctly marked with longitudinal rows of dark spots that often fuse to create dark stripes.

Similar Species: Northern Green Frogs and young American Bullfrogs are somewhat similar but lack the yellowish stripes. Dark Southern Leopard Frogs sometimes resemble Carpenter Frogs but have a light spot in the middle of the tympanum and only show 2 stripes on the body rather than 4.

Overall Range: Found on the Coastal Plain from New Jersey to extreme northern Florida.

Range and Status on Delmarva: Rare; found in isolated populations on the Coastal Plain. Records exist for Kent and Sussex Counties in Delaware, and Queen Anne's, Talbot, Caroline, Dorchester, Wicomico, and Worcester Counties in Maryland. However, field investigations in the 1990s indicate that the populations reported historically in Talbot County may have been extirpated, possibly because of habitat degradation (Given 1999). Absent from the barrier islands.

Habitat: Associated with acidic boggy or grassy freshwater wetlands, including Delmarva Bays and sphagnum bogs.

Voice: The advertisement call, produced through paired lateral vocal sacs, is a loud, double-noted *clack-clack* emitted by males up to 10 times in succession. From a distance the call resembles the sound of carpenters hammering on wood. M. Given (1987) identified 5 additional calls: 3 aggressive calls and 1 release call emitted by males, and 1 chirp note produced by courting females.

Reproduction and Development: Mating and egg laying take place from April through July. M. Given (1987, 1988a, 1993a) found that males establish and defend calling territories in shallow wetlands, usually in areas with partly submerged shrubs. Males defend their territories with upright posturing displays, aggressive vocalizations, and physical combat. Combat bouts consist of brief wrestling matches during which the males lock their front legs and attempt to mount each other in an amplexus-like embrace. These physical encounters may be accompanied by growl-like, aggressive calls. An interested female will approach a male, sometimes communicating with him by emitting a chirplike call, a behavior apparently unique among Delmarva's frog species. If mating ensues, the female deposits as many as 600 eggs in an oblong mass attached to submerged vegetation. The eggs hatch in about one week, depending on the water temperature (M. Given personal communication). The tadpoles are large and can grow to more than 8.8 cm (3.5 in.) in length before metamorphosing approximately one year after hatching.

Remarks: Although readily heard, this species is secretive and can be difficult to see or capture. Carpenter Frogs appear to thrive in wetlands that are too acidic for other species of the genus *Rana* (Given 1999). This species is apparently declining on Delmarva, possibly because of the neutralization of many historically acidic wetlands by agricultural runoff. Given (1999) has hypothesized that as a wetland becomes less acidic, more aggressive species of frogs, including the Northern Green Frog, are able to colonize and eventually displace the Carpenter Frog.

Reptiles (Class Reptilia)

The fossil record suggests that the first true reptiles evolved in the early Pennsylvanian period, about 300 million years ago. Reptiles were the first group of vertebrates to be able to live completely terrestrial lives. Although not all reptiles live on land, almost all species lay eggs or give birth on dry land. They are able to do this because of an evolutionary innovation: the amniotic egg. The amniotic egg is a fluid-filled envelope that surrounds the embryo and provides it with all the basic needs for its development. This mode of reproduction eliminates the aquatic, free-living larval stage found in most amphibians. In addition, *oviparous* (i.e., egg-laying) reptiles have amniotic eggs that are encased in a leathery or hard shell that protects the embryo from desiccation, damage from being buried in nests, and attack from small predators or infectious microorganisms.

Another adaptation that facilitates terrestrial existence is the relatively impermeable, scale-covered skin of reptiles. This scaly covering protects reptiles from abrasions and other injuries caused by contact with dry land and also greatly reduces the loss of body fluids in a terrestrial environment.

Reptiles, like amphibians, are ectothermic vertebrates. All but a few very large species obtain the vast majority of their body heat directly from the rays of the sun or indirectly from their surroundings. They can control their body temperature by moving from one area to another, such as moving from sun to shade. With the exception of the seaturtles, all reptiles on Delmarva hibernate during the cold winter months, seeking shelter from freezing temperatures by crawling into crevices or by burrowing underground or into the substrate at the bottom of a wetland or an aquatic habitat.

Unlike amphibians, reptiles have no larval stage. Both juvenile and adult reptiles have lungs, and the juveniles resemble the adults in body form although their coloration can be very different. In addition, except for the Leatherback Seaturtle, all reptiles with limbs have claws on their feet.

Living reptiles comprise the following groups:
- Order Testudines: turtles

- Order Squamata: lizards, snakes, and amphisbaenians (a specialized group of burrowing squamates that does not occur in North America north of Florida)
- Order Crocodylia: alligators, crocodiles, and gharials
- Order Rhynchocephalia: tuatara (found only on small islands in New Zealand)

Many scientists now believe that birds—traditionally considered to be the separate Class Aves—are actually a group within the reptiles (Pough et al. 2001). Nevertheless, only the traditional reptile groups are covered in this book.

There are approximately 7,134 living reptile species worldwide: about 260 turtles, some 6,850 squamates, 22 crocodilians, and 2 tuatara (Pough et al. 2001). Although reptiles occur on all continents except Antarctica, the greatest diversity is found in temperate to tropical climates. Reptiles known to occur on the Delmarva Peninsula include 17 turtle, 4 lizard, and 19 snake species.

Turtles (Order Testudines)

The Order Testudines (and the term *turtle* as used in this book) refers to all turtle species including those commonly referred to as tortoises, terrapins, cooters, and sliders.[2]

Turtles are not easily confused with any other type of animal. All have a protective covering or shell consisting of a *carapace* (upper shell) and a *plastron* (lower shell) that are connected by a bony or cartilaginous bridge (fig. 10). In some species the plastron is hinged. The carapace is formed from numerous bones that are usually fused to each other and to the underlying vertebrae and ribs. In most species the bones of the carapace and plastron are covered with large scales called *scutes* (fig. 11).

Turtles are also unique in having an anapsid skull (without a temporal opening), considered the most primitive reptile skull type. The only other reptile orders that share this anapsid skull structure are extinct orders. Turtles are indeed an ancient life form: paleontologists have found some fossil turtles that are nearly 200 million years old.

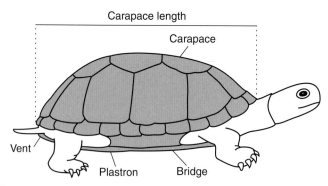

Figure 10. Generalized turtle

2. The term Chelonia is also often used for this order. Pough et al. (2001) explains that Chelonia is usually used to include only the extant (i.e., living) species, whereas Testudines includes both extant and extinct forms. This book uses Testudines because it is the term used by Conant and Collins (1998).

Another feature unique to turtles is that the shoulder and pelvic limb girdles are located inside the rib cage so that the limbs can be retracted inside the shell to a greater or lesser extent depending on the species. The limbs of terrestrial

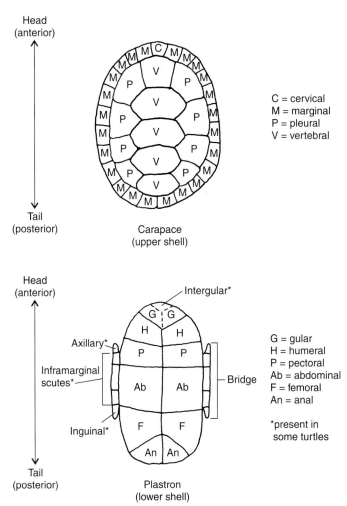

Head
(anterior)

Tail
(posterior)

Carapace
(upper shell)

C = cervical
M = marginal
P = pleural
V = vertebral

Head
(anterior)

Intergular*

Axillary*

Inframarginal
scutes*

Inguinal*

Bridge

Tail
(posterior)

Plastron
(lower shell)

G = gular
H = humeral
P = pectoral
Ab = abdominal
F = femoral
An = anal

*present in
some turtles

Figure 11. Turtle scutes

turtles are modified for walking, whereas the semiaquatic and aquatic turtles have varying degrees of webbing between the toes. Marine turtles have flattened limbs that serve as flippers. Most turtles have claws on the toes. Adult males typically have longer and thicker tails than females, and the vent is located beyond the edge of the carapace (fig. 12).

Except for the terrestrial Box Turtles in the genus *Terrapene* and tortoises in the Family Testudinidae, turtles are semiaquatic or aquatic animals. Most spend their entire lives in, or basking near, water (except at nesting time, when the females seek drier land). Most turtles are omnivorous, although with age some turtles' diets shift from omnivorous to herbivorous. Turtles do not have teeth but instead have a sharp, horny beak used for cutting or crushing.

Most turtles on Delmarva hibernate underwater through much of the colder months, taking refuge in the soft bottom of their wetland or aquatic habitat. One exception is the Eastern Box Turtle, which typically burrows on dry land in loose soil or decaying vegetation or hibernates in animal burrows. The seaturtles are another exception. These aquatic turtles generally migrate south to warmer waters for the winter, although some apparently hibernate on the ocean bottom (Ernst et al. 1994). Many turtles also burrow in the mud and become inactive during hot, dry summer weather (estivation). Like other reptiles, turtles have lungs and obtain oxygen from the air. However, many turtles also obtain oxygen from the water through the skin, throat lining, and terminal end of the digestive system (sacks in the cloaca), especially during hibernation and estivation (Halliday and Adler 1986).

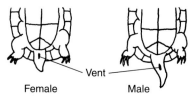

Figure 12. Tail length and location of vent in male and female turtles

Mating typically occurs in the spring, the fall, or both; it is preceded in many turtle species by courtship behavior that may include nudging, stroking, and/or biting of the female by the male. Internal fertilization of the eggs is accomplished when the male mounts the female and inserts his penis into her cloaca. All turtles lay their eggs on land. On Delmarva, between late May and late July, females typically lay their eggs in cavities that they dig in the soil or sand. Some species lay more than one clutch during the nesting season. There is no maternal care of the eggs or the hatchlings. It appears that in many turtles, including most on Delmarva, the temperature of the nest and eggs determines the sex of the hatchlings. In many turtle species low incubation temperatures produce males and higher temperatures produce females; in other species intermediate incubation temperatures produce males, whereas temperature extremes produce females. With the exception of an occasional Loggerhead Seaturtle, none of the various seaturtles (families Cheloniidae and Dermochelyidae) nest on Delmarva.

Hatching typically occurs in August or September on the Delmarva Peninsula. Hatchlings are small but grow rapidly for the first few years. Turtles are very long-lived, with many species documented to live twenty to forty years, and some, like the Eastern Box Turtle, sometimes living more than seventy-five years. Sexual maturity is reached in two to thirty years, depending on the species. Within each species, attainment of sexual maturity is more dependent on size and environmental conditions than on age. (Ernst et al. 1994.)

There are approximately 260 living species of turtles worldwide, belonging to 13 families (Pough et al. 2001). On the Delmarva Peninsula there are 17 species of turtles, representing 5 families: the Snapping Turtles (Family Chelydridae: 1 species); the Musk and Mud Turtles (Family Kinosternidae: 2 species); the Pond, Marsh, and Box Turtles (Family Emydidae: 9 species); the Seaturtles (Family Cheloniidae: 4 species); and the Leatherback Seaturtles (Family Dermochelyidae: 1 species).

Snapping Turtles (Family Chelydridae)

The Family Chelydridae is made up of only 3 genera, each containing only 1 species (Pough et al. 2001). These freshwater turtles are large-headed with powerful jaws and a long tail. One of the species, the Alligator Snapping Turtle, is probably the largest freshwater turtle in the world. Snapping Turtles are primarily aquatic and feed on living and dead animals and aquatic vegetation. Although they can swim, they usually walk along the bottom of their aquatic habitats. The head, neck, and limbs of these turtles cannot be retracted fully into the shell. There is 1 representative of this family on the Delmarva Peninsula: the Eastern Snapping Turtle.

Eastern Snapping Turtle   **Plate 45**
Chelydra serpentina serpentina (Linnaeus, 1758)

Other Names: Common Snapping Turtle; informally referred to as Snapper.
Description: 20.3 to 36.0 cm (8.0 to 14.0 in.); record 49.3 cm (19.4 in.).

A large, powerful turtle with a rough, brown to almost black carapace. The relatively flat carapace has distinct ridges and is strongly serrated along the back edge. The very large head is blunt with small eyes and a strongly hooked upper jaw. The neck is thick and long and is capable of extending from one-half to three-quarters of the length of the carapace. Strong, muscular limbs have webbed feet and heavy claws. The tail is long and is saw-toothed along the top, giving it a dinosaurian appearance. The skin on the head, neck, limbs, and tail is typically dark brown but sometimes tan or gray. The plastron is small, hingeless, cream-colored to light brown, and cross-shaped. Hatchlings have a dark plastron and 3 well-defined longitudinal ridges on the carapace that become smoother with age. Hatchlings also have a tail that is as long as, or longer than, the length of the carapace.
Similar Species: The Eastern Mud Turtle and Stinkpot are somewhat similar in appearance to the young Eastern Snapping

1. Deciduous Woodland, page 14

2. Maritime Woodland, page 14

3. Open Fields, page 14

4. Debris Pile, page 15

5. Coastal Dunes, page 15

6. Rocky Piedmont Stream, page 15

7. Coastal Plain Stream, page 15

8. Permanent Pond, page 15

9. Wooded Swamp, page 16

10. Freshwater Marsh, page 16

11. Delmarva Bays, aerial view showing both undisturbed and disturbed bays, page 16

12. Salt Marsh, page 18

R. S. SIMMONS

13. Eastern Hellbender *(Cryptobranchus alleganiensis alleganiensis),* specimen from Garrett County, Maryland, page 43

14. Spotted Salamander *(Ambystoma maculatum),* page 45

15. Marbled Salamander *(Ambystoma opacum),* male *(top)* and female *(bottom),* page 47

16. Eastern Tiger Salamander *(Ambystoma tigrinum tigrinum),* adult male, page 49

17. Eastern Tiger Salamander *(Ambystoma tigrinum tigrinum),* subadult, page 49

18. Red-spotted Newt *(Notophthalmus viridescens viridescens),* adult male, page 51

19. Red-spotted Newt *(Notophthalmus viridescens viridescens),* red eft stage, page 51

20. Northern Dusky Salamander *(Desmognathus fuscus),* page 55

21. Northern Two-lined Salamander *(Eurycea bislineata),* page 57

22. Long-tailed Salamander *(Eurycea longicauda longicauda)*, page 59

23. Four-toed Salamander *(Hemidactylium scutatum)*, page 60

24. Eastern Red-backed Salamander *(Plethodon cinereus)*, red-backed morph, page 61

25. Eastern Red-backed Salamander *(Plethodon cinereus),* lead-backed morph, page 61

26. Northern Slimy Salamander *(Plethodon glutinosus),* page 63

27. Eastern Mud Salamander *(Pseudotriton montanus montanus),* page 65

28. Northern Red Salamander *(Pseudotriton ruber ruber),*
page 67

29. Eastern Spadefoot *(Scaphiopus holbrookii),* page 73

30. Eastern American Toad *(Bufo americanus americanus),*
page 76

31. Fowler's Toad *(Bufo fowleri),* page 78

32. Eastern Cricket Frog *(Acris crepitans crepitans),* page 80

33. Gray Treefrog / Cope's Gray Treefrog *(Hyla versicolor / Hyla chrysoscelis),* page 82

34. Green Treefrog *(Hyla cinerea),* page 84

35. Barking Treefrog *(Hyla gratiosa),* page 86

36. Northern Spring Peeper *(Pseudacris crucifer crucifer),*
page 88

37. New Jersey Chorus Frog *(Pseudacris feriarum kalmi),* page 90

38. Eastern Narrow-mouthed Toad *(Gastrophryne carolinensis),* specimen from Georgia, page 92

39. American Bullfrog *(Rana catesbeiana),* page 94

40. Northern Green Frog *(Rana clamitans melanota),* page 96

41. Pickerel Frog *(Rana palustris),* page 98

42. Southern Leopard Frog *(Rana sphenocephala utricularia),* page 100

43. Wood Frog *(Rana sylvatica)*, page 101

44. Carpenter Frog *(Rana virgatipes)*, page 104

45. Eastern Snapping Turtle *(Chelydra serpentina serpentina)*, page 112

46. Eastern Mud Turtle *(Kinosternon subrubrum subrubrum)*, page 114

47. Stinkpot *(Sternotherus odoratus)*, page 116

48. Plastrons of Eastern Mud Turtle *(left)* and **Stinkpot** *(right)*, pages 114 and 116

49. Eastern Painted Turtle *(Chrysemys picta picta),* page 118

50. Spotted Turtle *(Clemmys guttata),* page 120

51. Wood Turtle *(Clemmys insculpta),* page 121

TURTLES

52. Bog Turtle *(Clemmys muhlenbergii),* page 123

53. Northern Map Turtle *(Graptemys geographica),* page 125

54. Northern Diamond-backed Terrapin *(Malaclemys terrapin terrapin),* page 127

55. Northern Red-bellied Cooter *(Pseudemys rubriventris),* young adult, page 129

56. Northern Red-bellied Cooter *(Pseudemys rubriventris),* old adult, page 129

57. Eastern Box Turtle *(Terrapene carolina carolina),* page 131

58. Red-eared Slider *(Trachemys scripta elegans)*, page 133

59. Loggerhead Seaturtle *(Caretta caretta),* specimen from the Gulf of Mexico, page 136

ANTHONY F. AMOS, THE UNIVERSITY OF TEXAS
MARINE SCIENCE INSTITUTE, PORT ARANSAS, TEXAS

60. Green Seaturtle *(Chelonia mydas),* specimen from Florida, page 140

R. S. SIMMONS

61. Atlantic Hawksbill Seaturtle *(Eretmochelys imbricata imbricata),* specimen from unknown location, page 142

ANTHONY F. AMOS, THE UNIVERSITY OF TEXAS
MARINE SCIENCE INSTITUTE, PORT ARANSAS, TEXAS

62. Kemp's Ridley Seaturtle *(Lepidochelys kempii),* specimen from the Gulf of Mexico, page 143

63. Leatherback Seaturtle *(Dermochelys coriacea),* specimen from Trinidad, page 145

64. Northern Fence Lizard *(Sceloporus undulatus hyacinthinus)*, page 150

65. Common Five-lined Skink *(Eumeces fasciatus)*, adult male, page 152

66. Common Five-lined Skink *(Eumeces fasciatus)*, juvenile, page 152

67. Broad-headed Skink *(Eumeces laticeps),* adult male, page 154

68. Little Brown Skink *(Scincella lateralis),* page 156

69. Red-bellied Watersnake *(Nerodia erythrogaster erythrogaster),* page 162

70. Common Watersnake *(Nerodia sipedon sipedon),* adult, page 164

71. Common Watersnake *(Nerodia sipedon sipedon),* juvenile, page 164

72. Queen Snake *(Regina septemvittata),* page 165

73. Northern Brownsnake *(Storeria dekayi dekayi),* adult female with young, page 167

74. Northern Red-bellied Snake *(Storeria occipitomaculata occipitomaculata),* page 168

75. Common Ribbonsnake *(Thamnophis sauritus sauritus),* page 170

SNAKES

SNAKES

76. Eastern Gartersnake *(Thamnophis sirtalis sirtalis),* page 171

77. Eastern Smooth Earthsnake *(Virginia valeriae valeriae),* adult female with young, page 172

78. Eastern Wormsnake *(Carphophis amoenus amoenus),* page 174

79. Ring-necked Snake *(Diadophis punctatus),* page 175

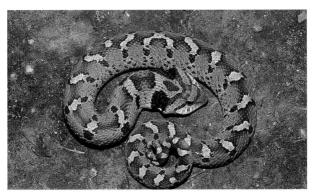

80. Eastern Hog-nosed Snake *(Heterodon platirhinos),* in defensive posture, page 177

81. Eastern Hog-nosed Snake *(Heterodon platirhinos),* color variations, page 177

R. S. SIMMONS

82. Northern Scarletsnake *(Cemophora coccinea copei),* specimen from Florida panhandle, page 180

83. Northern Black Racer *(Coluber constrictor constrictor),* adult, page 181

84. Northern Black Racer *(Coluber constrictor constrictor),* recently hatched juvenile, page 181

85. Cornsnake *(Elaphe guttata guttata),* page 183

86. Black Ratsnake *(Elaphe obsoleta obsoleta),* adult, page 185

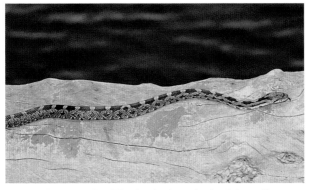

87. Black Ratsnake *(Elaphe obsoleta obsoleta),* juvenile, page 185

88. Eastern Kingsnake *(Lampropeltis getula getula),* page 187

89. Eastern Milksnake *(Lampropeltis triangulum triangulum),* page 188

90. Coastal Plain Milksnake *(Lampropeltis t. triangulum* x *Lampropeltis t. elapsoides),* page 188

91. Northern Rough Greensnake *(Opheodrys aestivus aestivus),* page 191

92. Copperhead *(Agkistrodon contortrix),* adult, specimen from northern Delaware, page 193

93. Copperhead *(Agkistrodon contortrix),* juvenile, specimen from southern Delaware, page 193

94. Eastern Six-lined Racerunner *(Cnemidophorus sexlineatus sexlineatus),* specimen from Georgia, page 197

95. Northern Pinesnake *(Pituophis melanoleucus melanoleucus),* specimen from Delaware but probably an escaped pet, page 198

96. Timber Rattlesnake *(Crotalus horridus),* specimen from western Maryland, page 199

Turtle, but they can be distinguished by their smooth, domed carapaces, hinged plastrons, and much shorter tails.

Overall Range: Found from Nova Scotia to extreme northern Florida and west to Saskatchewan and New Mexico. It has also been introduced farther west.

Range and Status on Delmarva: Very common throughout most of the peninsula, including several barrier islands. Recorded in all counties.

Habitat: Found in all freshwater and some brackish water habitats including streams, rivers, marshes, swamps, reservoirs, impoundments, millponds, Delmarva Bays, and other vernal wetlands.

Reproduction and Development: Mating occurs in the water between March and November. The males initiate and apparently force copulation with the females. During mating, the male grips the female's carapace with all four feet and conducts a series of violent muscular contractions of the legs, neck, and tail. The male may also bite the female on the head and neck while mating. Sperm may remain viable in the female for several years. (Ernst et al. 1994; Mitchell 1994.)

In late spring and early summer females leave the water to search for a nesting site, sometimes far from water. As the female searches, she may begin to dig several nest cavities, possibly testing the substrate before settling on a site. This behavior may also be a way to confuse nest predators. The female typically deposits 20 to 40 white, round eggs in a flask-shaped cavity that she then fills in with her hind feet. The eggs generally hatch in August and September. Sometimes the hatchlings overwinter in the nest, emerging the following spring. (Ernst et al. 1994.)

Remarks: The Eastern Snapping Turtle is by far the largest and most powerful reptile (aside from the seaturtles) on the Delmarva Peninsula. The adults are aggressive predators and scavengers and will eat anything that they can catch, including fish, amphibians, reptiles, birds, and mammals, as well as a wide variety of invertebrates. They also consume aquatic vegetation. Although Eastern Snapping Turtles sometimes eat young ducks and geese, their negative impact on waterfowl populations is probably exaggerated (Mitchell 1994). When out

---

Turtles   *113*

of the water this turtle aggressively defends itself against all predators or intruders, including humans. Its powerful jaws, extremely long neck, and lightning fast reflexes can inflict considerable damage to anything that comes within range. For this reason, people should avoid handling adult Eastern Snapping Turtles. In contrast, when encountered underwater this turtle is docile and very rarely attempts to bite.

The Eastern Snapping Turtle is commonly collected for human consumption, as its meat is the primary ingredient of the popular dish, snapper soup. Although this turtle appears to be doing very well on the peninsula, careful management of the resource will be needed to prevent overharvesting if the popularity of its meat ever increases.

Unlike most other aquatic turtles on Delmarva, Eastern Snapping Turtles are only rarely observed basking above the water surface.

Musk and Mud Turtles (Family Kinosternidae)

The Family Kinosternidae is an entirely New World family that contains 22 species (Pough et al. 2001). These semiaquatic turtles are poor swimmers; walking underwater or on land is the primary mode of locomotion. Members of this family usually have 23 marginal scutes (including the cervical scute) instead of 25, as in most other turtles. They also have musk glands in the skin under the carapace that release foul-smelling secretions. Two genera, *Kinosternon* and *Sternotherus,* are found in the United States and are each represented on Delmarva by 1 species. Turtles in these genera are small with a single- or double-hinged plastron that contains only 10 or 11 scutes instead of 12 or more, as in all other turtles.

Eastern Mud Turtle   **Plates 46, 48**
Kinosternon subrubrum subrubrum (Lacepède, 1788)

Description: 7.1 to 10.2 cm (2.8 to 4.0 in.); record 12.4 cm (4.9 in.).

A small turtle with a smooth, light to dark brown, domed carapace. The head and neck are brown with yellow mottling

or spotting (rarely with 2 yellow stripes). The limbs and tail are grayish brown. The yellowish brown plastron is double-hinged and nearly as long as the carapace. Hatchlings have a rough carapace with a mid-dorsal keel, and the carapace is very dark except for light spots along the marginal scutes. The plastron of young turtles is dark in the center and yellow, orange, or reddish near the sides.

Similar Species: The Stinkpot is very similar, but it has 2 yellowish stripes on each side of the head and a single-hinged plastron that is much smaller than the carapace.

Overall Range: Found from Long Island, New York, to northern Florida and west to Indiana and Mississippi.

Range and Status on Delmarva: Common on the Coastal Plain, including several barrier islands, but rare on the Piedmont. Recorded in all counties.

Habitat: Found in a variety of freshwater and brackish water habitats, including marshes with open water, slow-moving streams and rivers, millponds, Delmarva Bays, and ditches; it prefers shallow water.

Reproduction and Development: Courtship and mating typically take place in the spring, usually underwater but sometimes on land (Ernst et al. 1994). Courtship begins with the male, head extended, approaching the female from behind and touching or smelling her tail. The male then moves forward along her side nudging a musk gland on the bridge between the carapace and the plastron. If the female is unreceptive and moves away, the male may either give up or chase her, trying to bite her in the head region. If the female then becomes receptive, she stops and the male gently nudges her behind the eye. The male then mounts the female from above, grasping the rim of her carapace with all four feet. Intromission is accomplished when the male loops his tail around the female's tail and aligns his cloacal opening with hers. (Mahmound 1967.)

In spring or early summer the female lays up to 8 small, elliptical, pinkish white or bluish white eggs in a shallow nest in sand, loose soil, or rotting vegetation, or under logs or other debris. The eggs usually hatch in August or September, but the

hatchlings may remain at the nest until the following spring.
(Ernst et al. 1994.)

Remarks: Eastern Mud Turtles are semiaquatic and well
adapted for walking on land. They are frequently found moving
across upland areas, including roads, especially during or after
rain. In the water the preferred method of locomotion is
walking. They can be observed walking slowly on the bottoms
of aquatic habitats in search of food, which consists primarily
of invertebrates, carrion, and vegetation. Eastern Mud Turtles
are infrequently observed basking on logs.

A few Eastern Mud Turtles have been found in Sussex
County, Delaware, with 2 prominent yellow stripes on each
side of the head, as in the Stinkpot (J. McLaughlin personal
communication). These turtles appear to be very similar to the
Mississippi Mud Turtle, a subspecies found west of Alabama.
Further investigation may help determine the reason for, and
the extent of, this apparently aberrant form.

Stinkpot   Plates 47, 48
Sternotherus odoratus (Latreille, 1801)

Other Names: Common Musk Turtle; Eastern Musk
Turtle.
Description: 5.1 to 11.4 cm (2.0 to 4.5 in.); record
13.7 cm (5.4 in.).

A small, dark turtle with 2 yellowish stripes on
each side of the head that extend backward from the
snout, above and below the eyes. The smooth, highly domed
carapace is usually dark brown and is often covered with algae.
The skin on the head, neck, and limbs is typically grayish to
black. Barbels (fleshy protuberances) are present on the chin
and throat. The small plastron is yellowish to brown,
sometimes black, with a single hinge. Males have longer,
thicker tails, with a horny tip, and the male's plastron has
more soft flesh showing between the scutes than does the
female's. Hatchlings have a dark, rough carapace with a
prominent mid-dorsal keel and a light spot on the edge of each
marginal scute. The facial stripes are present from birth but
sometimes become obscured or faded in older turtles.

Similar Species: The Eastern Mud Turtle is similar, but it usually lacks the facial stripes and it has a large, doubly hinged plastron. The Eastern Snapping Turtle lacks the head stripes and has serrated marginal scutes.

Overall Range: Found from Maine to Florida and west to Wisconsin and Texas.

Range and Status on Delmarva: Common throughout the Delaware and Maryland portions of the peninsula, particularly on the Coastal Plain. Records are lacking from the barrier islands and from the Virginia counties on Delmarva (Mitchell and Reay 1999).

Habitat: Found in a wide variety of soft-bottomed, freshwater habitats including freshwater marshes, swamps, slow-moving streams, Delmarva Bays, and millponds. Usually encountered in shallow water.

Reproduction and Development: Courtship and mating take place in the water, primarily in the spring but also in the fall. Sperm from fall matings is apparently retained in the female until the following spring. Courtship and mating behaviors are as described for the Eastern Mud Turtle. Nesting occurs from midspring to midsummer, and several females often share the same nest site. Females lay 2 to 5 brittle, white, elliptical eggs in cavities or shallow depressions in loose soil, leaf litter, or decaying wood, often under logs, decaying stumps, or abandoned muskrat lodges. The eggs hatch from August to November. (Ernst et al. 1994.)

Remarks: The Stinkpot is named for the musky odor it produces when it is handled. The odorous secretions come from musk glands located underneath the carapace and are possibly used to warn off predators.

Stinkpots are active predators themselves and can be observed walking on the bottom of clear streams and ponds searching for small aquatic invertebrates, including insects, crayfish, worms, snails, and leeches. They also eat carrion and algae and other plants. This turtle is highly aquatic and is rarely found far from water. It is able to remain underwater for extended periods partly by reducing the amount of oxygen it consumes to one-eighth of what it consumes while above the surface (Root 1949). Basking, although relatively infrequently observed, is usually done on an overhanging branch, sometimes at a considerable height.

Pond, Marsh, and Box Turtles (Family Emydidae)

The Family Emydidae is a diverse group of turtles, containing approximately 10 genera and 35 species (Pough et al. 2001). Members of this family are found on all continents except Australia and Antarctica. Most of the species in this family are aquatic or semiaquatic and have relatively flat carapaces. An exception on the Delmarva Peninsula is the Eastern Box Turtle, which is terrestrial and has a domed carapace. All members of the Family Emydidae have a relatively large plastron, sometimes with a movable hinge. They also typically have small heads and tails, and many are habitual baskers. There are 9 species of the Family Emydidae represented on the Delmarva Peninsula.

Eastern Painted Turtle   Plate 49
Chrysemys picta picta (Schneider, 1783)

Description: 11.4 to 15.2 cm (4.5 to 6.0 in.); record 18.0 cm (7.1 in.).
    A small to medium-sized turtle with a smooth, flattened, oval carapace. The carapace is olive to almost black with large vertebral and pleural scutes that are aligned in rows across the back and have prominent, yellowish borders along the transverse seams. The marginal scutes have red markings that are especially bright on the underside. The plastron is yellowish, sometimes with a few dark spots. The head is black, with 2 bright yellow elongated spots on each side behind the eyes. Thin, yellow stripes on each side of the head extend back from the nose and eyes, becoming red on the neck. The limbs and tail are usually black with thin red stripes. Adult males have very long claws on the forelimbs. Hatchlings are similar in coloration to adults but have rounder shells.

Similar Species: Northern Red-bellied Cooters are much larger as adults, lack yellow spots on the side of the head, and have higher domed shells. Bog Turtles have a large, conspicuous, orange blotch on each side of the head and usually lack any light-colored markings on the carapace. Adult melanistic Red-eared Sliders may be confused with this species, but they lack yellow spots on the side of the head.

Overall Range: Found from Nova Scotia to Georgia. This subspecies does not extend west of the Appalachian Mountains.

Range and Status on Delmarva: Very common throughout most of the peninsula. Records are lacking from the barrier islands except for Assateague and Chincoteague Islands. Recorded in all counties.

Habitat: Found in all freshwater habitats that have soft bottoms, adequate basking sites, and ample aquatic vegetation. These habitats include rivers, streams, ponds, impoundments, open-water areas of marshes, vernal pools, and ditches. This turtle is especially common in millponds and slow-moving stretches of streams.

Reproduction and Development: Courtship and mating occur in the water, usually in the spring but sometimes in the summer or fall (Mitchell 1994). Courtship begins with the male pursuing and eventually overtaking the female. The male then turns and faces the female, stroking her face and neck with his enlarged forelimb claws. If receptive, she will stroke his forelimbs with hers. Between stroking episodes the male may swim off, apparently trying to entice the female to follow. This behavior may be repeated several times before the female sinks to the bottom and is mounted from behind by the male, who then initiates copulation. (Ernst et al. 1994.)

Females lay 1 or more clutches, each with 2 to 10 white to cream-colored, elliptical eggs, between late spring and early summer. The eggs are laid in flask-shaped cavities usually within 200 yards of the water. Hatching apparently occurs in August and September, but hatchlings often overwinter in the nest and emerge the following spring. (DePari 1996; Ernst et al. 1994; Mitchell 1994.)

Remarks: Eastern Painted Turtles are the most frequently observed turtles on the peninsula. It is not uncommon to observe many individuals of various sizes basking on logs and stumps or floating with their heads protruding above the water in areas of quiet freshwater. This species has been observed basking in every month of the year on Delmarva and has been seen active in ponds under the ice in the middle of winter (J. White personal observation). A few warm winter days are apparently enough to stir this turtle from hibernation.

Eastern Painted Turtles are omnivorous, feeding primarily on aquatic vegetation and invertebrates. Frogs and fish are also taken, probably mostly as carrion.

Spotted Turtle   Plate 50
Clemmys guttata (Schneider, 1792)

Description: 8.9 to 11.4 cm (3.5 to 4.5 in.); record 12.7 cm (5.0 in.).

A small turtle that typically has bright yellow spots on a smooth, dark brown to black carapace. In some individuals the spots are lacking or faded with age. The plastron is yellow to yellowish orange with large, black blotches toward the margins. The head, neck, and upper surfaces of the limbs are dark and have a variable number of scattered yellow or orange spots. The undersides of the limbs are orange to reddish. Males have brown eyes, a tan chin, and a slightly concave plastron. Females have orange eyes, a yellow chin, and a flat plastron. Hatchlings have a long tail and are typically black with a spotted carapace, although some hatchlings lack spots.

Similar Species: The Bog Turtle has a bright orange blotch on each side of the head and a slightly keeled carapace. The Eastern Painted Turtle has red markings on the marginal scutes and a striped head and neck.

Overall Range: Found on the Coastal Plain and Piedmont from southern Maine to central Florida and west through the Great Lakes region to Michigan and northeastern Illinois. Some isolated colonies occur just north and west of this range.

Range and Status on Delmarva: Uncommon on the Coastal Plain, although it may be locally common in some areas. Found on several barrier islands. Apparently very uncommon on the Piedmont. Recorded in all counties.

Habitat: Prefers shallow, quiet water habitats with a soft substrate and abundant aquatic vegetation in or near woodlands; found in bogs, swamps, marshes, wet meadows, slow-moving wooded streams, ditches, vernal pools, and pond edges. Relatively large populations can sometimes be found in open fields or young woodlands with natural or artificially created depressions that fill with water in late winter and spring.

Reproduction and Development: Courtship and mating occur in the spring. The courting male aggressively chases the female in shallow water and around wetland edges while trying to bite her head and limbs. If successful, the male mounts the female, grasping her carapace with his feet and sliding his tail under hers. Mating may last up to an hour. Egg laying takes place from late spring through early summer. Females may dig several test holes before depositing 1 to 8 white, elliptical eggs in a nest cavity often excavated in grass tussocks or mounds of sphagnum moss. Eggs hatch in August and September, but hatchlings may remain in the nest until the following spring. (Ernst et al. 1994; Mitchell 1994.)

Remarks: Spotted Turtles are most active in the spring. They often bask on logs, banks, and debris, especially in the morning on sunny spring days. They are rarely seen during the hot, dry summer months, and it is possible that they estivate during this period (Nemuras 1967a). Although this species is found fairly commonly in some parts of the peninsula, populations appear to be declining overall. The decline is largely due to habitat loss, as many of the wetland areas in which Spotted Turtles live have been destroyed for development. In addition, the Spotted Turtle is popular in the pet trade and is susceptible to overcollecting.

Wood Turtle   Plate 51
Clemmys insculpta (LeConte, 1830)

Description: 14.0 to 20.3 cm (5.5 to 8.0 in); record 23.4 cm (9.2 in.).

The Wood Turtle is a medium-sized turtle with a very rough, sculpted, brown carapace. Each large scute on the carapace has concentric grooves and ridges that rise upward in the center somewhat like a pyramid. These scutes often have yellow and black radiating lines that are especially noticeable when wet. The hingeless plastron is yellow, with a dark blotch on each scute, and is concave in males and flat in females. The head, neck, tail, and legs are black above and usually orange to red underneath. The forelegs in particular show bright orange to red coloration, as indicated by the colloquial name "redleg" (Conant 1975). Males have a longer, thicker tail and can grow slightly larger than females. Juveniles have flattened carapaces that lack the pyramidal-shaped scutes. They also lack the orange-red coloration of adults and have very long tails that may equal the length of the carapace. (Ernst et al. 1994; Hulse et al. 2001.)

Similar Species: The largely terrestrial Eastern Box Turtle can be distinguished by its hinged plastron and highly domed carapace. The Northern Diamond-backed Terrapin, which has a sculpted carapace, has large, webbed hind feet and is restricted to estuarine environments.

Overall Range: Found from Nova Scotia to Virginia and west through the Great Lakes region to Minnesota and Iowa.

Range and Status on Delmarva: Rare; established populations have been recorded only in the lower Susquehanna River watershed and at Elk Neck, Cecil County, Maryland. A single specimen found in Talbot County, Maryland (Norman 1939), and two specimens observed by author Jim White in New Castle County, Delaware, are likely escaped pets and are therefore not shown on the range map. Careful surveys are required to better establish the range and status of this species on Delmarva. It is listed as threatened in Virginia.

Habitat: Wood Turtles are semiaquatic and are usually found near streams or rivers, where they spend much of the early spring and fall. During the summer they are more terrestrial, venturing into floodplain meadows, shrub thickets, and even agricultural fields to feed, but they often return to the water at night on unseasonably cold summer days and during droughts (Kaufmann 1992a). Winter is spent hibernating underwater.

Reproduction and Development: Courtship and mating occur in the water in the spring and fall, with fall mating apparently the most productive. After some initial courtship behavior of head bobbing and swaying that may last an hour or more, the male becomes very aggressive, often forcing the female to mate. He suddenly mounts the female and grasps her underneath her carapace with his claws, holding on tenaciously, and then shakes her from side to side, sometimes for several hours. He then begins rubbing and thumping his plastron against her carapace, along with biting at her neck and shell. To initiate copulation the male curls his tail around the female's tail, aligning their vents. Males will aggressively drive off other males, and male-to-male combat is common. Many mountings apparently do not result in sperm transfer, and females may be mounted by males several times during one mating season. (Ernst et al. 1994; Kaufmann 1992b.)

Females lay from 3 to 13 eggs in late spring or early summer in open areas with loose soil and ample sun exposure. The female first prepares the nest by digging out a shallow depression with her forefeet before excavating the egg chamber with her hind feet. Hatchlings emerge in late summer or early fall. (Ernst et al. 1994; Hulse et al. 2001.)

Remarks: In many parts of its range, habitat destruction and deaths from motor vehicle hits appear to be hurting Wood Turtle populations. In addition, Wood Turtles are vulnerable to overcollecting because they are in relatively high demand in the illegal pet trade.

Bog Turtle   **Plate 52**
Clemmys muhlenbergii (Schoepff, 1801)

Other Names: Muhlenberg's Turtle.
Description: 7.6 to 8.9 cm (3.0 to 3.5 in.); record 11.4 cm (4.5 in.).

A small, dark turtle with a conspicuous, yellowish orange to reddish blotch on each side of the head, often extending toward the top of the head. The moderately domed carapace is brown to black, sometimes with faint reddish blotches that radiate out from the center of each scute. The plastron is dark brown to black, often irregularly marked with yellow. The skin is brown and may be mottled with orange or red. Hatchlings are similar in appearance to the adults except that the carapace usually has a conspicuous keel and the scutes are rougher. Older turtles typically develop very smooth carapaces.

Similar Species: The Spotted Turtle can be very similar, but it has numerous small, yellow or orange spots rather than large blotches on the head and neck, and it usually has small, yellowish spots on the carapace. The Eastern Painted Turtle has a flatter carapace with red markings on the marginal scutes and also lacks the large, yellowish orange to reddish head blotches.

Overall Range: Found from New York to extreme northern Georgia in disjunct populations.

Range and Status on Delmarva: Rare; found only in a dozen or so isolated populations in New Castle County, Delaware, and Cecil County, Maryland, both on the Piedmont and the Coastal Plain. This turtle may possibly occur in other counties on the peninsula but may not have been encountered because of its secretive nature. It is listed as endangered in Delaware and Virginia and threatened in Maryland.

Habitat: The Bog Turtle prefers soft-bottomed, spring-fed, freshwater wetlands with constantly flowing, slow-moving, shallow water (Arndt 1977b, 1986), including sphagnum bogs, very wet meadows, and large, open, spring-fed marshes. Often these wetlands occur on floodplains along streams and rivers, including the upper reaches of tidal creeks.

Reproduction and Development: Mating occurs in May or early June in shallow water or on land. During courtship the male circles the female, probing her tail and cloacal region with his snout and sometimes biting her neck and head. If the female is receptive, the male mounts her carapace and initiates copulation. Nesting occurs in June or early July. A shallow nest is made in moss or loose soil on slightly elevated sites, such as tussocks of vegetation within the wetland. Up to 6 elliptical, white eggs are laid and typically hatch in August and September. Some hatchlings spend the winter in the nest, emerging the following spring. (Arndt 1977b; Ernst et al. 1994; Mitchell et al. 1991; Nemuras 1967b; Zappalorti 1976, 1978.)

Remarks: The Bog Turtle is rarely seen in the wild because of both its secretive nature and the scarcity of suitable habitat. Habitat destruction and collecting for the pet trade are thought to be responsible for its declining numbers. In 1997 the Bog Turtle was designated as threatened under the U.S. Endangered Species Act, making it a crime for anyone to capture or harm the turtle or to transport it without special permits. The Bog Turtle is the only federally protected reptile species that nests regularly on Delmarva.

Bog Turtles are largely subterranean, spending a lot of time burrowing in the mud out of view (Arndt 1977b). Although they do bask frequently on tussocks or in shallow rivulets, they rarely expose the entire body to the sun at one time and they burrow quickly into the mud when danger threatens.

Northern Map Turtle   Plate 53
Graptemys geographica (LeSueur, 1817)

Other Names: Common Map Turtle.
Description: females 17.8 to 27.4 cm (7.0 to 10.8 in.); males 8.9 to 16.0 cm (3.5 to 6.3 in.).

A moderately large turtle with an olive to brownish carapace that is patterned with yellow reticulated lines loosely resembling a topographic map. The carapace is moderately keeled and the posterior edge is serrated. The underside of the marginal scutes is yellowish, with dark, circular patterns. The plastron is plain yellowish. The dark greenish head, neck, and limbs are heavily marked with yellow stripes, and a yellow spot is located behind each eye. The jaw surfaces are wide, smooth, and light-colored, giving the appearance of big lips. Adult females are much larger overall and have proportionally larger heads than males. Adult males have much longer claws on the forelimbs. Hatchlings are more boldly marked than adults and have

---

strongly keeled carapaces and dark borders on the plastral scutes.

Similar Species: The Northern Diamond-backed Terrapin lacks the yellow stripes and yellow spots on the head and does not have a serrated posterior edge of the carapace. It also lives in brackish or salt water rather than freshwater. The Northern Red-bellied Cooter has an unkeeled carapace and is typically much darker in overall appearance. The Eastern Painted Turtle has an unkeeled carapace and red markings on the marginal scutes.

Overall Range: Found from southern Quebec to central Alabama and west to Minnesota and Arkansas. There are also scattered colonies east of this range in New York, New Jersey, Pennsylvania, and Maryland.

Range and Status on Delmarva: Relatively common in the Susquehanna River and at the mouths of its larger tributaries in Cecil County, Maryland. Individuals occasionally seen in the upper Chesapeake Bay and Northeast River probably originated from the Susquehanna populations. Not found elsewhere on the peninsula. This turtle is listed as endangered in Maryland.

Habitat: On the Delmarva Peninsula the Northern Map Turtle is found in the freshwater portions of large rivers and the mouths of their tributaries. Adult turtles are more often observed in deep, relatively slow-moving water where there are ample basking sites (e.g., rocks and logs). Juveniles apparently prefer slow-moving, shallower water (Pluto and Bellis 1986).

Reproduction and Development: Mating has not been studied on the Delmarva Peninsula, but in other areas it occurs in the water in spring and/or late summer to fall. The male apparently courts the female by swimming in front of her, nudging her snout with his, and then rapidly bobbing his head. Females nest from late May to mid-July. The female deposits 9 to 20 dull white, elliptical eggs in a flask-shaped cavity that she excavates in soft soil or sand. Apparently, 2 clutches of eggs are often laid each year. The eggs typically hatch in August or September, but in some locations the hatchlings may spend the winter in the nest. (Ernst et al. 1994.)

Remarks: Northern Map Turtles feed primarily on freshwater mollusks, including snails and clams. They use their powerful jaws to crush and consume these hard-shelled animals. This species is also known to eat crayfish, fish, aquatic insects, and vegetation (Ernst et al. 1994). A good place to observe these turtles on Delmarva is in the Susquehanna River north of the town of Port Deposit, Maryland. Look for them basking on rocks just north of Steele Island on sunny spring and summer days (when water is not being released from Conowingo Dam). A pair of binoculars or a spotting scope is helpful as Northern Map Turtles are wary when basking and quickly retreat to the water when approached.

The Northern Map Turtle is usually relatively docile when handled; its strong jaws, however, can inflict a painful bite.

Northern Diamond-backed Terrapin   Plate 54
Malaclemys terrapin terrapin (Schoepff, 1793)

Other Names: Northern Diamondback Terrapin.
Description: females 15.2 to 22.9 cm (6.0 to 9.0 in.); males 10.1 to 14.0 cm (4.0 to 5.5 in.).
A medium-sized turtle that is highly variable in coloration. The carapace may be gray, brown, yellowish, greenish, bluish, or black, often with prominent concentric growth rings on the scutes that may be worn smooth in older specimens. The plastron is light yellowish to green and sometimes has dark marks or patterns on each scute. The head, neck, and limbs are usually light gray with dark flecks, and the upper and lower "lips" are light yellowish. Adult females are much larger than the males. Hatchlings have a mid-dorsal keel and are usually more brightly patterned than the adults.
Similar Species: The Northern Map Turtle also has light colored "lips," but it is not found in brackish water or salt marshes. The Eastern Snapping Turtle can live in brackish water, but it has a strongly serrated carapace and a long tail. The Eastern Mud Turtle also enters brackish water, but it can be distinguished by its small, brown carapace and hinged plastron. The seaturtles can be distinguished by their paddle-shaped flippers and large heads.

Turtles

Overall Range: Found in coastal areas from Cape Cod to Cape Hatteras.

Range and Status on Delmarva: Common along the coast of the Delaware Bay and the Delaware River south of Delaware City; along the coast of the Chesapeake Bay in Maryland and Virginia; and in back bays and inlets along the Atlantic Coast. Sometimes seen in the Atlantic Ocean. The Northern Diamond-backed Terrapin apparently also strays into the Chesapeake and Delaware Canal and its tributaries (J. McLaughlin personal communication). Recorded in all counties, although in land-locked Caroline County, Maryland, it is apparently limited to the lower Choptank River.

Habitat: This highly aquatic turtle lives in brackish estuarine habitats such as salt marshes and tidal creeks, rivers, bays, and sounds.

Reproduction and Development: Mating takes place in the water in the spring, usually in May. From early June to mid-July females make their way up onto sandy beaches, artificial dikes, and sand dunes in search of suitable nesting sites, often using the same sites year after year. Favored egg-laying sites along the Delmarva coast are often sandy beaches along estuaries that are isolated from uplands by salt marshes. The sides of raised roadbeds through salt marshes are also commonly used. Between 4 and 18 pinkish white, leathery eggs are laid just above mean high tide in cavities dug out by the female. The eggs hatch between August and October. Some hatchlings spend the winter in the nest and emerge the following spring. (Ernst et al. 1994; Mitchell 1994; Roosenburg 1994.)

Remarks: The Northern Diamond-backed Terrapin, together with the 6 other Diamond-backed Terrapin subspecies, is one of the few turtle species in the world that dwell exclusively in brackish water habitats; it is the only species in the Family Emydidae to possess a nasal salt gland, used for the excretion of excess salts (Dunson 1985). Large groups of these turtles can be observed in May and June swimming just off the sandy beaches of the Delaware and Chesapeake Bays; they are also often seen basking on the mudflats at low tide, sometimes on the backs of the horseshoe crabs that are abundant along bay beaches every spring (J. White personal observation). This turtle is almost entirely carnivorous, feeding on a variety of estuarine invertebrates, including fiddler and hermit crabs and also mud snails, periwinkles, mussels, clams, and other small mollusks. It may also eat horseshoe crab eggs, as suggested by the authors' finding about 300 eggs in the fecal material of a captured turtle.

From the late 1800s to the 1930s the Northern Diamond-backed Terrapin was highly sought after as the main ingredient in terrapin stew, a once popular gourmet dish. The demand for fresh turtle meat led to overharvesting, thereby severely reducing populations all along the mid-Atlantic coast. Luckily this food fad disappeared and the species made a dramatic comeback. Populations now appear to be stable on the Delmarva Peninsula, although recent increases in the demand for terrapins as a food item may again threaten populations. (Garber 1988, 1990.)

Other threats to this turtle by humans include destruction of nesting habitat, drowning of terrapins inadvertently caught in crab traps, and killing of females and juveniles on roadways. Large numbers are killed each year on roads along barrier beaches. In the spring of 2001 the State of Delaware erected low fencing along a stretch of Route 1 through Delaware Seashore State Park to prevent nesting turtles from moving across the dangerous highway. However, the overall effect of the fence on the reproductive success of this turtle in the project area is unknown at this time.

Northern Red-bellied Cooter   **Plates 55, 56**
Pseudemys rubriventris (LeConte, 1830)

Other Names: Redbelly Turtle; formerly classified as *Chrysemys rubriventris*.
Description: 25.4 to 31.2 cm (10.0 to 12.5 in.); record 40.1 cm (15.8 in.).

A large turtle with a smooth, elongated, slightly domed carapace of variable coloration. The adult carapace is olive-brown to black, typically with a reddish vertical line that is forked on one or both ends on each pleural scute and a reddish, vertical, unbranched line on the dorsal

---

Turtles   *129*

side of each marginal scute. Some individuals have more variable or less distinguishable reddish markings. The plastron is usually reddish (sometimes yellowish), with dark smudges. The head, neck, and limbs of most individuals are black with narrow, yellow stripes. A distinctive, yellow, arrow-shaped marking on the top of the head is formed by the junction at the snout of a median stripe and stripes that extend forward from both eyes. Adults often appear completely black when viewed from a distance; however, a close look usually reveals the presence of some reddish markings on the carapace. In general, the patterns on both the shell and the skin become less distinguishable with age, with some adults becoming mostly black. On the average, adult females are larger than adult males (Mitchell 1994). Adult males also have much longer claws on the forelimbs.

Hatchlings have brightly colored green carapaces with yellowish vertical lines on the pleural scutes. The hatchling plastron is red or yellowish with a large, dark pattern along the seams of the plastral scutes. The skin is greenish with greenish yellow stripes. As the juvenile matures, the markings on the carapace change to red, the dark pattern on the plastron fades, and the skin becomes darker.

Similar Species: The Eastern Painted Turtle has a somewhat flatter carapace and 2 bright yellow spots behind each eye and is much smaller than the adult Northern Red-bellied Cooter. The introduced Red-eared Slider can be distinguished by its overall greenish appearance and the presence of a conspicuous, broad, red stripe behind each eye.

Overall Range: Found from New Jersey to northeastern North Carolina and west to eastern West Virginia. A disjunct population occurs in Massachusetts.

Range and Status on Delmarva: Common on the Piedmont and very common on most of the Coastal Plain. Uncommon to absent on the barrier islands. Recorded in all counties.

Habitat: Prefers relatively deep aquatic habitats, including ponds, lakes, reservoirs, and slow-moving, brackish or freshwater rivers.

Reproduction and Development: Mating occurs in the spring. The females may have 1 or 2 clutches of eggs; egg laying occurs from mid-May into July. Females deposit up to 35 white, elliptical eggs in an oval-shaped cavity in loose soil, sometimes as much as several hundred yards from the water. The eggs hatch in late summer, but the hatchlings may remain in the nest until the following spring. (Mitchell 1994.)

Remarks: The Northern Red-bellied Cooter is a habitual basker and during warm weather can be observed sunning on logs, stumps, and other debris in the many ponds and rivers on the Delmarva Peninsula. It is probable that the numbers of this species increased dramatically with the creation and continued maintenance of the many millponds on the peninsula.

The hatchlings and juveniles are omnivorous but become almost exclusively herbivorous with age, feeding on various aquatic plants. Northern Red-bellied Cooters were sold for human consumption in the 1800s and are reportedly still consumed in some areas of Virginia (Mitchell 1994).

Eastern Box Turtle   Plate 57
Terrapene carolina carolina (Linnaeus, 1758)

Description: 11.4 to 15.2 cm (4.5 to 6.0 in.); record 19.8 cm (7.8 in.).

A small to medium-sized turtle with a highly domed, oval carapace. The carapace, plastron, head, neck, and limbs are brownish to nearly black, with highly variable patterns of yellow to orange lines, spots, or blotches. The plastron is large and is made up of 2 movable lobes that are connected by a transverse hinge. The turtle's shell closes completely shut when the head, limbs, and tail are retracted and the anterior lobe is pulled closed. The center of the posterior lobe of the plastron is concave in adult males and is flat or slightly convex in females. Adult males also have relatively long tails and often have red eyes, whereas adult females have short tails and usually have brown eyes. Hatchlings have a flattened carapace with a strong keel and an undeveloped plastral hinge. The carapace is grayish brown, with a faint yellow spot on each large scute, especially on the keel, and yellow crescents along the margin. The plastron is

---

pale yellow to orange with a large, grayish brown blotch in the center.

Similar Species: The Wood Turtle has a rough, sculpted carapace and lacks a hinge on the plastron.

Overall Range: Found from Massachusetts to Georgia and west to Michigan and Tennessee.

Range and Status on Delmarva: Common throughout the peninsula, but populations are apparently declining. Recorded in all counties and on several barrier islands.

Habitat: Usually found in woodlands, meadows, floodplains, or old fields. Although these turtles are primarily terrestrial, they sometimes occur in wet areas such as marshes, bogs, and shallow vernal pools and ponds.

Reproduction and Development: Courtship and mating take place on land between April and October (Mitchell 1994). Evans (1953) describes how the male first circles the female and pushes or bites her carapace. He then mounts and scratches her shell with his claws. If the female is receptive, she opens the space between the rear of her carapace and her plastron, allowing the male to place his hind feet into the opening, which she then clamps shut on his feet. The male then snaps at her head and/or carapace until she reopens the posterior portion of her plastron. He then rocks backward, rests the back end of his carapace on the ground, and places his cloacal opening against hers to initiate copulation. Females have been documented to store sperm for up to four years (Ewing 1943).

Nesting activity occurs in the evening from late May to late July. Females dig a flask-shaped cavity—often in a forest opening or at a field edge (N. Nazdrowicz personal communication)—into which they lay 2 to 7 white, elliptical eggs. Some females produce 2 clutches in one year. Hatching typically occurs between early August and late November, with some hatchlings overwintering in the nest. (Allard 1948; Mitchell 1994; Riemer 1981.)

Remarks: Eastern Box Turtles are often encountered crossing open areas such as hiking trails and roads after heavy rains. They have relatively small home ranges, most staying within an approximate 500-foot-diameter area (Stickel 1989). Author

Jim White has often encountered an individual turtle within 30 feet of where it was found several years earlier. The hatchlings, however, are very secretive and are rarely encountered by humans.

Eastern Box Turtles can be long-lived, some reaching seventy-five years or more of age although the majority live fifty years or less (Dodd 2001). Counting the concentric annual growth rings of any large scute on the carapace can give a fair approximation of an individual turtle's age. After about fifteen to twenty years, however, new growth rings become indiscernible. In very old turtles the growth rings can be worn smooth, which makes them difficult or impossible to count.

Eastern Box Turtles are omnivorous and are especially fond of slugs. N. Nazdrowicz (personal communication) has also observed turtles eating mushrooms, dead cicadas, and a dead Eastern Gartersnake. They may also be important dispersers of woodland plant seeds. The seeds of some plants, including jack-in-the-pulpit and mayapple, have been found to germinate better when passed through a box turtle's digestive system (Braun and Brooks 1987; Rust and Roth 1981).

Eastern Box Turtles are commonly kept as pets; however, removing them from their natural habitat often leads to an early death. If a wild turtle is collected for classroom or home study (in accordance with state laws, see section III), it should be returned to the exact location of capture as soon as possible. Populations of this turtle are apparently in decline because of several factors, including habitat loss and fragmentation, death from motor vehicles and lawnmowers, and overcollection for the pet trade.

Ecologists at the University of Delaware have been monitoring a population of marked turtles in Delaware since 1965. The data indicate that this population has declined over that time (N. Nazdrowicz and R. Roth personal communication).

Red-eared Slider   Plate 58
Trachemys scripta elegans (Wied-Neuwied, 1838)

Other Names: Formerly classified as *Chrysemys scripta elegans.*

Description: 12.7 to 20.3 cm (5.0 to 8.0 in.); record 29.0 cm (11.4 in.).

The Red-eared Slider is a medium-sized turtle with a weakly keeled, oval carapace that can be various shades of green to brown with transverse yellowish stripes on each pleural scute. Most individuals have a conspicuous, broad, red stripe behind each eye, for which the subspecies is named. The head, neck, limbs, and tail are green to brown with yellow stripes. As in the Northern Red-bellied Cooter, a yellow, arrow-shaped marking on the top of the head is formed by the junction at the snout of a median stripe and stripes that extend forward from both eyes. The plastron is yellow with 1 dark blotch on each scute. In adult males the bright red stripe behind the eye often becomes dull with age, and there are few, if any, markings on the carapace, making identification difficult. Adult males also have very long claws on the forelimbs. Hatchlings are patterned similarly to young adults but are greener overall.

Similar Species: The Northern Red-bellied Cooter has red pigment on the carapace and plastron, and the carapace is more domed. The Eastern Painted Turtle has 2 yellow spots behind each eye; red stripes on the neck, limbs, and tail; and red markings on the marginal scutes.

Overall Range: Found from West Virginia to Alabama and west to Kansas and New Mexico. Introduced colonies have been established in many areas outside its natural range, including parts of the United States, Japan, Germany, Israel, and South Africa.

Range and Status on Delmarva: The range and status of this turtle on Delmarva are poorly understood. Outside its natural range, the Red-eared Slider has been introduced into various locations on the peninsula, undoubtedly through the pet trade (see "Remarks"). Well-established (i.e., reproducing) colonies have been documented in Becks Pond in New Castle County, Delaware (J. McLaughlin personal communication); in Haven Lake in Kent and Sussex Counties, Delaware, and in Silver Lake, Rehoboth Beach, Delaware (authors' personal observations); and in the vicinity of Salisbury, Wicomico

County, Maryland (Grogan 1994). Individuals have been found in numerous other ponds on Delmarva, on both the Piedmont and the Coastal Plain, as well as in the Brandywine River (J. McLaughlin personal communication), although it is unknown which of these individuals are from established colonies. Additional colonies could turn up in any county on the peninsula.

Habitat: Prefers freshwater aquatic habitats with quiet water, muddy bottoms, abundant vegetation, and ample basking sites. Mill and farm ponds appear to be the preferred habitats on the peninsula.

Reproduction and Development: Courtship and mating behaviors of the Red-eared Slider have not been documented on Delmarva. In other parts of its range, courtship and mating occur in the water in the spring and fall. Through most of its range, eggs are laid in the spring or early summer with hatching in the late summer or early fall (Ernst et al. 1994).

Remarks: The Red-eared Slider is a familiar turtle to the baby boom generation. From the 1950s through the early 1970s, millions of hatchling Red-eared Sliders were sold as pets in variety stores and pet shops across the nation. These inexpensive pets (from around twenty-five cents to one dollar, not including the small plastic bowl and palm tree) were often purchased for small children, most of whom had very little knowledge of how to maintain healthy turtles in captivity. The vast majority of these turtles died shortly after purchase, although some survived long enough for the owners to tire of them or at least feel that the turtles would be better off in the wild. The result was that turtles were released in ponds and rivers all over the United States and other parts of the world. Some of these turtles were able to survive and in some places to breed and establish colonies.

Captive juvenile Red-eared Sliders were found to be able to transmit the disease salmonellosis to humans. In 1975 the U.S. Food and Drug Administration banned all sale of turtles with a shell length of less than 4 inches within the United States or to Canada, for all but educational or scientific purposes. The export of these turtles continues today, however, with millions being sold abroad.

A good place to see these turtles in abundance is in Silver Lake, Rehoboth Beach, Delaware, where they are relatively tame because people feed them regularly.

Seaturtles (Family Cheloniidae)

The Family Cheloniidae is composed entirely of marine turtles, which come ashore only to nest. There are 5 living genera and 6 species in this family. All have low, streamlined carapaces that are covered with horny epidermal scutes. Their forelimbs are flipper-like with long digits and produce powerful swimming strokes. The hind limbs are paddle-like and act as rudders. The neck is short and cannot be retracted into the carapace. Most species are primarily tropical but some forage and/or nest in temperate waters. Four members of the Family Cheloniidae may be seasonally found in the waters surrounding Delmarva: the Loggerhead Seaturtle, Green Seaturtle, Atlantic Hawksbill Seaturtle, and Kemp's Ridley Seaturtle.

Loggerhead Seaturtle   **Plate 59**
Caretta caretta (Linnaeus, 1758)

Other Names: Loggerhead.
Description: 79 to 114 cm (31 to 45 in.); record 122+ cm (48+ in.).

A large seaturtle with an elongated, roughly heart-shaped, reddish brown to dark brown carapace that is serrated posteriorly. In some turtles the scutes on the carapace have yellow borders. The carapace may also appear greenish if covered with epiphytic plant growth. The carapace typically has 5 pairs of pleural scutes, with the first pair touching the cervical scute (fig. 13). There are usually 3 (rarely 4) inframarginal scutes on the bridge, each lacking visible pores (fig. 14). The plastron, the underside of the neck, and much of the limbs are cream-colored to yellowish. The massive head can be various shades of red, yellow, or brown and has 2 pairs of prefrontal scales between the eyes (fig. 15). Adult males

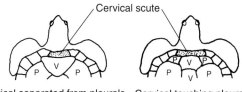

Cervical scute

Cervical separated from pleurals
(e.g., Green and
Atlantic Hawksbill)

Cervical touching pleurals
(e.g., Loggerhead
and Kemp's Ridley)

Figure 13. Relationship of cervical scute to pleural scutes in seaturtles

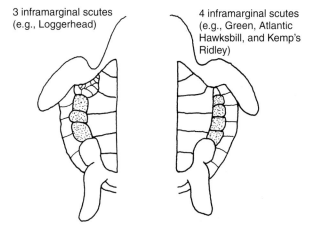

3 inframarginal scutes
(e.g., Loggerhead)

4 inframarginal scutes
(e.g., Green, Atlantic
Hawksbill, and Kemp's
Ridley)

Figure 14. Underside of seaturtles showing inframarginal scutes

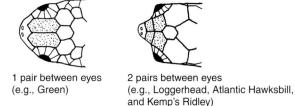

1 pair between eyes
(e.g., Green)

2 pairs between eyes
(e.g., Loggerhead, Atlantic Hawksbill,
and Kemp's Ridley)

Figure 15. Prefrontal scales on heads of seaturtles

have wider shells; longer, thicker tails; a longer and recurved nail on each forelimb; and yellower heads than the females. Juveniles are similar in coloration to the adults but have a mid-dorsal keel and 2 longitudinal ridges on the plastron that become progressively smoother with age (Mitchell 1994).

Similar Species: Kemp's Ridley Seaturtle has a nearly circular carapace, is usually grayish to green above and white below, and has 4 inframarginal scutes on the bridge, each with visible pores. The Green Seaturtle has only 1 pair of prefrontal scales between the eyes and has 4 pairs of pleural scutes, with the first pair not touching the cervical scute. The Atlantic Hawksbill Seaturtle has carapacial scutes that overlap posteriorly and has 4 pairs of pleural scutes, with the first pair not touching the cervical scute.

Overall Range: Found in many areas of the Pacific, Indian, and Atlantic Oceans. In the western Atlantic Ocean this species is found from the Canadian maritime provinces to Argentina; the majority of nesting activity along the East Coast of the United States occurs south of Virginia.

Range and Status on Delmarva: Relatively common in the warmer months along the coast of the Atlantic Ocean and into the Delaware and Chesapeake Bays. Nesting has occurred on Delmarva's Atlantic coastline, but it is extremely rare (see "Remarks"). This turtle is state-listed as endangered in Delaware and threatened in Virginia.

Habitat: Adult and subadult Loggerhead Seaturtles are found in coastal oceanic waters, estuaries, and occasionally the saline portions of tidal creeks. The hatchlings and young juveniles appear to live in or close to mats of floating sargassum in the ocean (Carr 1986).

Reproduction and Development: Mating of Loggerhead Seaturtles in North American waters has been recorded from mid-March to June and apparently occurs as the females migrate through the open-water territories of resident males on their way to the nesting beaches. Females typically undertake this migration every two to three years, sometimes traveling great distances, and often returning to the same beach where they nested previously. Mating pairs stay near the surface of the water and may stay joined for more than three hours. Nesting along the southeastern coast of North America occurs between May and August. Nests are usually located on open beaches between the sea and the primary dunes along the Atlantic coast and to a lesser extent on islands. The female digs a hole in the sand into which she deposits approximately 110 to 130 eggs. She then fills in the hole with sand and returns to the sea. A female may lay several clutches during a season. The eggs hatch in approximately sixty to sixty-five days. It takes ten to thirty years for the hatchlings to reach sexual maturity. (Ernst et al. 1994; Musick 1988.)

Remarks: The Loggerhead Seaturtle is by far the most commonly observed seaturtle in the Delaware and Chesapeake Bays and in the Atlantic Ocean off the Delmarva Peninsula. Research in the Chesapeake Bay indicates that the Bay is an important summer foraging area for juvenile Loggerhead Seaturtles, with the turtles feeding primarily on horseshoe crabs. It is estimated that several thousand turtles enter the Bay in May or early June and leave by November (Keinath et al. 1987; Keinath and Musick 1991; Klinger and Musick 1992; Lutcavage and Musick 1985; Musick 1988). Although research in the Delaware Bay has been more limited, preliminary findings indicate that the Delaware Bay is also an important resource for Loggerhead Seaturtles, both for adults and juveniles. Aerial surveys conducted in the Delaware Bay in 1997 indicate that this bay has densities of Loggerhead Seaturtles comparable to those in similar habitats as far south as Georgia (Spotila et al. 1998; P. Plotkin and E. Stetzar personal communications).

The Loggerhead Seaturtle is the only seaturtle that nests primarily outside the tropical oceans. Nesting on the East Coast of the United States occurs each year from North Carolina to Florida. Although occasional nesting has been documented on Delmarva, conditions are apparently too cold for the establishment of a breeding colony. From 1969 to 1972, researchers released 1,082 Loggerhead Seaturtle hatchlings on Assateague Island in an unsuccessful attempt to establish a breeding colony (Graham 1973).

This turtle is listed as threatened under the U.S. Endangered Species Act.

Green Seaturtle   **Plate 60**
Chelonia mydas (Linnaeus, 1758)

Other Names: Green Turtle
Description: 91 to 122 cm (36 to 48 in.); record 153.4 cm (60.4 in.).

A large seaturtle with an oval to heart-shaped carapace that is only slightly serrated posteriorly. The carapace can be olive, brown, gray, or black and is often mottled, blotched, or streaked. The carapace has 4 pairs of pleural scutes, with the first pair separated from the cervical scute by a vertebral scute (fig. 13). The plastron is white to yellowish and there are 4 inframarginal scutes on the bridge, each lacking visible pores (fig. 14). The head and limbs are olive, brown, gray, or black, and the scales are often rimmed with cream or yellow. There is 1 pair of prefrontal scales between the eyes (fig. 15). Males have a prehensile tail that extends beyond the carapace and a long, curved claw on each forelimb. Females have short tails and short, straight claws on the forelimbs. Juveniles are similar in coloration to the adults, but the carapace is keeled and the plastron has 2 longitudinal ridges (Mitchell 1994).

Similar Species: Both the Loggerhead Seaturtle and Kemp's Ridley Seaturtle have 5 pairs of pleural scutes, with the first pair touching the cervical scute, and 2 pairs of prefrontal scales between the eyes. The Atlantic Hawksbill Seaturtle also has 2 pairs of prefrontal scales, and it has carapacial scutes that overlap posteriorly.

Overall Range: Found primarily in tropical areas of the Atlantic, Pacific, and Indian Oceans. Green Seaturtles (especially juveniles) are also found to a lesser extent in more temperate areas. In the western Atlantic Ocean, the Green Seaturtle nests from Georgia south.

Range and Status on Delmarva: Very rare in the Chesapeake and Delaware Bays and along the Atlantic coast of the Delmarva Peninsula. Most individuals found here are juveniles (Mitchell 1994). This species does not nest on Delmarva. It is state-listed as endangered in Delaware and threatened in Maryland and Virginia.

Habitat: Apparently prefers shallow areas of warm seas. Juvenile and adult feeding grounds are usually near shore in shallow water with ample supplies of submerged vegetation and associated invertebrate diversity. However, individuals have been found far out to sea and some are known to migrate more than 1,200 miles across the open ocean (Carr and Coleman 1974). Hatchlings apparently drift in the open seas among mats of sargassum for one or more years (Carr 1987; Carr and Meylan 1980).

Reproduction and Development: Adult female Green Seaturtles generally nest every two to four years, with most females returning to the same beach where they nested previously. Some populations appear to spend their entire lives near their nesting beaches, whereas other populations migrate many hundreds of miles from their foraging sites to their nesting beaches and back. Most Green Seaturtles mate in shallow water off the nesting beaches. The prime nesting period in the western Atlantic Ocean is from May to September. It is estimated that this species requires nineteen to twenty-four years to reach sexual maturity in the wild. (Ernst et al. 1994.)

Remarks: Green Seaturtle populations appear to be declining as a result of exploitation by humans. This turtle gets its name from the greenish color of the fat in its flesh when butchered. The meat of the juvenile and adult turtles was, and in some areas still is, harvested and consumed at a rate that does not allow the population to be sustained. Leading seaturtle researcher Archie Carr described the Green Seaturtle as the most economically important reptile species in the world (Carr 1956). In addition, the collection of eggs for human consumption has led to the decline, and in some cases the eradication, of this species at many nesting beaches worldwide. The degradation of nesting beaches by development and light pollution at night as well as disturbance of nesting females by humans may also be contributing to the decline of the species. The Green Seaturtle is listed under the U.S. Endangered Species Act as endangered in its nesting areas in Florida and Mexico and as threatened in all other areas.

Unlike the other seaturtles, adult Green Seaturtles are largely herbivorous.

Atlantic Hawksbill Seaturtle   **Plate 61**
Eretmochelys imbricata imbricata (Linnaeus, 1766)

Other Names: Atlantic Hawksbill.
Description: 76 to 89 cm (30 to 35 in.); record 91+ cm (36+ in.).
A medium-sized seaturtle with a brown to greenish brown, flattened carapace that is shaped like a shield. The carapacial scutes overlap posteriorly (except in older adults) and the carapace is strongly serrated along the back edge. The carapace is keeled on the last 4 vertebral scutes and has 4 pairs of pleural scutes, with the first pair separated from the cervical scute by a triangular vertebral scute (fig. 13). The plastron is yellowish and has 2 distinct longitudinal ridges. There are 4 inframarginal scutes on the bridge, each lacking pores (fig. 14). The head is relatively small with smooth cutting edges on the jaws and a narrow snout that resembles a hawk's bill. Head scales are yellow with large, brown patches, and there are 2 pairs of prefrontal scales between the eyes (fig. 15). The underside of the limbs and head is yellowish. Juveniles and young adults have yellowish and dark brown markings on the carapace, creating the unique pattern from which the term *tortoiseshell* was derived (Mitchell 1994).
Similar Species: Both the Loggerhead Seaturtle and the Kemp's Ridley Seaturtle have 5 pairs of pleural scutes, with the first pair touching the cervical scute. The Green Seaturtle has only 1 pair of prefrontal scales between the eyes. None of the other seaturtles has overlapping carapacial scutes.
Overall Range: Found primarily in tropical areas of the western Atlantic Ocean but occasionally recorded as far north as Massachusetts. Also occasionally recorded in the eastern Atlantic Ocean between the British Isles and northwestern Africa. Nesting occurs primarily in the tropics, with limited nesting in southern Florida (Ernst et al. 1994).
Range and Status on Delmarva: Extremely rare to absent. Only one confirmed record—from the lower Chesapeake Bay (Mitchell 1994)—is known for the Delmarva region. This turtle is state-listed as endangered in Maryland and Virginia.
Habitat: Found primarily in tropical areas associated with rocky shorelines and coral reefs but may also enter lagoons,

mangrove shorelines, and tidal creeks. Hatchlings and small juveniles are found in or near floating mats of sargassum in the open ocean (Carr 1987).

Reproduction and Development: Mating usually takes place just offshore of the tropical nesting beaches. Unlike most other seaturtles, the Atlantic Hawksbill Seaturtle is usually a dispersed, solitary nester. This turtle is also unique in being able to "walk" rapidly over the beach instead of dragging its body with its forelimbs as is the habit of other seaturtles. Nesting in Florida has been recorded from April to August. Hatchlings grow quickly and may reach sexual maturity in as little as three years. (Carr 1952; Ernst et al. 1994.)

Remarks: As with the other seaturtles, populations of the Atlantic Hawksbill Seaturtle appear to be declining. Although this turtle was one of the first listed as endangered under the U.S. Endangered Species Act, exploitation by humans continues at an alarming rate. Collecting of younger turtles for the valuable carapace (tortoiseshell) to make combs, jewelry, and other ornaments may be the primary cause of this turtle's decline. In addition, the eggs and flesh are still consumed in some parts of the world.

Kemp's Ridley Seaturtle   Plate 62
Lepidochelys kempii (Garman, 1880)

Other Names: Atlantic Ridley.

Description: 58 to 71 cm (23 to 28 in.); record 74.9 cm (29.5 in.).

A small seaturtle with a gray (sometimes greenish or black), nearly circular, smooth carapace. The carapace is posteriorly serrated and has 5 pairs of pleural scutes, with the first pair touching the cervical scute (fig. 13). The plastron is white. The bridge has 4 (rarely, 5) inframarginal scutes (fig. 14), each with a small pore located toward the rear edge. The head and limbs are gray or olive. There are 2 pairs of prefrontal scales between the eyes (fig. 15). Juveniles are almost completely dark gray and have a knobby mid-dorsal ridge and 4 plastral ridges.

Similar Species: All other seaturtles in the Delmarva region have shells that are more elongated. The Loggerhead Seaturtle is reddish brown and has 3 poreless inframarginal scutes on the bridge. The Green Seaturtle and Atlantic Hawksbill Seaturtle each have 5 pairs of pleural scutes, with the first pair not touching the cervical scute.

Overall Range: Adults are found primarily in the Gulf of Mexico, but juveniles often appear as far north as Nova Scotia in the summer and fall.

Range and Status on Delmarva: Found in relatively high numbers each year between May and November in the Chesapeake Bay and along the Atlantic Coast, especially around barrier islands (Keinath et al. 1987; Keinath et al. 1991; Musick et al. 1984). It is estimated that the annual population of this species in the lower Chesapeake Bay is between 300 and 500 individuals (Keinath et al. 1991). The annual population of this species in the Delaware Bay is unknown. This turtle does not nest on Delmarva. It is state-listed as endangered in Delaware, Maryland, and Virginia.

Habitat: In the Delmarva region the Kemp's Ridley Seaturtle is found in shallower water than that inhabited by other seaturtles. In the Chesapeake Bay this species is often found in or near eelgrass meadows (Lutcavage and Musick 1985).

Reproduction and Development: Nesting occurs only on beaches in the Gulf of Mexico, with 95 percent of the population nesting on a single beach located at Rancho Nuevo in the Mexican state of Tamaulipas. Males and females congregate and mate just offshore of the nesting beach, and typically, large groups of females come up onto the beach together during daylight hours. These synchronized nestings have been termed *arribadas* (Spanish for "arrivals") by Archie Carr (1967) and occur between early April and late August. Hatchlings are thought to drift with the sea currents, some ending up in floating mats of sargassum in the Atlantic Ocean, where they spend the first few years of life. Juvenile turtles leave the open ocean and head to shallow coastal waters, where they may spend an estimated five to fifteen years in bays and estuaries, migrating seasonally along the coast (Carr 1967, 1986, 1987; Ross et al. 1989).

Remarks: The Kemp's Ridley Seaturtle is by far the most endangered seaturtle in the world. Its numbers have declined catastrophically since the late 1940s, when more than 42,000 females were observed coming ashore in one day on the beach at Rancho Nuevo, Mexico. By 1989 the estimated number of nesting females in an entire season had dropped below 700 (Ross et al. 1989). It is listed as endangered under the U.S. Endangered Species Act.

The Chesapeake Bay is a major summer feeding area for juvenile Kemp's Ridley Seaturtles. There are few places along the Atlantic Coast where such large concentrations of juveniles have been reported (Keinath et al. 1987). The preferred prey of this species is the blue crab *(Callinectes sapidus),* but marine mollusks and vegetation are also consumed (Lutcavage and Musick 1985).

Leatherback Seaturtles (Family Dermochelyidae)

The sole living member of the Family Dermochelyidae, the Leatherback Seaturtle *(Dermochelys coriacea),* is the largest turtle in the world today. This turtle differs from other seaturtles in its lack of a bony, shell-like carapace. The carapace and limbs are covered with a rigid, leathery skin imbedded with a mosaic of small, bony plates. The limbs lack claws and are either flipper-like (forelimbs) or paddle-like (hind limbs). Leatherback Seaturtles are primarily pelagic but are sometimes observed close to shore, often following schools of jellyfish, on which they feed.

Leatherback Seaturtle   **Plate 63**
Dermochelys coriacea (Vandelli, 1761)

Other Names: Leatherback.
Description: 135 to 178 cm (53 to 70 in.); record 188.7 cm (74.3 in.).

An extremely large seaturtle with a smooth, elongated, leathery carapace that is somewhat teardrop shaped. Present

---

on the carapace are 7 distinct longitudinal keels. The carapace, head, neck, and limbs are dark brown to black with scattered white to yellowish spots or blotches. Some individuals have pinkish blotches on top of the head. The forelimbs are very elongated, and none of the limbs have claws. The plastron is whitish and has 5 longitudinal ridges. Males have concave plastrons and have tails that are longer than their hind limbs. Hatchlings are dark brown to black with light coloration on each longitudinal keel and on the edges of the flippers.

Similar Species: The Leatherback Seaturtle is unmistakable; it is the only seaturtle without scutes or claws.

Overall Range: This is the most widespread reptile in the world and is found in all major oceans and seas except the Arctic Ocean. It occurs in the western Atlantic from Newfoundland south to Argentina and nests primarily in the tropics, from Brazil north through Central America and the Caribbean Islands and to a lesser extent in Florida and Georgia.

Range and Status on Delmarva: A few Leatherback Seaturtles are seen each year in the lower portion of the Chesapeake Bay and around the barrier islands along the Atlantic Ocean (Barnard et al. 1989; Musick 1988; Scarpulla 1989). They are less frequently seen in the lower Delaware Bay (E. Stetzar personal communication). This species does not nest on Delmarva. It is state-listed as endangered in Delaware, Maryland, and Virginia.

Habitat: Although occasionally found near shore and in estuaries, this is primarily a species of the open ocean. Even the juveniles are thought to be pelagic.

Reproduction and Development: Mating may take place in temperate waters prior to or during the females' migration to tropical nesting beaches. In the western Atlantic Ocean most females nest every two or three years and lay approximately 6 clutches of eggs at intervals through the nesting season, which may last from February to August. The eggs usually hatch in sixty to sixty-five days. Hatchlings usually emerge from the nest en masse, often near dawn, and head frantically to the sea. Those that are successful in making it past the gauntlet of predators that await them on land, in the air, and offshore swim quickly out to sea. Little is known about their development. (Pritchard 1971; Ernst et al. 1994.)

Remarks: The Leatherback Seaturtle is apparently closer to being endothermic than any other reptile. In cold water this turtle has been found to have an internal body temperature up to 18°C higher than the surrounding water temperature, which allows it to venture farther north than other marine reptiles. Research suggests that the Leatherback Seaturtle produces and maintains its body heat through a combination of muscle activity from swimming, specialized heat-producing fat tissue, a thick insulating fat layer, and modified blood-flow mechanisms in the flippers. The large body mass may also aid in heat retention. (Ernst et al. 1994.)

The Leatherback Seaturtle is a very powerful swimmer and can travel great distances in pursuit of its prey or to migrate to nesting areas. Jellyfish are a major component of the diet of this weak-jawed seaturtle. Although usually solitary, groups of up to one hundred Leatherback Seaturtles have been observed following large schools of jellyfish. In the Delmarva region Leatherback Seaturtles probably feed on sea nettle and the large, whitish moon jelly (Keinath et al. 1987; Musick 1988). This turtle has been known to mistakenly eat floating balloons, plastic bags, and other plastic debris that resemble jellyfish. The result is intestinal blockage and often death.

In many parts of the world, humans gather the eggs of this turtle for food, contributing to the decline of the species. This turtle is listed as endangered under the U.S. Endangered Species Act.

Lizards and Snakes (Order Squamata)

The Order Squamata includes the lizards, snakes, and amphisbaenians as well as several extinct groups. Traditional classification considered lizards and snakes as coequal suborders of Squamata (Suborder Lacertilia and Suborder Serpentes, respectively). Current understanding of evolution within this order, however, indicates that snakes are really only a type of legless lizard. Nevertheless, because of easily recognizable differences in appearance and behavior, and the fact that most people consider snakes as distinct from lizards, snakes and lizards are treated as two separate groups in this book.

Lizards (Formerly Considered Suborder Lacertilia)

The lizards are a diverse group of reptiles that inhabit a wide variety of habitats and geographical regions, although they are especially common in areas with warm, dry climates. Most species are terrestrial, arboreal, or fossorial; however, a few species are aquatic, and one species, the Galapagos Marine Iguana, lives at the edge of the ocean and feeds on submerged marine vegetation.

Most lizards have elongated bodies and 4 well-developed legs, each with 5 clawed toes (fig. 16). All are covered with scales, which may be smooth or keeled depending on the

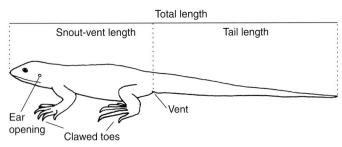

Figure 16. Generalized lizard

species. Unlike snakes, the majority of lizards have external ear openings and eyelids. Lizards hear well and most can also see well. They also have a good sense of smell. In addition to picking up odors through the nostrils, some lizards have a *Jacobson's organ* on the roof of the mouth (as in snakes), which facilitates sensing chemicals in the environment.

Many lizards have a breakaway tail that snaps off when grabbed by a predator. The broken-off tail continues to wiggle, often distracting the predator long enough to allow the lizard to escape. The lizard eventually grows a new tail, although it is usually not as long or as well shaped as the original. Lizards with incomplete tails are so frequently encountered that herpetologists measure the snout-vent (sometimes called head-body) length as well as the total body length (both measurements are provided for the lizard species in this book). The vent, or cloacal opening of lizards, is a transverse slit located at the base of the tail.

Most lizards are fast-moving, active predators, scavengers, or herbivores. Most have small teeth, and the vast majority of lizards, including all Delmarva species, are nonvenomous. Unlike snakes, the two halves of the lizard's lower jaw are fused together, limiting the size of prey that can be swallowed. All Delmarva lizards are predators of terrestrial invertebrates, including a wide variety of insects, arachnids, millipedes, centipedes, and isopods. As they grow, lizards periodically grow a new layer of skin under the old one; the old skin is typically shed in patches (not in a single piece as with snakes).

In colder regions, including on Delmarva, lizards spend the colder months inactively hibernating underground or in rotting logs, tree stumps, woodpiles, or other crevices.

Reproduction of lizards is accomplished by internal fertilization of the eggs. Males have a pair of saclike copulatory organs called *hemipenes* that are stored inside the cloaca except during copulation. In many species the males actively court the females (albeit briefly) before copulation. Courtship may include head bobbing, tongue flicking, chin rubbing, and other behaviors. After variable amounts of courtship, the male aligns his body lengthwise next to the female and wraps his tail around hers. Copulation occurs when the male everts a hemipenis and inserts it into the female cloaca. Worldwide, most lizards are *oviparous* (egg-laying) and, like other reptiles, lay their eggs on dry land. All Delmarva lizards are oviparous, laying their eggs under logs, stones, or other suitable cover or in soil or rotting vegetation.

There are more than 4,100 species of lizards worldwide, classified in approximately 18 families (Pough et al. 2001). Lizards are found on all continents except Antarctica. There are 4 species of lizards known to occur on the Delmarva Peninsula and these belong to 2 families: the Iguanids (Family Iguanidae: 1 species) and the Skinks (Family Scincidae: 3 species).

Iguanids (Family Iguanidae)

The Family Iguanidae contains more than 900 species and is divided into approximately 8 subfamilies (Pough et al. 2001). Only 1 species, a member of the Subfamily Phrynosomatinae, occurs on Delmarva. This subfamily contains a diverse group of small to medium-sized lizards that are found in a wide variety of habitats from southern Canada through Central America. Most are terrestrial or semi-arboreal. Some members of this subfamily have throat fans (dewlaps) or crests, and many use display patterns such as head bobbing, nodding, and push-ups to declare territory, determine sex, or discriminate species.

Northern Fence Lizard   **Plate 64**
Sceloporus undulatus hyacinthinus (Green, 1818)

Description: 10.2 to 18.5 cm (4.0 to 7.3 in.); snout-vent max. 8.6 cm (3.4 in.).

A medium-sized, stout lizard that is very rough in appearance. The roughness is due to the presence of keeled, overlapping scales, each adorned with a backward-pointing projection. Adult females are light brown to gray with undulating, dark brown or black crossbands on the back and tail. The female belly and throat are creamy with black specks, although some females have a tinge of blue on the throat. Adult males are also brown to gray above but have less distinct, sometimes obscure crossbands, and bright greenish blue patches on the throat and sides of the belly. Juveniles are similar to the females in pattern and coloration but are typically duller.

Similar Species: Because of its rough appearance, the Northern Fence Lizard is not easily confused with any other lizard on the Delmarva Peninsula.

Overall Range: Found from southern New Jersey to South Carolina and west to Kansas and Texas, with isolated populations in southeastern New York and northeastern Pennsylvania.

Range and Status on Delmarva: Common on the southern Coastal Plain with the exception of the barrier islands, where it is rare to absent. Uncommon on the northern part of the Coastal Plain. Absent from the Piedmont except possibly in the lower Susquehanna River watershed. Recorded in all counties.

Habitat: Found in old fields, hedgerows, and dry open areas of deciduous, coniferous, or mixed deciduous-coniferous woodlands. The Northern Fence Lizard avoids deep woods, preferring areas with abundant sunlight as in the edges of woods and fields. It is especially common around logs, woodpiles, stone piles, other human-deposited debris, and buildings.

Reproduction and Development: In the spring, shortly after emerging from hibernation, courting males set up and defend small territories. When another male or a female is encountered within his territory, the courting male performs display behavior, often from an elevated perch. This behavior includes push-ups to display his bright belly colors, head bobbing, and sometimes enlargement of the throat and extension of the dewlap to display his bright throat patches. A fast series of head bobs is thought to indicate arousal in males and may help to entice females to mate. (Mitchell 1994.)

Between early June and mid-July females deposit 6 to 13 elliptical eggs in a nest dug in the soil or within or under rotten logs, stumps, or other debris. The eggs usually hatch between early August and early September. (Mitchell 1994.)

Remarks: The Northern Fence Lizard is largely arboreal and is often seen climbing on fences, logs, or stumps. When threatened, it typically climbs the nearest tree or other vertical structure and hides on the far side, similar to the behavior seen in gray squirrels. Populations of this lizard appear to be declining in the northern portion of its Delmarva range because of habitat loss to residential and other development.

Skinks (Family Scincidae)

The Family Scincidae contains approximately 100 genera and over 1,000 species worldwide. Members of this family are found on all continents except Antarctica and are usually small to medium-sized lizards with smooth, often shiny scales. Most have cylindrical bodies, conical heads, and robust, medium-length tails. They are primarily terrestrial or semifossorial, although some are arboreal. Most are carnivorous, actively pursuing and feeding on invertebrates. Larger species may also eat small rodents and birds. There are 3 species of skinks on Delmarva.

Common Five-lined Skink   **Plates 65, 66**
Eumeces fasciatus (Linnaeus, 1758)

Other Names: Five-lined Skink.
Description: 12.7 to 21.6 cm (5.0 to 8.5 in.); snout-vent max. 8.6 cm (3.4 in.).

A medium-sized, smooth-scaled, slender lizard with coloration that varies with age and sex.

Juveniles are dark brown or black, with 5 bold, light-colored stripes and a bright blue tail. The stripes extend from the head to halfway down the tail, and the median stripe usually forks on top of the head and reunites again on the snout. The throat and upper belly are cream-colored fading to gray on the lower belly. As the lizard matures, the tail becomes grayish brown above and usually cream-colored underneath. Adult females retain the striping, although it becomes less conspicuous with age. In adult males the stripes are usually faint or obscured and the body takes on an olive brown coloration. During the breeding season the male's head turns orange red. This lizard usually has 4 upper labial scales in front of the subocular scale, 2 enlarged postlabial scales, and 26 to 30 scale rows around the midbody (fig. 17).

Similar Species: Broad-headed Skinks are very similar in coloration and can best be distinguished by their scales: they usually have 5 upper labial scales in front of the subocular scale, no enlarged postlabial scales, and usually 30 to 32 scale rows around midbody. Adult Broad-headed Skinks are also much larger than Common Five-lined Skinks.

Overall Range: Found from New England to northern Florida and west to Wisconsin and Texas. Isolated colonies occur north of this range.

Range and Status on Delmarva: Uncommon to common on the Coastal Plain, with the exception of the barrier islands, where it is absent. Apparently absent from the Piedmont. Recorded in all counties.

Habitat: Found in a wide variety of habitats but apparently prefers damp ones. Usually found in areas associated with moist deciduous, coniferous, or mixed deciduous-coniferous woodlands. This species also occurs in cutover areas, especially those with ample quantities of large logs and stumps, and it occurs near human dwellings, in and around woodpiles,

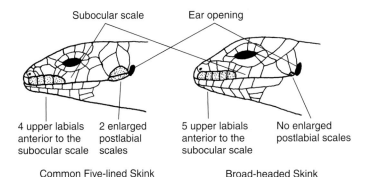

Figure 17. Comparison of skink head scales

compost heaps, or other debris. Although primarily terrestrial, this species sometimes climbs dead trees in search of prey.

Reproduction and Development: Mating probably occurs in late spring. During mating season the males are hostile to other males and will engage in violent combat, sometimes biting each other on the head and throwing each other through the air. Males reportedly locate females by following scent trails. Courtship is generally brief but may include some head bobbing, chin rubbing, or scratching. A receptive female may lower her head and allow the male to grasp her neck in his jaws. The male then wraps his tail around hers, and copulation ensues. Females deposit from 5 to 14 oval eggs in early summer. The eggs are deposited in or under rotting logs, stumps, or debris. The female remains with the eggs until hatching occurs in mid- to late summer. (Cooper and Vitt 1987; Fitch 1954; Mitchell 1994; Tyning 1990.)

Remarks: The Common Five-lined Skink is by far the most commonly encountered lizard on the Delmarva Peninsula. It is frequently found underneath loose bark and can be seen sunning on woodpiles on spring or fall mornings.

The juvenile's blue tail is apparently an adaptation to escape predators. Predators are attracted by the bright blue tail and grasp it instead of the lizard's vital areas. When grasped, the tail breaks off but keeps wiggling for a few minutes, distracting the predator and allowing the lizard to escape. (Cooper and Vitt 1985; Vitt and Cooper 1986.)

Broad-headed Skink   Plate 67
Eumeces laticeps (Schneider, 1801)

Other Names: Broadhead Skink.
Description: 16.5 to 32.5 cm (6.5 to 12.8 in.); snout-vent max. 14.2 cm (5.6 in.).

A relatively large, smooth-scaled, stout lizard, this is Delmarva's largest lizard. Coloration varies with age and sex. Juveniles are dark brown to black, with 5 (sometimes 7) bold, yellow stripes on the body, orangish stripes on the head, and a bright blue tail. The stripes extend from the head to halfway down the tail, and the median stripe usually forks on top of the head and reunites again on the snout. The throat and upper belly are cream-colored fading to gray-blue on the lower belly. As the lizard matures, the tail becomes grayish brown. Adult females retain faded striping. Adult males have a brown body that may show remnants of faint stripes on the back, and they have a wide, reddish head during the breeding season. This lizard usually has 5 upper labial scales in front of the subocular scale, no enlarged postlabial scales, and 30 to 32 scale rows around the midbody (fig. 17).

Similar Species: Common Five-lined Skinks are very similar in coloration (particularly the females and juveniles) and can best be distinguished by their scales: they usually have 4 upper labial scales in front of the subocular scale, 2 enlarged postlabial scales, and usually 26 to 30 scale rows around the midbody. In addition, adult Common Five-lined Skinks are smaller than adult Broad-headed Skinks and the adult male Common Five-lined Skink has a smaller head.

Overall Range: Found from southeastern Pennsylvania to Central Florida and west to Kansas and Texas.

Range and Status on Delmarva: Rare to very rare on the Coastal Plain and absent from the Piedmont. Records are lacking from all of Delaware and from Accomack County, Virginia. Apparently absent from the barrier islands.

Habitat: Found in mixed deciduous-coniferous or coniferous woodlands and cypress swamps, preferably large, open, mature stands. Broad-headed Skinks are largely arboreal and are often observed in trees and shrubs. They are also found around woodpiles, brush piles, trash, and other debris.

Reproduction and Development: Mating takes place in spring and early summer. During the breeding season, the female finds a suitable nesting site and emits a sexually attractive pheromone from the base of her tail. The male uses his tongue to detect this pheromone on the substrate, allowing him to track and locate the female. Once located, the male will mate with the female and then guard her and her nesting site, chasing away rival males. Males are apparently territorial only during the height of the breeding season. (Vitt and Cooper 1985.)

Between mid-June and late July the female deposits 9 to 20 eggs in a depression in loose soil or decaying logs or under leaf litter. The female stays with the eggs, encircling them with her body. The eggs hatch in about one month. (Green and Pauley 1987; Mitchell 1994.)

Remarks: The Broad-headed Skink's preference for large, mature woodlands, and the scarcity of this habitat on Delmarva, may explain the apparent rarity of this species on the peninsula. These skinks typically climb trees when approached by potential predators, including humans. They sometimes climb high in trees or hide in tree cavities.

The function of the juvenile's blue tail is to help escape predators, as described for the Common Five-lined Skink.

Little Brown Skink   Plate 68
Scincella lateralis (Say, 1823)

Other Names: Ground Skink; formerly classified as *Leiolopisma laterale.*
Description: 7.6 to 14.7 cm (3.0 to 5.8 in.); snout-vent max. 5.8 cm (2.3 in.).

A small, slender, smooth-scaled, short-legged lizard. The dorsal color is usually a shiny golden brown to bronze with tiny black flecks. A distinctive, dark dorsolateral stripe extends from the tip of the snout through the eye and well onto the long tail. A transparent "window" patch is present on the lower eyelid, through which the lizard can see with the eyes closed. The belly is white, yellowish, or gray. The juveniles are similar in coloration to the adults.
Similar Species: The only animal on Delmarva that superficially resembles this lizard is the Northern Two-lined Salamander, which is somewhat similar in coloration and body shape. However, the Northern Two-lined Salamander lacks scales and claws and moves much more slowly.
Overall Range: Found from southern New Jersey to the Florida Keys and west to Kansas and Texas. Isolated records exist just north of this range and in Mexico.
Range and Status on Delmarva: Found only on the Coastal Plain. Rare to absent on the northernmost portion of the

Coastal Plain and rare to uncommon in the middle portion. May be locally common in the southern part of the peninsula. On the barrier islands, it has been recorded only from Smith and Fisherman's Islands, Northampton County, Virginia. Records are lacking from New Castle County, Delaware, and the Piedmont of Cecil County, Maryland.

Habitat: Prefers deciduous to mixed deciduous-coniferous woodlands where the surface humus layer is well developed. Sometimes found in more open habitats such as dry fields and small, piney woodlots.

Reproduction and Development: Although not recorded, mating probably occurs in the spring on Delmarva. Females deposit up to 7 eggs under or in rotting logs or stumps; however, unlike Delmarva's two other skink species, female Little Brown Skinks do not remain to guard the nest (Fitch 1970). Observations by McCauley (1945) and Groves and Norden (1995), in Dorchester and Queen Anne's Counties, respectively, indicate that females on Delmarva may lay 2 clutches of eggs per year, with the second clutch hatching in late August or early September. This species reaches sexual maturity within one year of hatching and is short-lived, with most individuals living less than three years (Fitch 1970; Mitchell 1994).

Remarks: The Little Brown Skink rarely climbs, spending all of its active time on the ground in or on top of the leafy humus layer, in thick grass, or under logs and other debris. This lizard escapes predators by quickly scampering across the ground before disappearing under a log, leaves, or other cover. Observation of this species on Delmarva can be difficult because of both its secretive nature and its scarcity in some areas. However, walking slowly and very quietly along trails in suitable habitat while listening for the rustle of dry leaves, an observer may enjoy a brief sighting.

The tail of the Little Brown Skink is easily broken off when grabbed by a predator or careless human handler. The broken-off tail continues to wiggle erratically, often distracting the predator just long enough for the skink to make its escape. The tail will regenerate in time, but the temporary loss of the tail affects the skink's ability to perform courtship behavior, produce eggs, and escape future predators. (Mitchell 1994.)

Snakes (Formerly Considered Suborder Serpentes)

More than any other vertebrate group, snakes instill fear and disgust in many humans. Whether these emotions are manifestations of some deep-seated fears that remain from times when humans lived in closer contact with the natural world or are a result of myths and media hype passed down from generation to generation, the result is the same: many humans do not like snakes. Nevertheless, humans are also almost universally interested in these fascinating animals.

As mentioned at the beginning of the section on the Order Squamata, many herpetologists now believe that snakes are really only a type of legless lizard. Snakes are nevertheless treated in this book as a group separate from lizards, and their main characteristics, unique or otherwise, are described in the following pages.

All snakes have limbless, elongate bodies that are covered with scales (fig. 18). The vertebral column is also elongated, and the number of vertebrae ranges from 141 to 435, each body vertebra with a pair of ribs. Adult snakes range from just over 10 centimeters to nearly 10 meters (about 4 inches to 33 feet) in total length. The vent, or cloacal opening, separates the tail from the body of the snake and is covered by an anal scale, or plate. Most snake species have only one functional lung, which may be almost as long as the body.

All snakes lack external ear openings and eyelids. They have long, forked, protrusible tongues that are used to sample chemicals from the environment and deliver them to the Jacobson's organ, a specialized chemosensory organ located in the roof of the mouth. Through the use of the tongue and

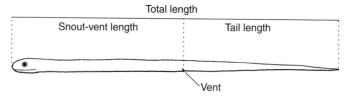

Figure 18. Generalized snake

Jacobson's organ, snakes can locate prey, detect danger, and identify other snakes within their species. Unique to snakes is the mechanism by which they focus their eyes. All other terrestrial vertebrates have eyes that are focused by changing the curvature of the lens using muscles that support the lens peripherally. Snake eyes, however, are focused by muscles within the iris that move the lens in relation to the retina.

Leglessness has not prevented snakes from exploiting a large variety of habitats. Some snakes spend most of their lives on the ground surface, whereas others are largely fossorial, arboreal, or aquatic. A few snakes are even marine. Snakes can be diurnal, nocturnal, crepuscular, or a combination of these.

Snakes cannot tolerate freezing temperatures, and therefore in colder regions (including Delmarva), they spend the winter months inactive in a winter resting place, or *hibernaculum*. The hibernaculum may be located underground below the frost line or in a crevice or hole in a rotting log, tree stump, or debris pile out of reach of freezing temperatures. Some snakes hibernate solitarily whereas others congregate in communal dens. Individuals of several different species sometimes use the same hibernaculum, and some snakes return to the same hibernaculum year after year (Linzey and Clifford 1981).

Snakes are strict carnivores and are known to eat a wide variety of prey, including bird and reptile eggs. Small species tend to feed on invertebrates, whereas larger species often feed on fish, amphibians, reptiles, birds, or mammals. Some snakes eat their prey alive; others kill prey first by constricting with their bodies. Still others have specialized teeth (fangs) that can deliver venom to help subdue their prey. Snake teeth are pointed and curved backward and cannot be used for chewing; therefore, snakes must eat their prey whole. Many snakes have jaw modifications that allow them to swallow relatively large prey whole. In these snakes the jaw parts are less rigid than those of most other reptiles and are loosely connected to each other and to the cranium. An elastic ligament allows separation of the lower jaw halves, permitting an extra-wide gape.

Snakes reproduce through internal fertilization of the eggs. Like other squamates, male snakes have a pair of saclike copulatory organs (hemipenes) that are kept inside the cloaca except during copulation. Only one hemipenis is used at a time during mating. Snakes are either *viviparous* (live-bearing) or *oviparous* (egg-laying), depending on the species. Parental care of offspring is limited, although some species do attend the eggs after deposition, offering protection from predators. Pythons are unusual in that they use their own body heat to incubate the eggs.

As snakes grow, they shed their skin periodically, usually in one piece from head to tail. Many species, including those on the Delmarva Peninsula, reach sexual maturity between one and four years of age.

Field marks that are useful in identifying snakes include the following: (1) the number of dorsal scale rows at midbody, (2) keeled versus smooth dorsal scales, (3) divided versus undivided anal plate, and (4) the overall coloration and patterning (figs. 19, 20, and 21).

Contrary to popular belief, most snakes are not aggressive and will flee when approached by a human. If cornered, however, many snakes will resort to defensive striking or biting. When captured, some snakes thrash about and secrete a foul-smelling fluid, known as musk, from the anal scent glands near the base of the tail.

There are more than 2,500 living species of snakes worldwide, belonging to approximately 15 families (Pough et al. 2001). Snakes are found on all continents except Antarctica. On the Delmarva Peninsula there are 19 species of snakes,

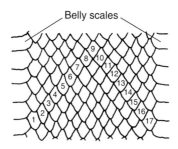

Figure 19. Expanded top view of snake showing numbering of dorsal scale rows

representing 2 families: the Colubrid Snakes (Family Colubridae: 18 species) and the Vipers (Family Viperidae: 1 species).

Colubrid Snakes (Family Colubridae)

The Family Colubridae is by far the largest family of snakes, with more than 1,700 species in approximately 320 genera worldwide (Pough et al. 2001). This diverse family is divided by many authorities into subfamilies, 3 of which are represented on Delmarva: Harmless Live-bearing Snakes (Subfamily Natricinae: 8 species); Harmless Rear-fanged Snakes (Subfamily Xenodontinae: 3 species); and Harmless Egg-laying Snakes (Subfamily Colubrinae: 7 species). Some authorities accord these groupings family status, rather than subfamily. This book follows the nomenclature used by Pough et al. (2001) for the scientific names. The common English names for the subfamilies are those presented by Joseph T. Collins on his

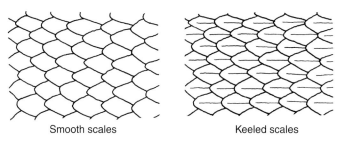

Smooth scales   Keeled scales

Figure 20. Smooth versus keeled scales

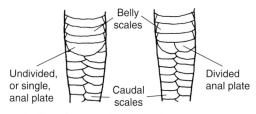

Figure 21. Underside of snakes near the vent

Web site (www.naherpetology.org), although Collins considers these groupings to have family status.

Because the Family Colubridae is very diverse and is represented on Delmarva by so many species (18), the pattern followed in this section is different from the rest of this book; species are grouped by subfamily and arranged alphabetically within each subfamily.

Harmless Live-bearing Snakes (Subfamily Natricinae)

The Subfamily Natricinae are small to moderately large snakes that may be aquatic, terrestrial, or semifossorial (Pough et al. 2001). They are all viviparous. Those on Delmarva feed primarily on cold-blooded prey such as frogs, salamanders, fish, and invertebrates, and they are not constrictors. Many are noted for discharging foul-smelling musk when handled. There are 8 species in 5 genera (*Nerodia, Regina, Storeria, Thamnophis,* and *Virginia*) known to occur on Delmarva.

Red-bellied Watersnake   **Plate 69**
Nerodia erythrogaster erythrogaster (Forster, 1771)

Other Names: Redbelly Water Snake; formerly classified as *Natrix erythrogaster erythrogaster.*
Description: 76 to 122 cm (30 to 48 in.); record 157.5 cm (62.0 in.).

A moderately large, thick-bodied snake that is reddish brown to chocolate brown above (sometimes appearing shiny black) with a plain red to reddish orange belly. The dark dorsal color often extends onto the sides of the belly. The lower half of the head is usually orangish, and a white or yellow patch is present on the throat. The dorsal scales are strongly keeled, and the anal plate is divided. Juveniles are boldly patterned with brown dorsal blotches that alternate with smaller lateral blotches on a pinkish ground color. The dorsal blotches often form bands on the anterior part of the body. The juvenile belly can be cream, yellow, pinkish, or pale orange.

Similar Species: The Common Watersnake usually has a bold pattern of 2 irregular rows of brown to reddish half-moon-shaped spots on a yellowish belly.

Overall Range: Found from southeastern Virginia to northern Florida and west to southeastern Alabama. An isolated population occurs on the Delmarva Peninsula.

Range and Status on Delmarva: Very rare overall; found only in southern Sussex County, Delaware, and Dorchester, eastern Wicomico, and northern Worcester Counties, Maryland. Apparently more common locally in southern Dorchester and northern Worcester Counties (W. Grogan personal communication). Absent from the barrier islands.

Habitat: Found in or adjacent to headwater swamps, freshwater and brackish portions of tidal swamps and marshes, slow-moving streams, and ditches. Typically associated with bald cypress or Atlantic white cedar swamps. Unlike the Common Watersnake, it has rarely been seen in water on Delmarva and may wander far from water, particularly in hot, dry weather.

Reproduction and Development: Reproduction and development have not yet been documented on Delmarva. In other parts of its range, mating occurs from April through June (Ernst and Barbour 1989b). Up to 50 young are born alive in late summer or early fall (Linzey and Clifford 1981).

Remarks: Little is known about the natural history and range of this species on Delmarva. Although this snake is fairly common and relatively easy to observe in the southern part of its overall range, it is rarely seen on the peninsula and may be declining because of habitat destruction. Any sighting of this snake should be documented by a combination of photograph or specimen along with detailed notes.

Red-bellied Watersnakes feed on aquatic and semiaquatic prey, including crayfish, frogs, salamanders, and fish. The prey is eaten alive. (Mitchell 1994.)

In comparison to the Common Watersnake this snake is usually less apt to bite when encountered or initially picked up (W. Grogan personal communication).

Common Watersnake   Plates 70, 71
Nerodia sipedon sipedon (Linnaeus, 1758)

Other Names: Northern Water Snake; formerly
classified as *Natrix sipedon sipedon.*
Description: 61 to 107 cm (24 to 42 in.); record 140.0
cm (55.1 in.).
     A moderately large, thick-bodied snake that is
highly variable in coloration. Adults usually have
reddish brown to black markings on the back and sides on a
pale gray to dark brown background. The markings usually
form crossbands on the anterior part of the body and blotches
that alternate on the back and sides on the posterior part of
the body. Two irregular rows of brownish or reddish
half-moon-shaped spots are usually present on the yellowish
belly. The dorsal scales are strongly keeled, and the anal plate
is divided. Juveniles have more pronounced markings on a pale
gray or light brown background. The markings gradually fade
with age and are sometimes obscured in older, larger snakes,
giving them an almost uniform black appearance.
Similar Species: Because of its large size, blotchy markings,
and sometimes aggressive behavior, this snake is very often
misidentified as a venomous species such as the Copperhead or
Cottonmouth. However, the Copperhead has hourglass-shaped
crossbands that are narrowest on the dorsal surface of the
body, vertical pupils, and facial pits below and between the
eyes and nostrils. The Cottonmouth *(Agkistrodon piscivorus)*
can also be distinguished by its vertical pupils and facial pits,
but it is not found on the Delmarva Peninsula. Adult
Red-bellied Watersnakes are uniformly brown on the dorsal
surface and have reddish, usually unmarked, bellies. Juvenile
Red-bellied Watersnakes have markings above but usually
have unmarked bellies.
Overall Range: Found from Maine to North Carolina and west
to Minnesota and Colorado.
Range and Status on Delmarva: Very common throughout
the peninsula. Reported on many barrier islands.
Habitat: Found in or near virtually all freshwater habitats,
including rivers, streams, ponds, ditches, vernal pools,

---

freshwater marshes, and swamps; and in brackish habitats, including tidal streams and the edges of salt marshes.

Reproduction and Development: Mating takes place in the spring, usually out of the water on logs, snags, vegetation, or the ground. Common Watersnakes bear their young alive, from mid-August to mid-October. Litter sizes ranging from 8 to 46 young have been reported. (Fitch 1970.)

Remarks: The Common Watersnake is one of the most frequently encountered snakes on the peninsula. It is usually observed basking near water or swimming on the surface. This snake can be very bold, allowing an observer to get very close before slithering away into the brush or water. When cornered, it often flattens its body and strikes aggressively. Although not dangerous to humans, it will readily bite if handled. In addition, it discharges a malodorous musk from its anal glands when handled.

The Common Watersnake feeds primarily on fish and amphibians. All prey are swallowed whole and alive, including catfish with their mildly venomous fin spines (W. Grogan personal communication). This snake often preys upon American and Fowler's Toads and is apparently immune to their toxic skin secretions.

Queen Snake   Plate 72
Regina septemvittata (Say, 1825)

Other Names: Formerly classified as *Natrix septemvittata.*

Description: 38 to 61 cm (15 to 24 in.); record 92.2 cm (36.3 in.).

A small to medium-sized, slender snake that is olive brown to dark brown above. A yellowish lateral stripe on the first and second scale rows extends from nose to tail. Some individuals also have 3 indistinct, dark stripes on the back. The belly is yellowish, with 4 dark brown stripes that converge near the throat and converge or break up on the tail. The two outer belly stripes are on the lower half of the first scale row. The dorsal scales are keeled, and the anal plate is divided. Juveniles are similar to adults but have more clearly defined belly stripes.

Similar Species: Common Ribbonsnakes and Eastern Gartersnakes usually have a light mid-dorsal stripe and lack stripes on the belly.

Overall Range: Found from Ontario, southwestern New York, and southeastern Pennsylvania south to the Florida panhandle and west to Michigan and Mississippi. A few isolated populations occur west of this range.

Range and Status on Delmarva: Uncommon; found on the Piedmont and on the northern portion of the Coastal Plain. Records exist only from New Castle County, Delaware, and Cecil and Kent Counties, Maryland.

Habitat: The Queen Snake prefers rocky, relatively unpolluted streams but is also sometimes found in soft-bottomed, slow-moving streams (including freshwater tidal ones), bogs, or freshwater marshes or along the edges of ponds or lakes. It is usually found where there is ample scrubby vegetation on the banks.

Reproduction and Development: Queen Snake mating has been reported in spring and fall. Queen Snakes are viviparous, giving live birth to up to 18 young in August or September. Sexual maturity is reached in two to three years. (Branson and Baker 1974; Linzey and Clifford 1981.)

Remarks: The Queen Snake is the most aquatic snake on the Delmarva Peninsula and is rarely found far from the water's edge. This diurnal snake spends most of its time searching under submerged rocks and crevices for its prey or basking while draped over streamside vegetation. Although the Queen Snake may eat some small fish, salamanders, and frogs, its principle food is crayfish that have recently molted (soft-shelled).

The Queen Snake appears to be declining on Delmarva as streams continue to be degraded. Stream degradation has resulted in the reduction, and in some places the elimination, of the crayfish populations on which the snake depends.

If captured, this snake often thrashes around vigorously and discharges a large quantity of musk, but it rarely attempts to bite. Charles Schultz's *Peanuts* characters Charlie Brown and Lucy had an unfounded fear of the harmless Queen Snake.

Northern Brownsnake   **Plate 73**
Storeria dekayi dekayi (Holbrook, 1836)

Other Names: Northern Brown Snake; DeKay's
Snake.

Description: 23 to 33 cm (9 to 13 in.); record 49.3 cm
(19.4 in.).

   A small snake that is light to dark brown above
with 2 parallel rows of dark spots down the back.
The dark spots are sometimes connected by narrow, dark lines
to form the impression of 2 dark dorsal stripes. A mid-dorsal
stripe that is slightly lighter than the rest of the body runs
between the 2 rows of dark dorsal spots. The scales on the side
of the body are often tipped in black. A nearly vertical black
streak is found on the side of the head behind the eye. The
belly is cream-colored to slightly pinkish and is unmarked
except for black specks at the side of each ventral scale in some
individuals. The dorsal scales are keeled, and the anal plate is
divided. Juveniles are dark brown to black with a conspicuous
cream to yellowish collar band on the neck.

Similar Species: Five other snakes might be confused with
either the adult or the juvenile Northern Brownsnake. Eastern
Smooth Earthsnakes and Eastern Wormsnakes can be
distinguished by their smooth scales and the absence of a dark
streak on the side of the head. The Northern Red-bellied Snake
has a reddish belly and 3 light spots on the neck. The Eastern
Gartersnake usually has light lateral stripes and an undivided
anal plate. The Ring-necked Snake has smooth scales and a
brighter yellowish or orangish neck collar than the juvenile
Northern Brownsnake.

Overall Range: Found from southern Maine to North Carolina
and west to the Great Lakes region and eastern Tennessee.

Range and Status on Delmarva: Uncommon throughout most
of the peninsula, although relatively abundant in some isolated
locations, particularly in urban areas. Reported from several
barrier islands. Recorded in all counties.

Habitat: Found in a wide variety of habitats ranging from
undisturbed to urban and from dry to moist. Habitats include
deciduous, mixed deciduous-coniferous, and coniferous

Snakes   *167*

woodlands and fields, marshes, swamps, suburban yards, and abandoned lots in urban areas.

Reproduction and Development: Northern Brownsnakes apparently mate in the spring. They are viviparous, bearing up to 41 live young between July and September. Sexual maturity is attained at about two years of age. (Ernst and Barbour 1989b; Fitch 1970.)

Remarks: The Northern Brownsnake is terrestrial and spends most of its life in leaf litter and under logs, rocks, or man-made debris. Its primary prey includes earthworms, slugs, and other soft-bodied invertebrates, although small frogs, snails, and fish may also be eaten. (Mitchell 1994.)

Sometimes called the "City Snake," the Northern Brownsnake is often found in disturbed areas, including abandoned city lots, city parks, and yards. Author James White has found this snake in several locations within the city of Wilmington, Delaware. However, urban populations of this snake may be declining, because of the use of pesticides that kill the snake's prey and city cleanup projects that destroy the snake's debris habitat. Free-roaming cats also reduce Northern Brownsnake numbers. (Mitchell 1994.)

Northern Red-bellied Snake   Plate 74
Storeria occipitomaculata occipitomaculata (Storer, 1839)

Other Names: Northern Redbelly Snake.
Description: 20 to 25 cm (8 to 10 in.); record 40.6 cm (16.0 in.).

A small snake with 3 cream to orange spots on the nape of the neck and usually a reddish belly. The dorsal surface can be brown, gray, or black, often with 2 to 4 thin, dark longitudinal stripes. A broad, tan to black mid-dorsal stripe is usually present, bordered by thin, dark stripes. Scales of the second scale row are sometimes edged in white and may appear as white lines down the sides. A light spot bordered below with black is found behind and below the eye. The belly is usually bright orange to red and is sometimes edged with black. The dorsal scales are keeled, and the anal plate is divided. Juveniles are similar to the adults but are darker overall with more conspicuous light spots on the neck.

Similar Species: The Northern Brownsnake has 2 rows of dark spots down the back, and like the smooth-scaled Eastern Wormsnake and Eastern Smooth Earthsnake, it lacks both a reddish belly and 3 light spots on the neck. The Eastern Gartersnake usually has light lateral stripes and an undivided anal plate. Ring-necked Snakes with incomplete neck collars may cause confusion, but they have smooth scales and typically have much brighter color on the neck.

Overall Range: Found in spotty distribution from Nova Scotia to Georgia and west to Saskatchewan and eastern Oklahoma.

Range and Status on Delmarva: Rare on the Coastal Plain; absent from the Piedmont. Specimens have been found in Kent and Sussex Counties, Delaware, and Cecil, Queen Anne's, Dorchester, Wicomico, Somerset, and Worcester Counties, Maryland. Absent from the barrier islands. More field surveys are required to better define the range of this snake on Delmarva.

Habitat: Usually found in or near deciduous, mixed deciduous-coniferous, and coniferous woodlands with adequate cover such as rocks and logs. Sometimes found in more open habitats such as shrubby edges and fields, especially near freshwater wetlands.

Reproduction and Development: Northern Red-bellied Snakes mate in the spring and fall. Females that mate in the fall apparently store the spermatozoa in the oviducts over winter to be used for spring fertilization (Fitch 1970). This snake is viviparous, with up to 21 live young born in summer or early fall. Sexual maturity is apparently reached at two years of age. (Ernst and Barbour 1989b; Fitch 1970.)

Remarks: Because the Northern Red-bellied Snake is one of Delmarva's rarest snakes, all observations should be documented. This secretive snake is primarily nocturnal, feeding mostly on slugs, but earthworms and other soft-bodied invertebrates are also eaten. Most specimens have been found underneath logs, stones, and man-made debris, whereas others have been observed on roadways on rainy nights. Although this snake does not bite when handled, it does emit musk and has

---

Snakes

been reported to sometimes curl back its upper lip in a sneer (Green and Pauley 1987).

Common Ribbonsnake   Plate 75
Thamnophis sauritus sauritus (Linnaeus, 1766)

Other Names: Eastern Ribbon Snake.
Description: 46 to 66 cm (18 to 26 in.); record 96.5 cm (38.0 in.).

A medium-sized, slender snake with a very long tail. The dorsal color is dark brown, with 3 bold, cream to yellow (sometimes greenish) stripes extending from the back of the head to near the tip of the tail. The lateral stripes are on the third and fourth scale rows. A yellowish spot is in front of each eye. The belly is unmarked yellowish to bluish green. The exceptionally long tail is about one-third of the total length of the snake. Dorsal scales are keeled, and the anal plate is undivided. Juveniles are similar to the adults.

Similar Species: The Eastern Gartersnake is heavier-bodied and has lateral stripes on the second and third scale rows, black spots on the lateral margins of the belly, and a tail that is less than one-fourth the total length of the snake.

Overall Range: Found along the eastern seaboard from central New England to South Carolina and west to Mississippi. Also found in parts of Ohio, Indiana, Illinois, Kentucky, and Tennessee.

Range and Status on Delmarva: Uncommon on the Coastal Plain; very rare to absent on the Piedmont. Records are lacking from Wicomico County, Maryland; Accomack County, Virginia; and most of the Piedmont of New Castle County, Delaware (encroachment onto the Piedmont has apparently occurred along some stream valleys [J. McLaughlin personal communication]). Also absent from the barrier islands.

Habitat: This semiaquatic snake can be found in or near a variety of freshwater aquatic and wetland habitats, including marshes, swamps, wet meadows, floodplains, streams, vernal pools, and pond edges. It is often found in bushes and shrubby trees overhanging the water.

Reproduction and Development: Mating occurs mostly in the spring. Females are viviparous, with live young born in late July through early September (Mitchell 1994). Litter sizes of up to 26 young have been reported (Ernst and Barbour 1989b).

Remarks: Common Ribbonsnakes feed almost exclusively on amphibians, especially frogs (Ernst and Barbour 1989b). Author Jim White has observed these snakes searching for prey among groups of chorusing Eastern Cricket Frogs. The prey is normally swallowed alive.

The Common Ribbonsnake is an active and extremely agile snake. It disappears quickly when alarmed, often swimming across the surface of the water and disappearing into vegetation. If caught, it thrashes about and emits quantities of musk but rarely bites.

Eastern Gartersnake   **Plate 76**
Thamnophis sirtalis sirtalis (Linnaeus, 1758)

Other Names: Eastern Garter Snake.

Description: 46 to 66 cm (18 to 26 in.); record 124.0 cm (48.8 in.).

A medium-sized snake with highly variable coloration. The dorsal background color is usually brown or greenish. There is typically a conspicuous yellow or white mid-dorsal stripe, with less prominent pale lateral stripes on the second and third scale rows and 2 rows of alternating dark spots between the stripes, which form a checkered pattern. Some individuals, however, have very obscure stripes. The belly is yellowish, light green, or light gray, with small, black spots along the edges. The dorsal scales are strongly keeled, and the anal plate is undivided. Juveniles are similar to the adults but are usually more boldly patterned.

Similar Species: The Common Ribbonsnake has a more slender body, longer tail, and very distinct yellow lateral stripes on the third and fourth scale rows. It also lacks dorsal spots. The Northern Brownsnake has a nearly vertical black streak behind the eye, and its anal plate is divided.

Overall Range: Found from Quebec to Florida and west to Minnesota and eastern Texas.

Range and Status on Delmarva: Very common throughout most of the peninsula, although records are lacking from Accomack County, Virginia. Absent from the barrier islands.

Habitat: Found in a wide variety of terrestrial and semiaquatic habitats, including deciduous, mixed deciduous-coniferous, and coniferous woodlands; fields and freshwater wetlands; and the edges of streams, rivers, and ponds. Often found around human dwellings and gardens and sometimes in city lots.

Reproduction and Development: Mating usually occurs in spring not long after the snake emerges from hibernation although fall mating has also been documented. The male uses his olfactory senses to detect the female and follows her scent trail prior to courtship. Females give birth to up to approximately 85 live young between early July and late September. (Ernst and Barbour 1989b; Fitch 1970.)

Remarks: The Eastern Gartersnake is one of the most commonly encountered snakes on the peninsula. One common misconception is that the Eastern Gartersnake does not bite. Although it is not venomous and cannot cause serious injury, this snake is often aggressive and will readily bite anyone who handles it improperly. It also produces a strong, malodorous musk from its anal glands when alarmed, and it often flattens its body in defensive posture.

The Eastern Gartersnake eats earthworms, millipedes, spiders, insects, amphibians (especially frogs), and fish. It sometimes eats small birds and rodents. This snake is one of the last to enter hibernation in the fall and one of the first to emerge in the late winter or early spring. It is often active on unusually warm days in winter and early spring.

Eastern Smooth Earthsnake   Plate 77

Virginia valeriae valeriae (Baird and Girard, 1853)

Other Names: Eastern Earth Snake.

Description: 18 to 25 cm (7 to 10 in.); record 39.1 cm (15.4 in.).

A small, moderately stout-bodied snake that is uniformly dark gray or brownish above. Tiny, dark spots may be present

on the back. The underside of the head, body, and
tail is plain white, grayish, or yellowish. The dorsal
scales are smooth except for faint keels on the back
above the cloacal region. There are 15 dorsal scale
rows at midbody, and the anal scale is divided.
Juveniles are similar to the adults in coloration
although they may be a darker or lighter shade.

Similar Species: The Eastern Wormsnake has a
pinkish belly and 13 dorsal scale rows at midbody.
The Northern Brownsnake has 2 rows of black spots down the
back and keeled scales. The Northern Red-bellied Snake has
keeled scales, 3 light spots on the neck, and usually a reddish
belly.

Overall Range: Found from New Jersey to Florida and west to
Ohio and Alabama.

Range and Status on Delmarva: Uncommon; spotty
distribution on Delmarva. There are only a few records—all
prior to 1975—from the Piedmont. Records are lacking from
Queen Anne's, Talbot, Caroline, Dorchester, and Somerset
Counties, Maryland. There are a few historic records from
Accomack and Northampton Counties, Virginia, including Hog
and Cobb's Islands (Dunn 1918; Fowler 1925b; Reed 1956e);
however, the validity of these records has been questioned
(Conant et al. 1990).

Habitat: Found in or near deciduous, mixed
deciduous-coniferous, or coniferous woodlands that have sandy
or otherwise loose soil in which to burrow. This snake may be
found in more open habitats such as fields, roadsides, and
dump sites. Most Delmarva specimens are found under logs,
stones, and other natural or man-made debris.

Reproduction and Development: Eastern Smooth
Earthsnakes probably mate in spring and fall (Mitchell 1994).
They are viviparous with litters of 2 to 14 live young born from
late July to September (Ernst and Barbour 1989b).

Remarks: Although uncommonly encountered, the Eastern
Smooth Earthsnake may actually be quite common in some
areas. Its fossorial nature, however, makes it difficult to find in
areas where boards, logs, trash, and other suitable cover
materials are lacking. This snake feeds primarily on

Snakes

earthworms but may take other soft-bodied invertebrates such as slugs and grubs.

The Eastern Smooth Earthsnake does not bite but will often give off musk when handled.

Harmless Rear-fanged Snakes (Subfamily Xenodontinae)

The term *rear-fanged* is used for this subfamily because most members have 2 enlarged, faintly grooved rear teeth, and some, like the Eastern Hog-nosed Snake, can apparently deliver mildly venomous saliva. Members of this subfamily on Delmarva are terrestrial or fossorial, and they prey mostly on cold-blooded vertebrates or invertebrates. Some species apparently use constriction to subdue their larger prey. All species on Delmarva are oviparous. On Delmarva, 3 species in 3 genera (*Carphophis, Diadophis,* and *Heterodon*) are known to occur.

Eastern Wormsnake   **Plate 78**
Carphophis amoenus amoenus (Say, 1825)

Other Names: Eastern Worm Snake.
Description: 19 to 28 cm (7.5 to 11 in.); record 33.8 cm (13.3 in.).

A small, slender snake that resembles a large earthworm. The dorsal surface is plain brown, and the belly and first and second dorsal scale rows are pinkish. The head is small, pointed, and not distinct from the neck. The tail is short, ending in a sharp spine. The scales are smooth with an iridescent sheen. There are 13 dorsal scale rows at midbody, and the anal plate is divided. Juveniles are similar to adults except that their backs are darker brown and bellies a brighter shade of pink.

Similar Species: The Northern Brownsnake has strongly keeled scales and 2 rows of black spots on the back. The Eastern Smooth Earthsnake has a white, grayish, or yellowish belly; 15 dorsal scale rows at midbody; and scattered black dots

---

on the back. The Northern Red-bellied Snake has keeled scales, usually a bright orange to red belly, and 3 light spots on the neck.

Overall Range: Found from southern New England to South Carolina and west to Ohio and Alabama.

Range and Status on Delmarva: Fairly common throughout the Coastal Plain with the exception of the barrier islands, where it is absent. Also absent from the Piedmont. Recorded in all counties.

Habitat: Prefers moist deciduous, coniferous, or mixed deciduous-coniferous woodlands and open areas with soft, loamy soil that is suitable for burrowing. This snake is fossorial, living under logs, rocks, or debris or burrowing in soil.

Reproduction and Development: Mating behavior of the Eastern Wormsnake has not been observed in the field but there is evidence that it takes place in the spring and possibly also the fall. Females deposit 2 to 6 eggs under rocks or rotten logs or in decaying vegetation between late spring and midsummer. The eggs hatch in late summer. (Mitchell 1994.)

Remarks: The Eastern Wormsnake is very secretive and is rarely encountered in the open. However, observers can commonly find it by turning over logs, rocks, and debris in or near woodlands. This snake does not bite when handled but will try to escape by probing its head and tail into the captor's hand searching for a way out. Juveniles and adults feed primarily on earthworms and soft-bodied insects, searching for them under leaf litter, in loose soil or decaying logs and stumps, and under natural or man-made debris.

Ring-necked Snake   Plate 79
Diadophis punctatus (Linnaeus, 1766)

Other Names: Ringneck Snake.

Most of the Ring-necked Snakes found on the Delmarva Peninsula are believed to be intergrades between the following 2 subspecies (see "Overall Range" and "Remarks"):

- **Northern Ring-necked Snake** *(Diadophis punctatus edwardsii)* (Merrem, 1820)

- **Southern Ring-necked Snake** *(Diadophis punctatus punctatus)* (Linnaeus, 1766)

Description: 25 to 38 cm (10 to 15 in.); record 70.4 cm (27.7 in.).

A small, slender, shiny, bluish gray or dark brown to black snake with a cream to bright yellow or orange neck collar. The Northern Ring-necked Snake usually has a complete collar, and the yellowish belly is either plain or has small, black spots down the midline. The Southern Ring-necked Snake usually has an incomplete neck collar, interrupted on top of the neck, and the yellowish belly has a row of large, black, half-moon-shaped spots along the midline. Intergrades *(Diadophis punctatus punctatus* x *edwardsii)* often show a mixture of these traits. The scales of both subspecies are smooth, and the anal plate is divided. Juveniles appear similar to the adults but are darker at hatching.

Similar Species: Because of its distinct neck collar, the Ring-necked Snake is not easily confused with other snakes in the Delmarva area. Juvenile Northern Brownsnakes do have a thin neck collar, and Northern Red-bellied Snakes have 3 light neck spots, but both of these other snakes have keeled scales.

Overall Range: The Northern Ring-necked Snake is found from Nova Scotia to the northern portion of the Delmarva Peninsula and west to Minnesota and the uplands of northern Georgia and northeastern Alabama. The Southern Ring-necked Snake is found from southern New Jersey and most of the Delmarva Peninsula to Florida and west to the Appalachian Mountains.

Range and Status on Delmarva: Common throughout most of the Coastal Plain with the exception of the barrier islands, where only one specimen, from Chincoteague Island, has been documented. Relatively uncommon on the Piedmont. Recorded in all counties except Northampton County, Virginia.

Habitat: Prefers moist areas in or near deciduous, coniferous, or mixed deciduous-coniferous woodlands. It spends its life in the leaf litter or under surface objects such as rotting logs, stones, and other natural or man-made debris.

Reproduction and Development: Mating may take place in both spring and fall as in other parts of its range. In June and July the females lay up to 10 eggs, often under rotting logs, stones, or other natural or man-made debris. The nest sites are often communal. Hatching occurs in August and early September, and sexual maturity is reached within two or three years. (Ernst and Barbour 1989b; Mitchell 1994.)

Remarks: It is believed that the Ring-necked Snakes found on most of the Delmarva Peninsula, especially on the Coastal Plain, are intergrades between the 2 subspecies (Conant 1946; Conant and Collins 1998). Individuals found often show a mix of traits of both. Individuals from the Piedmont, however, usually appear to be typical Northern Ring-necked Snakes. (Conant 1946; J. White personal observation.)

Ring-necked Snakes feed largely on salamanders, including Eastern Redback and Northern Two-lined Salamanders, and also on earthworms, frogs, lizards, and small snakes (Mitchell 1994). Apparently most prey is eaten alive or held in the mouth until it stops moving, although the use of constriction to subdue vertebrate prey has also been reported.

Although this snake is secretive and is rarely found in the open except at night, when some are found on roadways, it may be the most commonly encountered snake on Delmarva when an observer is turning over surface cover, especially debris in roadside dumps. Ring-necked Snakes do not bite when handled but will emit musk.

Eastern Hog-nosed Snake   **Plates 80, 81**
Heterodon platirhinos (Latreille, 1801)

Other Names: Eastern Hognose Snake.
Description: 51 to 84 cm (20 to 33 in.); record 115.6 cm (45.5 in.).

A medium-sized, stout-bodied snake with an upturned, shovel-like snout for which it is named. This species is highly variable in color. Most individuals have dark blotches on the back alternating with smaller dark blotches on the sides on a background of varying

---

Snakes   177

combinations of beige, pink, orange, or brown. However, some individuals become entirely black or dark gray as adults and are therefore termed *melanistic.* The belly is usually mottled with gray or greenish on yellow, light gray, or pink. The head and neck are flattened when the snake is in defensive posture. The dorsal scales are keeled, and the anal plate is divided. Juveniles are similar to the adults in appearance except that any melanistic coloration is absent.

Similar Species: This snake is most often mistaken for a Copperhead, although the latter species can be distinguished by its hourglass-shaped dorsal crossbands, vertical pupils, and heat-sensing pit on each side of the head. Melanistic individuals may be confused with the Northern Black Racer or Black Ratsnake, but the Northern Black Racer has smooth scales and the Black Ratsnake has a body shaped like a typical mailbox in cross section: flat on the bottom and sides and rounded on top. (See figure 22, shown with the Cornsnake species account.)

Overall Range: Found from New Hampshire to Florida and west to South Dakota and Texas.

Range and Status on Delmarva: Relatively common on the Coastal Plain, including several barrier islands. Apparently very rare on the Piedmont of Cecil County, Maryland, and absent from the Piedmont of New Castle County, Delaware. Recorded in all counties.

Habitat: Typically found in sandy habitats such as sandy soil areas in deciduous, mixed deciduous-coniferous, and coniferous woodlands as well as sandy fields, dunes, or sandy beaches.

Reproduction and Development: Mating occurs in the spring and possibly the fall. The female lays 4 to 61 eggs in loose or sandy soil, usually in June or July but sometimes in August. The eggs hatch in August and September. (Ernst and Barbour 1989b; Hulse et al 2001.)

Remarks: Throughout its range, the Eastern Hog-nosed Snake feeds primarily on toads of the Family Bufonidae. On the Delmarva Peninsula this snake feeds almost exclusively on Fowler's Toads, rarely American Toads. It also eats other frogs and salamanders and occasionally insects and small mammals. A diurnal predator, the Eastern Hog-nosed Snake can often be observed searching for prey under logs and other debris or using its snout to burrow for toads in the soil. Once captured, prey is swallowed alive. A pair of enlarged rear teeth is used to puncture inflated toads before swallowing. The enlarged rear teeth also have faint traces of an anterior groove similar to the groove present in some venomous snakes. Although the Eastern Hog-nosed Snake rarely bites in defense, the saliva of this species is mildly venomous to some mammals, including some humans (Bragg 1960; Grogan 1974a). The toxins in the saliva are also venomous to toads and other amphibians, the snake's prey animals (Grogan 1974a).

When disturbed by a predator or a curious human, the Eastern Hog-nosed Snake usually responds with bluffing behavior by puffing up with air, widening its head and neck, and raising its head in cobralike fashion while emitting a loud hissing sound in an attempt to scare the intruder away. If this tactic does not succeed, the snake typically feigns death by writhing rapidly, turning over on its back, opening its mouth, extending its tongue, and sometimes even regurgitating its last meal before finally lying still. If picked up, the snake feels flaccid as if the body has started to decay. However, if the snake is placed back on the ground right side up, it will again turn over onto its back, revealing that it is indeed still alive.

Harmless Egg-laying Snakes (Subfamily Colubrinae)

The Subfamily Colubrinae represents the largest and most diverse group of Colubrids. They are all oviparous. Those on Delmarva may be terrestrial, semifossorial, or largely arboreal. Some species are constrictors, and many feed on small mammals, although a variety of cold-blooded vertebrates and invertebrates are also eaten. On Delmarva, 7 species in 5 genera (*Cemophora, Coluber, Elaphe, Lampropeltis,* and *Opheodrys*) are known to occur.

Northern Scarletsnake   **Plate 82**
Cemophora coccinea copei (Jan, 1863)

Other Names: Northern Scarlet Snake.
Description: 36 to 51 cm (14 to 20 in.); record 82.6
cm (32.5 in.).

A small to medium-sized, slender, strikingly
colored snake. The dorsal surface is patterned with
black-bordered, bold red blotches on a background of
yellow, cream, or gray. The underside is white to yellowish and
unpatterned. The pointed red snout projects well beyond the
lower jaw. The scales are smooth, and the anal plate is
undivided. Juveniles are similar to adults in coloration.
Similar Species: The Milksnake has black belly markings.
The venomous Eastern Coralsnake, which does *not* occur on
Delmarva, has a black snout and wide bands of red and black
on the dorsal surface separated by narrow yellow bands.
Overall Range: Found from extreme southern Delaware to
northern Florida and west to Oklahoma and eastern Texas.
Isolated colonies in New Jersey and central Missouri.
Range and Status on Delmarva: Extremely rare. Only four
confirmed Delmarva records exist, all on the Coastal Plain: one
from southern Sussex County, Delaware, found in 1963 (Arndt
1985); one from Wicomico County, Maryland, found in 1923
(Fowler 1945); and two from Worcester County, Maryland,
found in 1975 and 1991 (Grogan 1985, 1994). Absent from the
barrier islands.
Habitat: Found in areas of loose, usually sandy soil in
coniferous and mixed deciduous-coniferous woodlands.
Sometimes found in open areas adjacent to woodlands.
Reproduction and Development: Very little is known about
the reproductive behavior of the Northern Scarletsnake. In
other parts of its range, it lays 2 to 9 eggs in early to
midsummer. Hatching probably occurs in late August or
September. It is possible that some hatchlings overwinter in
the nest. (Ernst and Barbour 1989b; Mitchell 1994.)
Remarks: This secretive snake spends much of its time
burrowing underground or under the cover of logs, loose bark,
or debris searching for prey. It is rarely encountered in the

open except when found crossing roads at night, especially after heavy rains.

Northern Scarletsnakes primarily eat reptile eggs, but live prey, including frogs, skinks, small snakes, mice, and insects, are also taken. Enlarged back teeth puncture the eggs, and the contents are squeezed into the mouth through chewing action and external pressure from a body coil. Live prey are killed by constriction. (Mitchell 1994.)

The Northern Scarletsnake may be the rarest snake on Delmarva, and therefore all sightings should be reported and documented by a photograph. The vivid coloration of this snake resembles that of the venomous Coralsnakes of the genus *Micrurus,* which are not found north of North Carolina. Although not proven, it is thought that this mimicry may give the Northern Scarletsnake some degree of protection from visual predators that mistake it for a dangerous species.

Northern Black Racer   Plates 83, 84
Coluber constrictor constrictor (Linnaeus, 1758)

Description: 91 to 152 cm (36 to 60 in.); record 185.4 cm (73.0 in.).

A large, smooth, slender, black snake. The dorsal surface of the adult is satiny black, and the underside of the head and part of the neck are white. The belly is dark gray, and the undersurface of the tail is light gray. Like most other snakes the body is nearly circular in cross section. The scales are smooth, and the anal plate is divided. Juveniles have reddish brown to dark gray dorsal blotches on a light gray background except for the tail, which is uniformly brown above and white below. The eyes of the juvenile are relatively large. Adult coloration is attained by about three years of age and at a total length of approximately 40 to 45 cm (16 to 18 in.). (Hulse et al. 2001; Mitchell 1994.)

Similar Species: Black Ratsnakes have keeled scales, white markings on the belly, and a body shaped like a typical mailbox in cross section: flat on the bottom and sides and rounded on top. (See figure 22, shown with the Cornsnake species account.) Melanistic Eastern Hog-nosed Snakes have stout, often flat bodies, with upturned snouts. Cornsnakes and juvenile Black Ratsnakes have checkered bellies, a dark stripe from eye to jaw or beyond, and brown or red blotches on the tail.

Overall Range: Found from Maine to South Carolina and west to Ohio and Alabama.

Range and Status on Delmarva: Common throughout the peninsula, including some of the barrier islands. Particularly common on the Coastal Plain. Recorded in all counties.

Habitat: Found in all terrestrial habitats, including woodlands, fields, agricultural areas, and around rural buildings. This snake can also be found along the perimeters of freshwater, brackish, and saltwater wetlands and in sand dunes and is often observed under roadside debris and in dump piles.

Reproduction and Development: Mating takes place in the spring not long after emergence from hibernation. In late spring or early summer the females deposit up to 40 granular, somewhat oblong eggs under logs, rocks, or human-deposited debris, including mulch and sawdust piles. The eggs hatch in mid- to late summer. Hatchlings mature in two or three years. (Hunter et al. 1992; McCauley 1945; Mitchell 1994.)

Remarks: The Northern Black Racer is a fast-moving snake, as its English name implies. When encountered in open terrain it usually slithers away at great speed eluding all but the quickest snake hunter. If cornered, it will stand its ground, strike and bite aggressively, and sometimes vibrate its tail vigorously. Sometimes it rears up high to strike, lifting its head as much as two feet above the ground. This snake also tends to bite repeatedly, leaving painful lacerations each time it pulls away.

Northern Black Racers appear to rely on vision more than many other snakes do, and are often observed with the head and forward part of the body lifted straight up off the ground searching for prey or danger. They eat a wide variety of prey, including birds and their eggs, small mammals, lizards, snakes, frogs, salamanders, and insects. Contrary to the specific name of this snake *(constrictor),* the Northern Black Racer does not use constriction to subdue its prey. Instead it grabs prey with its mouth, pins it down with its body, and either suffocates it with its weight or swallows it alive. (Green and Pauley 1987; Mitchell 1994.)

Cornsnake   **Plate 85**
Elaphe guttata guttata (Linnaeus, 1766)

Other Names: Corn Snake; Red Rat Snake.
Description: 76 to 122 cm (30 to 48 in.); record 182.9 cm (72 in.).

A moderately large, colorful snake. This snake has a background color of gray, brown, or orangish brown and irregularly oval to rectangular, red to reddish brown blotches that are usually bordered with black on the dorsal surface. Smaller and more irregular blotches are present on the sides. The first dorsal blotch is divided into 2 long branches that extend from the neck forward, meeting on top of the head to form a spearpoint-shaped mark between the eyes. A bold red to reddish brown stripe extends from the back of the eye to the corner of the mouth and onto the neck. Like other snakes in the genus *Elaphe,* the body is shaped like a typical mailbox in cross section: it is flat on the bottom and sides and rounded on the top. See figure 22. The belly is heavily checkered with black on white, and the underside of the tail usually has black lateral stripes. The dorsal scales are weakly keeled, although the keels are difficult to see without magnification. The anal plate is divided. Juveniles are patterned like the adults, but the blotches are usually brighter red.
Similar Species: The Cornsnake is often confused with several other snakes, including the Milksnake, the Black Ratsnake, and the Copperhead. The Milksnake can be distinguished by its smooth scales, undivided anal plate, and possession of either a light Y-, U-, or V-shaped marking within the dark blotch on the back of the head or a light neck collar. Juvenile Black Ratsnakes lack the spearpoint-shaped marking on top of the head, and the stripe behind the eye stops at the corner of the mouth. Copperheads have hourglass-shaped crossbands on the dorsal surface and do not have a checkered belly.

Snakes   *183*

Overall Range: Populations are widely but sporadically distributed from the Pine Barrens in southern New Jersey to the Florida Everglades and west to Kentucky and Louisiana.

Range and Status on Delmarva: Uncommon to very rare. Records are only known from southern Sussex County, Delaware, and Talbot, Caroline, Dorchester, Wicomico, and Somerset Counties, Maryland. However, undiscovered populations may be scattered in suitable habitat throughout the southern part of the peninsula. This snake is listed as endangered in Delaware.

Habitat: Found on Delmarva in sandy, coniferous, or mixed deciduous-coniferous woodlands, including coastal maritime forests. Also ventures out into more open habitats such as fields and the vicinity of farm buildings in search of prey.

Reproduction and Development: Cornsnakes mate in the spring, not long after emerging from winter hibernation. The eggs, which usually number between 7 and 20 , are laid in June or July in or underneath rotting stumps, logs, and sawdust piles (Linzey and Clifford 1981; Mitchell 1994). The eggs hatch in August and September, and the hatchlings mature within three years (Green and Pauley 1987).

Remarks: The Cornsnake, despite its bold coloration, is one of Delmarva's most secretive and difficult-to-observe vertebrates. In addition to being uncommon and generally solitary, the Cornsnake spends much of its life out of sight, underground among tree roots or in animal burrows. Its aboveground movements appear to occur mainly at dusk and in early evening (W. Grogan personal communication). This snake is a constrictor, feeding primarily on small mammals as well as birds and their eggs.

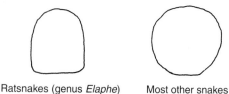

Ratsnakes (genus *Elaphe*)   Most other snakes

Figure 22. Cross sections of snake bodies

Cornsnakes are commonly sold in the pet trade because they are easily bred in captivity and they make fairly good pets, tending to be rather docile. However, wild Cornsnakes should never be collected on the Delmarva Peninsula because of their low population levels. In addition, in Delaware it is illegal to collect this snake because of its designation as endangered.

Black Ratsnake   Plates 86, 87
Elaphe obsoleta obsoleta (Say, 1823)

Other Names: Black Rat Snake, Black Snake, or Pilot Black Snake.
Description: 107 to 183 cm (42 to 72 in.); record 256.5 cm (101.0 in.).

A large, relatively thick-bodied, shiny, black snake. The body is shaped like a typical mailbox in cross section: flat on the bottom and sides and rounded on top (fig. 22). The entire back, sides, and top of the head are usually uniformly shiny black, sometimes with white speckling. The chin and throat are white. The belly is checkered black and white near the head, often fading to gray toward the tail. The mid-dorsal scales are weakly keeled, and the anal scale is usually divided. Juveniles are boldly marked on the dorsal surface with dark brown or black blotches on a gray or peppered black and white background. With age, this pattern becomes partially to totally obscured by black. Juveniles also have a dark stripe that runs from behind the eye to the back corner of the mouth. The juvenile chin and throat are white, and the belly is brown and white checkered.
Similar Species: Adult Black Ratsnakes may be confused with Northern Black Racers, melanistic Eastern Hog-nosed Snakes, or older dark Common Watersnakes; however, these other snakes have bodies that are more circular in cross section. In addition, Northern Black Racers have smooth scales and a uniformly dark belly from neck to tail; melanistic Eastern Hog-nosed Snakes have an upturned shovel-like snout; and Common Watersnakes have strongly keeled scales, and although old individuals are typically dark, they are rarely

---

uniformly black. Juvenile Black Ratsnakes are often confused
with other snakes, especially the Northern Black Racer and
the Cornsnake. Juvenile Northern Black Racers lack the dark
stripe between the eye and the jaw and the checkerboard
pattern on the belly and have 1½ to 2 times as many blotches
on the back. Juvenile Cornsnakes have a spear-shaped
marking on the top of the head, and the stripe from the eye to
the jaw extends onto the neck.

Overall Range: Found from Vermont to Georgia and west to
southern Minnesota and Oklahoma.

Range and Status on Delmarva: Relatively common
throughout the peninsula, including some of the barrier
islands. Recorded in all counties.

Habitat: Found in a wide range of terrestrial habitats,
including deciduous, mixed deciduous-coniferous, and
coniferous woodlands; hedgerows, old fields, and agricultural
areas; forested wetlands; and in and around barns and other
buildings.

Reproduction and Development: Mating usually occurs in
mid- to late spring. The females lay 5 to 44 elongate to oval,
leathery eggs between late spring and midsummer, depositing
them in rotten logs and stumps, loose soil, or decomposing
vegetation, or around human structures or debris, including
mulch and sawdust piles. The eggs hatch in late summer and
early fall, and hatchlings reach sexual maturity in the fourth
year. (Fitch 1970; Mitchell 1994.)

Remarks: The Black Ratsnake is the longest snake recorded
on the peninsula. It is an excellent climber and is often
observed moving high in tree branches in search of prey. This
snake feeds primarily on warm-blooded animals, including
Southern Flying Squirrels, Gray Squirrels, Eastern
Chipmunks, Cottontail Rabbits, Meadow Voles, White-footed
Mice, and Norway Rats (Mitchell 1994; J. White personal
observation). Birds of many species are also preyed upon, with
bird eggs, nestlings, and adults sometimes captured high in
the trees. Juvenile Black Ratsnakes have also been observed
feeding on frogs (N. Nazdrowicz personal communication).
Black Ratsnakes locate their prey by using their senses of sight
and smell (Mitchell 1994). They use a slow, methodical

approach, a lightning-quick strike, and powerful constriction to secure and kill the often relatively large prey.

A common myth concerning this snake is that it sometimes breeds with venomous species, such as the Copperhead, to produce viable offspring that resemble Black Ratsnakes but are venomous. Venomous snakes are in different families from the Black Ratsnake and therefore not closely related; hence, crossbreeding is impossible.

Some researchers (Burbrink 2001; Burbrink et al. 2000) have suggested a regrouping of the *Elaphe obsoleta* complex into 3 separate species, with those snakes found along the East Coast to be renamed Eastern Ratsnake *(Elaphe alleghaniensis)*. However, additional research is apparently needed to support the proposed reclassification.

Eastern Kingsnake   **Plate 88**
Lampropeltis getula getula (Linnaeus, 1766)

Other Names: Chain Kingsnake.
Description: 91 to 122 cm (36 to 48 in.); record 208.3 cm (82.0 in.).

A moderately large, shiny, black snake with narrow, white to cream-colored crossbands that fork on the sides just above the belly and connect to form a chainlike pattern. The belly, chin, and throat are irregularly checkered with black and white or yellow. The scales are smooth, and the anal plate is undivided. Juveniles are similar to the adults.
Similar Species: Juvenile Northern Black Racers and Black Ratsnakes appear somewhat similar to juvenile Eastern Kingsnakes, but they have dark blotches on a gray background and have a divided anal plate.
Overall Range: Found from southern New Jersey to northern Florida and west to the Appalachians and southern Alabama.
Range and Status on Delmarva: Uncommon throughout most of the Coastal Plain. Apparently absent from all of the barrier islands except Smith Island, Northampton County, Virginia. Absent from the Piedmont except in the Susquehanna River watershed. Recorded in all counties.

Habitat: Found in deciduous, mixed deciduous-coniferous, and coniferous woodlands and in fields and the edges of freshwater wetlands. Also found around old farm buildings and sawdust piles and under boards and other human-deposited debris.

Reproduction and Development: Eastern Kingsnakes probably mate in the spring. In June or July a clutch of 3 to 24 eggs is laid in rotten logs, sawdust, or soil. Hatching occurs in August or September. (Ernst and Barbour 1989b.)

Remarks: Eastern Kingsnakes are primarily diurnal but can also be seen crossing roads just after dark. Most specimens are found by turning over boards and other human-deposited debris. When threatened, this snake may coil, strike, and vibrate its tail. It discharges musk from its anal glands when first handled.

The Eastern Kingsnake feeds very aggressively on other species of snakes and will eat snakes nearly its own size, including the venomous Copperhead. It also eats lizards, amphibians, bird and turtle eggs, and small mammals. It is a strong constrictor.

Milksnake Plates 89, 90

Lampropeltis triangulum (Lacepède, 1788)

Other Names: Milk Snake.

Classification of the Milksnakes on Delmarva is part of an ongoing debate that will require further study to be resolved (see "Remarks"). To be consistent with the rest of this field guide, the scientific classification used by Crother et al. (2000) is followed here. Therefore this species is presented as being represented on Delmarva by two forms—1 subspecies and 1 intergrade between 2 subspecies:

- **Eastern Milksnake** *(Lampropeltis triangulum triangulum)* (Lacepede, 1788)
- **Coastal Plain Milksnake:** thought to be an intergrade between the Eastern Milksnake and the Scarlet Kingsnake *(Lampropeltis triangulum elapsoides)* (Holbrook, 1838), a more southern subspecies not found on Delmarva.

Description: Both the Eastern Milksnake and the Coastal Plain Milksnake are medium-sized snakes with brown or red blotches bordered in black along the entire length of the body and tail. Both have smooth dorsal scales and an undivided anal plate. Distinguishing traits are discussed below.

- **Eastern Milksnake:** 61 to 91 cm (24 to 36 in.); record 132.1 cm (52.0 in.). The Eastern Milksnake has 3 (rarely, 5) rows of 32 or more reddish brown to olive brown blotches on a gray or tan background. The dorsal blotches are much larger than, and alternate with, the lateral blotches. A Y-, U-, or V-shaped marking the same color as the body's background can usually be found within the large dorsal blotch on the nape of the neck. The belly is irregularly checkered with black and white. Juvenile snakes resemble the adults but have brighter, more reddish blotches on a light background.
- **Coastal Plain Milksnake:** 53 to 89 cm (21 to 35 in.). (W. Grogan personal communication.) The Coastal Plain Milksnake has 24 to 31 black-bordered red dorsal blotches that typically extend laterally down to or onto the belly scales, creating the appearance of rings when viewed from above or from the side. The background color is yellow, cream, or white. This snake lacks the Y-, U-, or V-shaped neck marking and instead has a full or partial neck collar the same color as the body's background. The belly has dark blotches that sometimes coalesce with the dorsal blotches, creating nearly complete body rings in some specimens (Grogan and Forester 1998).

Similar Species: The Cornsnake, Common Watersnake, Copperhead, juvenile Black Ratsnake, and juvenile Northern Black Racer all have blotchy markings, but they all lack both a Y-, U-, or V-shaped mark on the nape of the neck and a neck collar. The Cornsnake, Common Watersnake, Black Ratsnake, and Northern Black Racer can also be distinguished by the presence of a divided anal plate, whereas the Copperhead can be distinguished by the presence of hourglass-shaped dorsal crossbands and vertical pupils. In addition, the Cornsnake, the snake most often confused with the Milksnake, has a distinctive spearpoint-shaped mark on top of the head between the eyes, and the body is shaped like a typical mailbox in cross section.

Overall Range: The Eastern Milksnake is found from Maine to North Carolina and west to Minnesota and Alabama. The Coastal Plain Milksnake apparently ranges from southern New Jersey to northeastern North Carolina.

Range and Status on Delmarva: The Eastern Milksnake is fairly common on the Piedmont and the Fall Line region of northern New Castle County, Delaware, and northern Cecil County, Maryland, but it is absent from the Coastal Plain except near the Fall Line. The Coastal Plain Milksnake occurs only on the Coastal Plain, where it is rare. It has been documented in New Castle County, Delaware, and in Cecil, Kent, Dorchester, Wicomico, Somerset, and Worcester Counties, Maryland (Grogan and Forester 1998; J. McLaughlin personal communication). No confirmed records exist from the barrier islands or from the two Virginia counties. Further study is needed for researchers to understand the range of this snake on Delmarva.

Habitat: The Eastern Milksnake occurs in fields and deciduous woodlands, where it hides under rocks and fallen trees. It is also found in and around old farm buildings and can be especially common around stone structures. In contrast, the Coastal Plain Milksnake is found in sandy, mixed deciduous-coniferous woodlands where it spends much time burrowing and is rarely found above ground (Grogan and Forester 1998).

Reproduction and Development: The Eastern Milksnake usually mates in the spring and lays from 5 to 20 eggs in decaying logs or under rocks or debris in June or July (Williams 1988). The authors have observed hatchlings on Delmarva in August and September.

Reproductive data available for the Coastal Plain Milksnake is from St. Mary's and Kent Counties, Maryland (Grogan and Forester 1998; Miller and Grall 1978). Mating has been documented in mid-May and egg-laying in mid-June, with 5 eggs laid in each of 2 clutches observed. Hatching occurs in August and September.

Remarks: The classification of the Milksnakes on the mid-Atlantic Coastal Plain may be the most debated herpetological issue on Delmarva. Grogan and Forester (1998) summarize this ongoing debate and provide compelling arguments for recognizing the Coastal Plain Milksnake as a distinct subspecies *(Lampropeltis t. temporalis)*. They and many other scientists (e.g., Conant 1943; McCauley 1941; Miller and Grall 1978) challenge the currently accepted view put forth by Williams (1988) that the Coastal Plain Milksnake form is not a subspecies but is rather an intergrade between *L. t. triangulum* and *L. t. elapsoides.* Although the authors agree with the arguments presented by Grogan and Forester, the subspecies *temporalis* has not been included in this account because it is not recognized by Crother et al. (2000).

The Milksnake's common name may have resulted from the preposterous myth that these snakes seek out cows, somehow climb up to the teats, and proceed to suck milk. Although Milksnakes often frequent farm buildings in search of prey and therefore can be found around cows, the act of milking a cow is beyond the snake's needs and abilities.

Milksnakes are constrictors, and like other members of the genus *Lampropeltis,* they sometimes prey on other snakes. The Eastern Milksnake feeds primarily on small mammals, especially mice, whereas the more moderately sized Coastal Plain Milksnake apparently prefers lizards and snakes (Grogan and Forester 1998).

The striking dorsal patterns of some Milksnakes cause some people to mistake them for Copperheads, and hence, the Milksnakes are often killed.

Northern Rough Greensnake   Plate 91
Opheodrys aestivus aestivus (Linnaeus, 1766)

Other Names: Rough Green Snake.
Description: 56 to 81 cm (22 to 32 in.); record 115.8 cm (45.6 in.).

A medium-sized, very slender snake with a bright green head, body, and tail. The belly, chin, and underside of the tail are white, yellowish, or pale

---

Snakes   *191*

green. The dorsal scales are keeled, and the anal plate is divided. Juveniles resemble the adults except that they are paler green and have proportionally larger heads. The color of dead specimens rapidly fades to light blue.

Similar Species: Because of its unique, bright green coloration, this snake is not easily confused with any other snake on the peninsula.

Overall Range: Found from southern New Jersey to Florida and west to Kansas and northern Mexico.

Range and Status on Delmarva: Uncommon to rare on the Coastal Plain with the exception of some of the barrier islands, where it is common. Absent from the Piedmont except in the Susquehanna River watershed in Cecil County, Maryland, where it is apparently rare. Recorded in all counties.

Habitat: Found in areas of dense, green vegetation (small trees, shrubs, brier patches, and tangles of vines), particularly the edge habitat of deciduous and mixed woodlands. This snake is often observed in the foliage of shrubs and small trees near the edge of, or overhanging, ponds, streams, and marshes. It is also reportedly found in the debris that accumulates at the high tide zone along barrier beaches (Mitchell 1994).

Reproduction and Development: Northern Rough Greensnakes mate primarily in the spring but sometimes in the fall. The females lay 2 to 14 smooth, capsule-shaped eggs in June or July, depositing them inside decaying logs, stumps, and trees or under rocks, boards, and other debris. The eggs hatch in August and September. Sexual maturity is reached in one to two years. (Ernst and Barbour 1989b.)

Remarks: The scientific name *Opheodrys* is derived from the Greek words *ophios* (serpent) and *drys* (tree) and refers to the arboreal nature of snakes in this genus. The Northern Rough Greensnake is an excellent climber that spends most of its life in the branches of shrubs and small trees. It feeds mainly on terrestrial invertebrates such as grasshoppers and crickets, spiders, and insect larvae, although it may also feed on young lizards (Groves 1941). This snake is often overlooked because its long, slender, green body blends in perfectly with green leaves, twigs, and vines (particularly greenbrier). When handled, the Northern Rough Greensnake may display defensively by opening its mouth to show off its purple-black interior, but it rarely attempts to bite.

Northern Rough Greensnakes appear to be especially active in early fall and are often found crossing roads. Unfortunately most observations are of snakes that have already been hit by cars (personal communications with J. McLaughlin, N. Nazdrowicz, and A. Norden).

Some authors (Grobman 1984; Linzey and Clifford 1981) recognize a separate subspecies, *Opheodrys aestivus conanti,* on the barrier islands of Delmarva; however, this subspecies has not been recognized by most other authorities in the herpetological community.

Vipers (Family Viperidae)

The Family Viperidae contains approximately 227 species in 20 to 27 genera worldwide (Pough et al. 2001). Most members of this family are heavy-bodied, venomous snakes with a broad, triangular head and vertical pupils. All have a pair of hollow fangs on the upper jaw that are used to deliver venom to their prey or to ward off predators. The fangs are located near the front of the mouth and are hinged at the base so that they fold back along the roof of the mouth when the snake is at rest and move forward as the mouth opens to strike. All New World species have a pair of heat-sensing pits between the eyes and nostrils. These pits contain cells that can detect differences in temperature of 0.001°C, an adaption that allows these "pit vipers" to locate and track warm-blooded prey in total darkness, such as in a rodent burrow (Mitchell 1994). This family is represented on Delmarva by only 1 species, the Copperhead.

Copperhead   **Plates 92, 93**
Agkistrodon contortrix (Linnaeus, 1766)

Copperheads are apparently represented on the Delmarva Peninsula by 1 subspecies and an intergrade between 2 subspecies:

- **Northern Copperhead** *(Agkistrodon contortrix mokasen)* (Palisot de Beauvois, 1799)
- Intergrade of the Southern Copperhead and the Northern Copperhead *(Agkistrodon contortrix contortrix* x *mokasen)*

Description: 61 to 91 cm (24 to 36 in.); record 134.6 cm (53.0 in.).

A medium-sized, relatively thick-bodied snake with a thin neck and a large, somewhat flattened, triangular head. The Northern Copperhead has approximately 15 chestnut brown, hourglass-shaped crossbands on a light to medium brown dorsal background. The crossbands have lighter brown interiors and are widest on the sides and narrowest on the midline of the back. On some individuals a few of the crossbands are separated at the midline, offsetting the two sides of the hourglass. Small, dark spots are frequently present between the crossbands. The belly is light-colored and may be flecked or smudged with black. The head is tan, reddish, or copper-colored, with a heat-sensing pit located between the eye and the nostril. The eyes are light with dark vertical pupils. The dorsal scales are keeled, and the anal plate is undivided. Juveniles are usually paler than adults and have a bright yellow tail and a narrow dark line through the eye that divides the dark head from pale "lips."

Intergrades of the Southern and Northern Copperhead are often lighter (sometimes pinkish) in overall coloration and have narrower crossbands, many of which are separated at the midline.

Similar Species: Many of the area's nonvenomous snakes, especially those with boldly patterned backs (e.g., the Cornsnake, Eastern Hog-nosed Snake, Milksnake, and Common Watersnake), are commonly confused with Copperheads. However, no other snake on Delmarva has hourglass-shaped dorsal crossbands, vertical pupils, and a heat-sensing pit on each side of the head.

Overall Range: The Northern Copperhead is found from Massachusetts to Virginia, west to Illinois, and south to the uplands of Georgia and northern Alabama. Intergrades of the Southern and Northern Copperhead are apparently found in a broad band from the Delmarva Peninsula through eastern Virginia and the Carolinas, westward through central Georgia and central Alabama, and north to Illinois (Gloyd and Conant 1990).

Range and Status on Delmarva: Uncommon to rare overall but may be locally common. The Northern Copperhead is found in isolated populations in the Piedmont region of the peninsula along the Brandywine River in northern New Castle County, Delaware, and in Cecil County, Maryland. Intergrade populations are found in the southern half of the peninsula in southern Sussex County, Delaware; Dorchester, Wicomico, Somerset, and Worcester Counties, Maryland; and Accomack and Northampton Counties, Virginia. Copperheads are apparently absent from the middle portion of the peninsula and from the barrier islands.

Habitat: Found in a wide variety of terrestrial habitats. The Northern Copperhead prefers rocky areas in deciduous woodlands, often on steep, rocky slopes or in river valleys. Intergrade populations are found in mixed deciduous-coniferous woodlands or near bald cypress swamps and stream valleys.

Reproduction and Development: Copperheads usually mate in the spring just after emerging from hibernation, but fall mating has also been observed. Females give birth to up to 18 live young between mid-August and early October (Gloyd and Conant 1990). A female captured in northern Delaware gave birth to 9 young in late August 2000 (J. White personal observation). Two females from Wicomico County, Maryland, gave birth to litters of 13 and 14 young (W. Grogan personal communication). Sexual maturity is reached in two or three years (Mitchell 1994).

Remarks: The Copperhead is the only extant venomous snake on the Delmarva Peninsula. The vast majority of Delmarva residents will never see a Copperhead, although the authors receive many calls each year from people mistakenly reporting sightings. This species is relatively docile and reluctant to strike unless directly stepped on or otherwise provoked. Cases of humans being bitten on Delmarva are very rare; the authors know of no reported deaths directly attributable to

---

envenomization by a Copperhead on the peninsula in recent times. Nevertheless, this snake should never be handled, and caution should be taken when in Copperhead habitat because the bite, though rarely fatal, is still dangerous, particularly for young children and the elderly.

Adult Copperheads feed mainly on small mammals and birds, although lizards, frogs, small snakes, and insects are also taken. Juvenile Copperheads also feed on small mammals but a larger percentage of their food consists of invertebrates, salamanders, and frogs. The pit between the eye and nostril is an opening into a heat-sensitive organ that enables Copperheads to detect warm-blooded prey in the dark. This species is nocturnal or crepuscular in summer but largely diurnal in spring and fall. (Ernst and Barbour 1989b.)

Species of Possible Occurrence

Species included here have been reported in recent years but never confirmed (i.e., properly documented) on Delmarva. These species are considered to be "possible," based on their presence in nearby locations and the presence of suitable habitat on Delmarva. Currently, no amphibians fit this category, but 2 reptile species are included.

Eastern Six-lined Racerunner   Plate 94

Cnemidophorus sexlineatus sexlineatus (Linnaeus, 1766); Family Teiidae

The Eastern Six-lined Racerunner measures 15.2 to 24.1 cm (6.0 to 9.5 in.), with a snout-vent maximum of 7.6 cm (3.0 in.). This is a medium-sized, slender lizard with 6 light stripes extending from the head to the tip of the tail. The background color is dark brown to black. The tail is very long and slender and is rough to the touch. The belly scales are large, rectangular, and arranged in 8 regular rows. Males have a bluish belly, and juveniles have a light blue tail. This lizard is very active and bold but extremely difficult to catch because of its quickness. Similar species include the Common Five-lined Skink and Broad-headed Skink, which may be confusing particularly as juveniles. However, these two skinks have much brighter blue tails as juveniles, they are shiny, and their ventral scales are like their dorsal scales in size and shape.

This lizard prefers open, well-drained areas with sandy or loose soil. It ranges from the western shore of Maryland to Florida and west to Missouri and Texas and is the only member of the Family Teiidae native to the eastern United States. A single record exists from Delmarva, in extreme southern Northampton County, Virginia (Mitchell and Reay 1999). This record, however, is questionable (J. Mitchell personal communication).

Northern Pinesnake

Plate 95

Pituophis melanoleucus melanoleucus (Daudin, 1803); Family
Colubridae, Subfamily Colubrinae

The Northern Pinesnake measures 122 to 168 cm (48 to 66 in.),
with a record of 210.8 cm (83.0 in.). It is a large "black and
white" snake with a loud hiss. The background color is white,
yellowish, or pale gray, and there are black or dark brown
blotches on the back and sides from the head to the tip of the
tail. The belly is white with dark spots along each side. The
scales are keeled, and the anal plate is undivided. Juveniles
are similar to the adults in coloration and patterning. This
secretive snake spends much time burrowing. It also hisses
loudly when disturbed and may bite when first caught. Similar
species include the Eastern Hog-nosed Snake, which also
hisses but is usually multicolored and smaller and has an
upturned, shovel-like snout; and the juvenile Black Ratsnake,
which has a divided anal plate and a checkered belly.

The Northern Pinesnake prefers mixed pine-oak
habitats, particularly those with Virginia pine or pitch pine
(Burger and Zappalorti 1986, 1988). Its overall range includes
widely scattered populations in many southeastern states from
western Virginia south, as well as populations in southern
New Jersey. The only existing specimen collected on Delmarva
is considered highly likely to be an escaped pet, based on its
capture in a residential area in Kent County, Delaware
(Grogan and Heckscher 2001). Several sightings are known
from more suitable habitat in Sussex County, Delaware, and
Wicomico and Worcester Counties, Maryland, but they are not
confirmed by specimens or photographs (Harris 1975; Grogan
and Heckscher 2001). It is quite possible that populations of
this snake exist on Delmarva but have been overlooked
because of its secretive nature.

Extirpated Species

Extirpated species are those that previously occurred, but no longer occur, in a given area. On Delmarva, the Timber Rattlesnake is the only amphibian or reptile species that the authors believe is likely to have been extirpated in recent times (i.e., in the last two hundred years). It is possible that the Eastern Hellbender has also been extirpated; however, this salamander is included with the full species accounts because there have been sightings (albeit unconfirmed) within the last twenty years.

Timber Rattlesnake   Plate 96
Crotalus horridus (Linnaeus, 1758); Family Viperidae

Old newspaper articles report that rattlesnakes were found in Dorchester and Wicomico Counties, Maryland, and Accomack County, Virginia, in the 1800s and early 1900s. (Special Dispatch to the *Baltimore Sun,* Cambridge, Maryland, June 27, 1897. *Peninsula Enterprise,* Accomac Court House, Virginia, August 4, 1894; September 30, 1899; July 13, 1901.) Mitchell (1994) also provides several anecdotal accounts for Accomack and Northampton Counties, Virginia. In addition, there are several old place names on Delmarva that refer to rattlesnakes, such as Rattlesnake Hill east of Milton, Sussex County, Delaware; Rattlesnake Island in Worcester County, Maryland; and Rattlesnake Ridge on Chincoteague Island, Accomack County, Virginia.

Although there are no museum specimens to confirm the old accounts, it is quite possible that they are valid reports of the Timber Rattlesnake—a species that still occurs today in parts of New Jersey, Pennsylvania, Maryland, and Virginia as well as many other eastern states. Suitable habitat is present on the peninsula, but there have been no reports in about one hundred years. Therefore it is assumed that this species, if it indeed occurred, has been extirpated from the peninsula.

V. CONSERVATION OF DELMARVA'S HERPETOFAUNA

Amphibian and reptile populations have been dramatically affected by land development and other human activities. Although a few species have actually increased in number (e.g., the American Bullfrog, Northern Red-bellied Cooter [formerly Redbelly Turtle], and Black Ratsnake), most species have suffered, and a few have been, or are nearly, eradicated. The Eastern Tiger Salamander, Barking Treefrog, Eastern Narrow-mouthed Toad, Carpenter Frog, Wood Turtle, Bog Turtle, Cornsnake, Queen Snake, and Copperhead have been reduced to very small, isolated populations as a result of human activities. The Eastern Hellbender and possibly the Northern Pinesnake and Eastern Timber Rattlesnake have been, or are on the verge of being, extirpated from the peninsula.

Causes of Amphibian and Reptile Decline

By far the major cause of amphibian and reptile declines on the Delmarva Peninsula is habitat loss and degradation. Although native peoples altered natural habitats somewhat throughout the peninsula, it was not until the Europeans arrived that profound changes to the natural landscape began. Progressive clearing (e.g., for agriculture and wood products) of the dense forest that covered nearly all of the peninsula's uplands resulted in tremendous loss of natural habitat.

Equally devastating was the filling and draining of wetlands to increase tillable acreage.

Unfortunately habitat loss continues today. Woodlands are still being clearcut or fragmented for commercial, residential, and industrial development. The woodland patches that remain are often degraded by overuse, mismanagement, and invasion by nonnative plant species. Although they receive some legal protection, wetlands—particularly inland, freshwater wetlands—continue to be lost or degraded. Filling of small vernal pools is still relatively commonplace and results in the obliteration of critical amphibian breeding habitat. The removal of natural vegetation buffers around wetlands quickly degrades the quality of the wetland habitats. Also a threat to wetland herpetofauna is the common practice of enlarging and deepening vernal pools to create permanent ponds. Most amphibian species that use vernal pools cannot survive in permanent ponds that have predator fish populations.

In addition, various types of pollution continue to degrade amphibian and reptile habitat. Sediment runoff from agricultural fields and construction projects increases the turbidity of streams, reducing the aquatic invertebrate populations, the principal food of many stream-dwelling species. Chemical pollutants, including industrial wastes, fertilizers, pesticides, and herbicides, still find their way into wetlands and other aquatic habitats, causing reductions in reproductive success, malformations, and even death in some species, particularly amphibians.

The collection of amphibians and reptiles from the wild can also harm populations. The biggest impact is collection for sale in the pet trade. The prospect of easy money sometimes entices people to take large numbers of amphibians and reptiles from the wild, a practice that can be devastating to already troubled populations. Even the collection of just one or a few animals for home or school study may have a negative effect when the species is uncommon or rare.

Two other factors that adversely affect amphibian and reptile populations are nonnative animals and motor vehicle traffic. The introduction of nonnative animals, such as feral cats, decreases native amphibian and reptile populations through predation. Vehicles traveling Delmarva's roadways kill countless numbers of amphibians and reptiles each year. Those that are particularly susceptible to roadkill include amphibians that migrate across roadways to breeding areas on warm, rainy nights; snakes that warm themselves on road surfaces; and the Northern Diamond-backed Terrapin, which frequently crosses coastal roadways to nest.

Conservation and Management of Amphibians and Reptiles

Several actions must be taken if people wish to protect and possibly increase the remaining amphibian and reptile populations on the Delmarva Peninsula. These include the following:

- Set aside and protect as much area of woodlands, stream corridors, and wetlands as possible, on both private and public lands.
- Manage natural areas to maximize biodiversity, providing quality habitat for the complete spectrum of native species, including amphibians and reptiles. Especially important is the retention of microhabitats, including unmowed areas, logs, stumps, rocks, and leaf litter. When possible, management programs should integrate regular monitoring protocols to ensure that objectives are being met.
- Enact and strictly enforce laws to reduce habitat loss and degradation. Many freshwater wetland habitats have inadequate or no legal protection and consequently are at high risk for degradation or destruction for development. Upland forests are also insufficiently protected. Unless stricter laws are enacted, only habitats that lie within protected areas such as parks, wildlife areas, refuges, or preserves will sustain healthy amphibian and reptile populations.
- Enact and strictly enforce laws to prevent commercial collecting of all nongame herpetofauna. Collection of native amphibians and reptiles for sale in the pet trade

should be made illegal everywhere, with no exceptions. (Delaware, Maryland, and Virginia regulations pertaining to the collection of amphibians and reptiles can be found through government agencies such as state fish, game, and wildlife departments; some regulations are also available at the Web sites listed in section III.)

- Support and strengthen existing federal, state, and local laws that protect rare or endangered species and fully protect their habitats.
- Conduct research and maintain databases on species distribution, life history, and causes of decline, and apply the findings to land management practices. Support agencies and organizations (e.g., state nongame and Natural Heritage programs) that coordinate this work.
- Promote environmental and science education programs that include the importance of protecting amphibians and reptiles and their critical habitats. Emphasize what each person can do to increase protection.
- Publicize the values and needs of Delmarva's amphibians and reptiles to raise consciousness and gain support for their protection.

Species of Special Conservation Concern

Delaware, Maryland, and Virginia each have laws and regulations that designate and protect endangered and threatened species. The state-protected amphibians and reptiles, along with federally protected amphibians and reptiles, are listed in the following table under the heading "State and Federal Status." In general, it is illegal to collect, possess, or sell any species (or its parts) that is designated as endangered (abbreviated as E in the table) or threatened (T) without appropriate state or federal (and in some cases, local) permits. In addition, the habitats of federally designated endangered or threatened species are protected from destruction, whereas current state laws provide little, if any, protection for the habitats of state-designated endangered or threatened species.

Each state also has a Natural Heritage Program that ranks the state's plant and animal species according to the number of known populations or occurrences in the state. The protocol for this ranking was developed by the Nature Conservancy. Those species of greatest conservation concern, designated by rankings of S1, S2, or S3, are included in the table under the heading "Natural Heritage Rank." This table also indicates the global ranking for each of those species, as designated by the Natural Heritage Network and Natureserve. Unlike the federal and state endangered and threatened designations, the global and state natural heritage rankings have no legal standing, but are instead used to set inventory, protection, and management priorities.

The status and rank designations listed in the table are current as of August 1, 2002, but are subject to change. Contact the Natural Heritage Programs listed in section III for updated information.

Delmarva's Amphibian and Reptile Species of Special Conservation Concern

Common Name	Scientific Name	State and Federal Status[1]				Natural Heritage Rank[6]			
		DE[2]	MD[3]	VA[4]	US[5]	DE[7]	MD[8]	VA[9]	Global[10]
Salamanders									
Eastern Hellbender	Cryptobranchus a. alleganiensis		E	SC			S1	S2S3	G4
Spotted Salamander	Ambystoma maculatum					S2			G5
Marbled Salamander	Ambystoma opacum					S3			G5
Eastern Tiger Salamander	Ambystoma t. tigrinum	E	E	E		S1	S2	S1	G5
Long-tailed Salamander	Eurycea l. longicauda					S1			G5
Four-toed Salamander	Hemidactylium scutatum					S1			G5
Eastern Mud Salamander	Pseudotriton m. montanus					S1			G5
Northern Red Salamander	Pseudotriton r. ruber					S3			G5
Frogs									
Cope's Gray Treefrog	Hyla chrysoscelis					S2			G5
Green Treefrog	Hyla cinerea					S3			G5
Barking Treefrog	Hyla gratiosa	E	E	T		S1	S1	S1	G5
Eastern Narrow-mouthed Toad	Gastrophryne carolinensis		E				S1S2		G5
Carpenter Frog	Rana virgatipes		I	SC		S1	S2	S3	G5
Turtles									
Spotted Turtle	Clemmys guttata					S3			G5
Wood Turtle	Clemmys insculpta			T		SR		S2	G4
Bog Turtle	Clemmys muhlenbergii	E	T	E	T	S1	S2	S1S2	G3
Northern Map Turtle	Graptemys geographica		E				S1	S2S3	G5
Loggerhead Seaturtle	Caretta caretta	E		T	T	SZN	S1B	S1B/S1N	G3
Green Seaturtle	Chelonia mydas	E		T	T	SZN	S1N	SZN	G3

Continued on following page

Delmarva's Amphibian and Reptile Species of Special Conservation Concern—Continued

Common Name	Scientific Name	State and Federal Status[1]				Natural Heritage Rank[6]			
		DE[2]	MD[3]	VA[4]	US[5]	DE[7]	MD[8]	VA[9]	Global[10]
Turtles (continued)									
Atlantic Hawksbill Seaturtle	Eretmochelys i. imbricata		E	E	E	SZN	SRN	SA	G3
Kemp's Ridley Seaturtle	Lepidochelys kempii	E	E	E	E	SZN	S1N	S1N	G1
Leatherback Seaturtle	Dermochelys coriacea	E	E	E	E	SZN	S1	SZN	G3
Lizards									
Broad-headed Skink	Eumeces laticeps					SH			5
Little Brown Skink	Scincella lateralis					S1			G5
Snakes									
Red-bellied Watersnake	Nerodia e. erythrogaster					S1	S2S3		G5
Queen Snake	Regina septemvittata					S1			G5
Northern Brownsnake	Storeria d. dekayi					S3			G5
Northern Red-bellied Snake	Storeria o. occipitomaculata					S1			G5
Common Ribbonsnake	Thamnophis s. sauritus					S2			G5
Eastern Smooth Earthsnake	Virginia v. valeriae					S1			G5
Northern Scarletsnake	Cemophora coccinea copei					SH	S3		G5
Cornsnake	Elaphe g. guttata	E				S1			G5
Eastern Kingsnake	Lampropeltis g. getula					S2			G5
Milksnake	Lampropeltis triangulum					S2			G5
Northern Rough Greensnake	Opheodrys a. aestivus					S2			G5
Northern Pinesnake	Pituophis m. melanoleucus					SR	SR	S1S3	G4
Copperhead	Agkistrodon contortrix					S1			G5
Timber Rattlesnake	Crotalus horridus						S3		G4

Notes to Table

[1] State and federal status: **E** = endangered; **T** = threatened; **I** = in need of conservation; population is limited or declining and may become threatened if current trends or conditions continue; **SC** = merits special concern; not a regulatory category.

Blank spaces indicate (1) species not known to occur in the area, or (2) species not designated as endangered or threatened.

[2] Reference: Delaware Wildlife and Non-Tidal Fishing Regulations; authority: 7 DelCode, Chap. 1, Sec. 103.

[3] Reference: Maryland Nongame and Endangered Species Conservation Act, Annotated Code of Maryland sections 10-2A-01 to 10-2A-09; also, State Threatened and Endangered Species regulations, COMAR 08.03.11.01 to 08.03.11.14; authority: Title 8: DNR, Subtitle 03, Chap. 11.

[4] Reference: Virginia Endangered Species Act, Code of Virginia, Section 29.1-564-570.

[5] Reference: "Endangered and Threatened Wildlife and Plants," 50 CFR 17.11 and 17.12, determined by U.S. Fish and Wildlife Service, Department of the Interior; authority: federal Endangered Species Act of 1973, as amended, 16 U.S.C. 1531-1543.

[6] Natural Heritage rank, state rank key: **S1** = extremely rare, typically 5 or fewer known populations or occurrences; often especially vulnerable to extirpation; **S2** = very rare, typically 6 to 20 known populations or occurrences; often susceptible to extirpation; **S3** = rare to uncommon, typically 21 to 100 known populations or occurrences; not immediately threatened with extirpation but may be if additional populations are destroyed; **SA** = accidental occurrence; **S#B** = breeding status; **SH** = historically known, but not verified for an extended period, usually more than 15 years; **S#N** = non-breeding status; **SR** = reported, but no evidence exists for accepting or rejecting the report; **SZN** = long distance migrant with occurrences too irregular, transitory, or dispersed to be reliably identified, mapped, and protected.

Where two ranks are shown, the rank is uncertain but considered to be within the indicated range.

Blank spaces indicate (1) species not known to occur in that state, or (2) species not considered rare in that state (although it may be rare on the Delmarva Peninsula portion of that state).

National Heritage rank, global rank key: **G1** = critically imperiled; **G2** = imperiled; **G3** = rare; **G4** = apparently secure but uncommon in parts of its range; **G5** = secure.

[7] Reference: Delaware Natural Heritage Program, Division of Fish and Wildlife, Department of Natural Resources and Environmental Control.

[8] Reference: Maryland Wildlife and Heritage Division, Department of Natural Resources.

[9] Reference: Virginia Division of Natural Heritage, Department of Conservation and Recreation.

[10] Reference: Natural Heritage Network and Natureserve.

APPENDIX: CHECKLIST OF DELMARVA AMPHIBIANS AND REPTILES

English Name	Scientific Name	Notes (date, location)

Salamanders

Eastern Hellbender	*Cryptobranchus a. alleganiensis* _____
Spotted Salamander	*Ambystoma maculatum* _____
Marbled Salamander	*Ambystoma opacum* _____
Eastern Tiger Salamander	*Ambystoma t. tigrinum* _____
Red-spotted Newt	*Notophthalmus v. viridescens* _____
Northern Dusky Salamander	*Desmognathus fuscus* _____
Northern Two-lined Salamander	*Eurycea bislineata* _____
Long-tailed Salamander	*Eurycea l. longicauda* _____
Four-toed Salamander	*Hemidactylium scutatum* _____
Eastern Red-backed Salamander	*Plethodon cinereus* _____
Northern Slimy Salamander	*Plethodon glutinosus* _____
Eastern Mud Salamander	*Pseudotriton m. montanus* _____
Northern Red Salamander	*Pseudotriton r. ruber* _____

Frogs

Eastern Spadefoot	*Scaphiopus holbrookii* _____
Eastern American Toad	*Bufo a. americanus* _____
Fowler's Toad	*Bufo fowleri* _____
Eastern Cricket Frog	*Acris c. crepitans* _____
Cope's Gray Treefrog	*Hyla chrysoscelis* _____
Green Treefrog	*Hyla cinerea* _____

English Name	Scientific Name	Notes (date, location)
Barking Treefrog	*Hyla gratiosa* _____
	_____
Gray Treefrog	*Hyla versicolor* _____
	_____
Northern Spring Peeper	*Pseudacris c. crucifer* _____
	_____
New Jersey Chorus Frog	*Pseudacris feriarum kalmi* _____
	_____
Eastern Narrow-mouthed Toad	*Gastrophryne carolinensis* _____
	_____
American Bullfrog	*Rana catesbeiana* _____
	_____
Northern Green Frog	*Rana clamitans melanota* _____
	_____
Pickerel Frog	*Rana palustris* _____
	_____
Southern Leopard Frog	*Rana sphenocephala utricularia* _____
	_____
Wood Frog	*Rana sylvatica* _____
	_____
Carpenter Frog	*Rana virgatipes* _____
	_____

Turtles

Eastern Snapping Turtle	*Chelydra s. serpentina* _____
	_____
Eastern Mud Turtle	*Kinosternon s. subrubrum* _____
	_____
Stinkpot	*Sternotherus odoratus* _____
	_____
Eastern Painted Turtle	*Chrysemys p. picta* _____
	_____
Spotted Turtle	*Clemmys guttata* _____
	_____
Wood Turtle	*Clemmys insculpta* _____
	_____
Bog Turtle	*Clemmys muhlenbergii* _____
	_____
Northern Map Turtle	*Graptemys geographica* _____
	_____
Northern Diamond- backed Terrapin	*Malaclemys t. terrapin* _____
	_____
Northern Red-bellied Cooter	*Pseudemys rubriventris* _____
	_____
Eastern Box Turtle	*Terrapene c. carolina* _____
	_____

English Name	Scientific Name	Notes (date, location)
Red-eared Slider	*Trachemys scripta elegans* _____	
Loggerhead Seaturtle	*Caretta caretta* _____	
Green Seaturtle	*Chelonia mydas* _____	
Atlantic Hawksbill Seaturtle	*Eretmochelys i. imbricata* _____	
Kemp's Ridley Seaturtle	*Lepidochelys kempii* _____	
Leatherback Seaturtle	*Dermochelys coriacea* _____	

Lizards

Northern Fence Lizard	*Sceloporus undulatus hyacinthinus* _____	
Common Five-lined Skink	*Eumeces fasciatus* _____	
Broad-headed Skink	*Eumeces laticeps* _____	
Little Brown Skink	*Scincella lateralis* _____	

Snakes

Red-bellied Watersnake	*Nerodia e. erythrogaster* _____	
Common Watersnake	*Nerodia s. sipedon* _____	
Queen Snake	*Regina septemvittata* _____	
Northern Brownsnake	*Storeria d. dekayi* _____	
Northern Red-bellied Snake	*Storeria o. occipitomaculata* _____	
Common Ribbonsnake	*Thamnophis s. sauritus* _____	
Eastern Gartersnake	*Thamnophis s. sirtalis* _____	
Eastern Smooth Earthsnake	*Virginia v. valeriae* _____	
Eastern Wormsnake	*Carphophis a. amoenus* _____	
Ring-necked Snake	*Diadophis punctatus* _____	
Eastern Hog-nosed Snake	*Heterodon platirhinos* _____	
Northern Scarletsnake	*Cemophora coccinea copei* _____	

English Name	Scientific Name	Notes (date, location)
Northern Black Racer	*Coluber c. constrictor* _____ _____	
Cornsnake	*Elaphe g. guttata* _____ _____	
Black Ratsnake	*Elaphe o. obsoleta* _____ _____	
Eastern Kingsnake	*Lampropeltis g. getula* _____ _____	
Milksnake	*Lampropeltis triangulum* _____ _____	
Northern Rough Greensnake	*Opheodrys a. aestivus* _____ _____	
Copperhead	*Agkistrodon contortrix* _____ _____	

GLOSSARY

amphisbaenians: A specialized group of burrowing squamates with rings of scales encircling the body and tail and usually without visible limbs. Sometimes called worm lizards.

amplexus: The mating embrace of frogs. In Delmarva species, occurs when the male climbs onto the female's back and clasps her just behind her front legs (axillary amplexus) or just in front of her hind legs (inguinal amplexus).

anal plate: In some lizards and all snakes, the large scale immediately in front of and covering the vent that marks the beginning of the tail. May be single (undivided) or divided by a diagonal suture. Figure 21.

anterior: Toward the head or front end.

aquatic: Living in water.

arboreal: Living in trees.

autotomy: Reflex separation of body parts; breakage of a lizard's or salamander's tail as an escape mechanism without the tail being grasped.

axillary: Related to or near the axilla or armpit.

bask: To lie in, or expose the body to, the warmth of the sun's rays.

biodiversity: Biological diversity; the variety of species of plants, fungi, bacteria, animals, and other life forms in an ecosystem.

blotch: A large, usually rounded or squarish spot.

bridge: In turtles, the portion of the shell that connects the carapace and the plastron on each side. Figure 10.

caecilian: An elongate, limbless amphibian that is highly specialized for burrowing and occurs only in the tropics. Order Gymnophiona.

carapace: The upper shell of a turtle, including its bones and horny scutes. Figures 10 and 11.

carnivorous: Feeding on animals.

cervical scute: In turtles, the single platelike scale located at the anterior margin of the carapace, immediately over the neck. Figure 11.

cloaca: The common chamber into which the digestive, urinary, and reproductive ducts discharge their contents, and that opens to the exterior through the vent.

costal grooves: Parallel, vertical grooves on the sides of salamanders between the front and back legs. Figure 2.

cranial crest: A bony, raised ridge between or behind the eyes on some toads. Figures 8 and 9.

crepuscular: Active at dawn and/or dusk.

crossband: A transverse band of color differing from the background color that is oriented with its long axis perpendicular to the animal's body axis.

diurnal: Active during the daytime.

dorsal: Pertaining to the back or upper surface of the body.

dorsolateral: Pertaining to an area between the middle of the back and the side of the body.

dorsolateral ridge: A fold or ridge of raised skin along each side of the back in some frogs of the genus *Rana*. Figure 4.

ectothermic: Dependent on external heat to warm its body; "cold-blooded."

eft: The terrestrial, often brightly colored subadult life stage of a newt.

endangered: A species whose abundance is so low that it could soon be extirpated in all or a designated portion of its natural range.

estivate: To become inactive or dormant during hot and dry periods.

estuary: A partially enclosed, tidally influenced body of water, such as the Delaware Bay and the Chesapeake Bay, that contains a mixture of freshwater received from its tributaries and saltwater received from the ocean.

extant: Currently existing; not extinct.

Fall Line (Fall Zone): The boundary, marked by falls or rapids along streams, between the Appalachian Piedmont and the Atlantic Coastal Plain physiographic provinces.

family: The taxonomic category ranked between the order and the genus; composed of related genera.

fauna: All of the animals living in a particular area.

fertilization: The combining of egg and sperm that leads to the development of an embryo.

flagellum: In some tadpoles, the narrow, terminal part of the tail that has greatly reduced fins and is capable of moving independently from the rest of the tail. Figure 6.

---

flora: All of the plants growing in a particular area.

fossorial: Adapted for digging or burrowing; living underground.

genus (pl., **genera**): The taxonomic category ranked between the family and the species; forms the first part of the scientific name.

gravid: Pregnant with eggs or young.

groin: The juncture of the lower abdomen and the inner part of the thigh.

ground color: The primary background coloration on an animal.

habitat: A place or environment where an organism naturally or normally lives its entire life or portions of its life.

hemipenis (pl., **hemipenes**): One of the paired copulatory organs in male lizards and snakes.

herbivorous: Feeding on plants.

herpetofauna: The amphibians and reptiles inhabiting a particular area.

herpetology: The study of amphibians and reptiles.

hinge: In some turtles, a flexible area of articulation between the anterior and posterior parts of the plastron.

hybrid: The offspring of parents from two closely related species.

inframarginal scutes: In seaturtles, a series of small scutes between the marginals of the carapace and the sides of the adjacent plastral scutes. Figures 11 and 14.

inguinal: Pertaining to the groin area.

intergrade: The offspring of parents from two closely related subspecies usually exhibiting a combination of their characteristics.

invertebrate: An animal without a backbone.

keel: A longitudinal ridge on the dorsal scales of some snakes giving the snake a rough appearance (fig. 20); a longitudinal ridge on the carapace or plastron of some turtles; or a thin, raised edge along the back and tail of some salamanders.

labial scales: In some reptiles, the scales of the upper and lower lips. Figure 17.

larva (pl., **larvae**): In amphibians, the immature, gilled stage occurring prior to metamorphosis. Figures 3 and 6.

lateral: Pertaining to the side of an organism.

longitudinal: Extending along the length; lengthwise.

marginal scutes: In turtles, the scutes around the outer edge of the carapace. Figure 11.

melanistic: Having more than the normal amount of the dark pigment melanin, often resulting in an all-black or nearly all-black animal.

mental gland: In some salamanders, a gland on the chin that secretes a substance that is sexually stimulating to females of the same species.

---

metamorphosis: In amphibians, transformation from the larval to the subadult stage, as when a tadpole transforms into a subadult frog.

mid-dorsal: Pertaining to the center of the back.

morphology: The form and structure of an organism.

nasolabial groove: A thin groove extending from the nostril to the upper lip in the lungless salamanders; enhances the sense of smell. Figure 2.

nocturnal: Active during the night.

omnivorous: Feeding on both plants and animals.

oviparous: Pertaining to species which lay eggs that develop and hatch outside the female's body.

parotoid glands: A pair of external, wartlike glands, located behind the eyes of some toads, which secrete noxious or poisonous compounds and aid in defense. Figures 8 and 9.

pelagic: Living in or pertaining to the open waters of the ocean.

phylogenetic: Pertaining to natural evolutionary relationships and lines of descent.

physiographic: Pertaining to physical geography, the study of the earth's surface.

plastron: The lower shell of a turtle, including its bones and horny scutes. Figures 10 and 11.

pleural: Referring to the lungs or the chest wall.

pleural scutes: In turtles, the large scales of the carapace located between the vertebral and marginal scutes; called *costals* by some authors. Figures 11 and 13.

pond-type morphology: In salamanders, a larval form with bushy external gills and a long, prominent dorsal fin that extends from behind the head to the tip of the tail. Figure 3.

population: A group of organisms that belong to the same species and live in the same area at the same time.

posterior: Toward the back or rear end of the body.

postlabial scales: In lizards, the scales lying immediately in front of the ear openings and in line with the upper labial scales. Figure 17.

prefrontal scales: In reptiles, the pair(s) of scales on top of the head in front of or between the eyes. Figure 15.

prehensile: Adapted for wrapping around or holding.

primitive: Referring to traits that evolved early and later gave rise to other traits; ancestral.

sargassum: A type of seaweed concentrated by ocean currents in the Sargasso Sea in the Gulf Stream of the Atlantic Ocean and used as a nursery area by some juvenile seaturtles.

scale rows: The longitudinal rows of dorsal scales around the bodies of lizards and snakes. They are counted just in front of the middle of the body. Figure 19.

scales: The thin, flattened, horny epidermal structures that cover a reptile's body.

scute: A large, platelike scale on a reptile, particularly turtles. Figures 11, 13, and 14.

serrated: Notched or toothed like a saw.

smooth scale: In snakes, a scale without a keel or ridge. Figure 20.

snout: The part of the head anterior to the eyes.

sonogram: A graphic analysis of sounds used to study the calls of animals such as frogs.

spade: In some toads, the horny tubercle on the inside of each hind foot that is used for digging. Figure 7.

species: A population, or group of populations, of organisms that can interbreed to produce fertile offspring; the basic taxonomic category that together with the genus forms an organism's scientific name.

spermatophore: A small, gelatinous, pyramid-shaped structure capped with sperm cells that is deposited on substrates by courting male salamanders.

sphagnum: A genus of mosses that grow in wet, acid areas.

spiracle: In tadpoles, a small, tubelike external opening, usually on the left side, for the exit of respiratory water. Figure 6.

squamates: A group of reptiles that includes the snakes, lizards, and amphisbaenians; Order Squamata.

stream-type morphology: In salamanders, a larval form with short, reduced gills and a narrow dorsal fin that extends from near the hind limbs to the tip of the tail. Figure 3.

subadult: In amphibians, an individual that has transformed but is not yet sexually mature.

subocular scales: In reptiles, the scales located beneath the eye. Figure 17.

subspecies: A race or a subdivision of a species that is distinct in appearance and geographic location but that can still interbreed with other subspecies of that species.

tadpole: The aquatic, gilled larval stage of a frog. Figure 6.

taxonomy: The science of the classification and naming of organisms according to their presumed natural relationships.

terrestrial: Living on land.

territorial: Pertaining to an animal that defends an area against the entry of other animals, especially members of the same species and sex.

territory: An area occupied and defended by an animal, as in a breeding territory that is occupied by a breeding male and defended against entry by other males of the same species.

threatened: Any species that is declining in numbers and is likely to become endangered within the foreseeable future.

transform: Metamorphose; to change from the larval to the subadult form.

transverse: Crosswise; at right angles to the longitudinal axis of the body.

tubercle: A small, knoblike projection or wart.

tympanum: The eardrum; on frogs a round, smooth structure on each side of the head, behind the eye. Figure 4.

vent: The cloacal opening located at the rear of the body or base of the tail. Figures 2, 4, 6, 10, 12, 16, and 18.

ventral: Pertaining to the underside of an animal.

vernal pool: A seasonally flooded depression that typically fills with water during winter or spring and dries by late summer or early fall.

vertebral scutes: The large medial scutes of a turtle's carapace that overlie the vertebral column. Figure 11.

viviparous: Pertaining to species that do not lay eggs but instead give birth to fully developed young, all embryonic development occurring inside the mother's body.

vocal sac: An inflatable pouch on the throat or at the sides of the neck in male frogs used to produce resonance when calling, thus increasing the quality and volume of the call. Figure 5.

wart: A hard projection on the skin. Figure 8.

REFERENCES

Allard, H. A. 1948. The eastern box turtle and its behavior. *J. Tenn. Acad. Sci.* 23:307–321.

Altig, R. 1970. A key to the tadpoles of the continental United States and Canada. *Herpetologica* 26:180–207.

Anderson, K., and H. G. Dowling. 1982. Geographic distribution: *Hyla gratiosa* (Barking Treefrog). *SSAR Herp. Review* 13(4):130.

Anderson, P. K. 1954. Studies in the ecology of the narrow-mouthed toad, *Microhyla carolinensis carolinensis. Tulane Stud. Zool.* 2(2):15–46.

Arndt, R. G. 1972. Additional records of *Clemmys muhlenbergii* in Delaware, with notes on reproduction. *Bull. Md. Herp. Soc.* 8(1):1–5.

———. 1975a. Meet our turtles. *Del. Conserv.* 19(1):11–14.

———. 1975b. The occurrence of barnacles and algae on the red-bellied turtle, *Chrysemys r. rubriventris* (Le Conte). *J. Herpetol.* 9:357–359.

———. 1975c. Turtles of Delaware. *Del. Conserv.* 19(1):10, 15.

———. 1976a. Delaware snakes. *Del. Conserv.* 20(1):11–14.

———. 1976b. The most maligned creatures: snakes. *Del. Conserv.* 20(1):10, 15–20.

———. 1977a. A blue variant of the green frog, *Rana clamitans melanota,* (Amphibia, Anura, Ranidae) from Delaware. *J. Herpetol.* 11(1):102–103.

———. 1977b. Notes on the natural history of the bog turtle, *Clemmys muhlenbergii* (Schoepff), in Delaware. *Chesapeake Sci.* 18:67–76.

———. 1978. The bog turtle . . . an endangered species? *Del. Conserv.* 22(2):18–25.

———. 1983. *Ambystoma tigrinum tigrinum* (Eastern tiger salamander). *Herp. Review* 14(3):83.

———. 1985. Distributional notes on some Delaware snakes, with two first records for the state. *Bull. Md. Herp. Soc.* 21(2):67–73.

———. 1986. Notes on the bog turtle, *Clemmys muhlenbergii,* in Warren County, New Jersey. *Bull. Md. Herp. Soc.* 22:56–61.

———. 1989. Notes on the natural history and status of the tiger salamander, *Ambystoma tigrinum,* in Delaware. *Bull. Md. Herp. Soc.* 25(1):1–21.

Arndt, R. G., and W. A. Potter. 1973. A population of the map turtle, *Graptemys geographica,* in the Delaware River, Pennsylvania. *J. Herpetol.* 7:375–377.

Arndt, R. G., and J. F. White. 1988. Geographic distribution: *Hyla gratiosa* (Barking Treefrog). *Herp. Review* 9(1):16.

Arnold, S. J. 1976. Sexual behavior, sexual interference, and sexual defense in the salamanders *Ambystoma maculatum, Ambystoma tigrinum,* and *Plethodon jordani. Z. Tierpsychol.* 42:247–300.

———. 1977. The evolution of courtship behavior in New World salamanders with some comments on Old World salamandrids. In *The Reproductive Biology of Amphibians,* ed. D. H. Taylor and S. I. Guttman, 141–183. New York: Plenum Press.

Barnard, D. E., J. A. Keinath, and J. A. Musick. 1989. Distribution of ridley, green, and leatherback turtles in Chesapeake Bay and adjacent waters. In *Proceedings of the 9th Annual Workshop on Sea Turtle Conservation Biology, Jekyll Island, Ga.,* comp. S. Eckert, K. Eckert, and J. Richardson, 201–203. Natl. Oceanic Atmos. Admin. Tech. Mem. NMFS-SEFC-232.

Behler, J. L., and F. W. King. 1979. *The Audubon Society Field Guide to North American Reptiles and Amphibians.* New York: Knopf.

Bell, E. L. 1956. Some aspects of the life history of the red salamander, *Pseudotriton r. ruber,* in Huntington County, Pa. *Mengel Naturalist* 1956:10–13.

Berger-Bishop, L. E., and R. N. Harris. 1996. A study of caudal allometry in the salamander *Hemidactylium scutatum* (Caudata: Plethodontidae). *Herpetologica* 52:515–525.

Bishop, S. C. 1941. Salamanders of New York. *N.Y. State Mus. Bull.* 324:1–365.

Black, I. H., and K. L. Gosner. 1958. The barking tree frog, *Hyla gratiosa* in New Jersey. *Herpetologica* 13(4):254–255.

Blanchard, F. N. 1923. The life history of the four-toed salamander. *Amer. Nat.* 57:262–268.

Brady, M. K. 1925. Notes on the herpetology of Hog Island. *Copeia* 1925(137):110–111.

Bragg, A. N. 1960. Is *Heterodon* venomous? *Herpetologica* 16:121–123.

Branin, M. L. 1935. Courtship activities and extra-seasonal ovulation in the four-toed salamander, *Hemidactylium scutatum* (Schlegel). *Copeia* 1935:172–175.

Branson, B. A., and E. C. Baker. 1974. An ecological study of the queen snake, *Regina septemvittata* (Say) in Kentucky. *Tulane Stud. Zool. Botany* 18:153–171.

Braun, J., and G. R. Brooks, Jr. 1987. Box turtles *(Terrapene carolina)* as potential agents for seed dispersal. *Amer. Midl. Nat.* 117:312–318.

Brodie, E. D., Jr., R. T. Nowak, and W. R. Harvey. 1979. The effectiveness of antipredator secretions and behavior of selected salamanders against shrews. *Copeia* 1979:270–274.

Bruce, R. C. 1974. Larval development of the salamanders *Pseudotriton montanus* and *P. ruber. Amer. Midl. Nat.* 92:173–190.

———. 1975. Reproductive biology of the mud salamander, *Pseudotriton montanus,* in western South Carolina. *Copeia* 1975:129–137.

———. 1978. A comparison of the larval periods of Blue Ridge and Piedmont mud salamanders *(Pseudotriton montanus). Herpetologica* 34:325–332.

———. 1985. Larval period and metamorphosis in the salamander *Eurycea bislineata. Herpetologica* 41:19–28.

Brundage, H. M. III. 1982. Ocean travelers. *Del. Conserv.* 25(1):24–25.

Burbrink, F. T. 2001. Systematics of the eastern ratsnake complex *(Elaphe obsoleta). Herpetol. Monogr.* 15:1–53.

Burbrink, F. T., R. Lawson, and J. B. Slowinski. 2000. Mitochondrial DNA phylogeography of the polytipic North American rat snake *(Elaphe obsoleta):* a critique of the subspecies concept. *Evolution* 54(6):2107–2118.

Burger, J., and R. T. Zappalorti. 1986. Nest site selection by pine snakes, *Pituophis melanoleucus,* in the New Jersey pine barrens. *Copeia* 1986(1):116–121.

———. 1988. Habitat use in free-ranging pine snakes, *Pituophis melanoleucus,* in the New Jersey pine barrens. *Herpetologica* 44:48–55.

Burger, W. L. 1958. List of Virginian amphibians and reptiles. Virginia Fisheries Lab (now VIMS), Gloucester Point, Va. In A checklist of Virginia's mammals, birds, fishes, reptiles, and amphibians. Reprinted from *Virginia Wildlife,* September 1959.

Burton, T. M. 1977. The natural history of the red-backed salamander. *Bull. Chicago Herp. Soc.* 12(1):13–20.

Bury, R. B. 1976. Report on the distribution and status of reptiles and amphibians of the Delmarva Peninsula. National Fish and Wildlife Laboratory, Herpetology Section. U.S. Gov. Memo. July 2, 1976.

Carr, A. F., Jr. 1952. *Handbook of Turtles: The Turtles of the United States, Canada, and Baja California*. Ithaca, N.Y.: Comstock Publishing Associates, Cornell University Press.

———. 1956. *The Windward Road: Adventures of a Naturalist on Remote Caribbean Shores*. New York: A. Knopf. Cited in Mitchell 1994.

———. 1967. *So Excellent a Fishe: A Natural History of Sea Turtles*. Garden City, N.Y.: Natural History Press.

———. 1986. Rips, FADS, and little loggerheads. *Bioscience* 36:92–100.

———. 1987. New perspectives on the pelagic stage of sea turtle development. *Conserv. Biol.* 1:103–121.

Carr, A. F., Jr., and P. J. Coleman. 1974. Seafloor spreading theory and the odyssey of the green turtle. *Nature* 249:128–130.

Carr, A. F., Jr., and A. B. Meylan. 1980. Evidence of passive migration of green turtle hatchlings in Sargassum. *Copeia* 1980:366–368.

Collins, J. T. 2001. The Center for North American Herpetology Web site. http://www.naherpetology.org.

Conant, R. 1940. *Rana virgatipes* in Delaware. *Herpetologica* 1:176–177.

———. 1943a. The milk snakes of the Atlantic coastal plain. *Proc. New England Zool. Club* 22:3–24.

———. 1943b. *Natrix erythrogaster erythrogaster* in the northeastern part of its range. *Herpetologica* 2(5):83–86.

———. 1945. *An Annotated Check List of the Amphibians and Reptiles of the Del-Mar-Va Peninsula*. Wilmington, Del.: Society of Natural History of Delaware.

———. 1946. Intergradation among ring-necked snakes from southern New Jersey and the Del-Mar-Va Peninsula. *Bull. Chicago Acad. Sci.* 7(10):473–482.

———. 1947a. The carpenter frog in Maryland. *Md. J. Nat. Hist.* 17(4):72–73.

———. 1947b. Reptiles and amphibians in Delaware. In *Delaware, A History of the First State*, ed. H. Clay Reed, 23–25. New York: Lewis Historical Publishing.

———. 1951. The red-bellied terrapin, *Pseudemys rubriventris* (Le Conte), in Pennsylvania. *Annals Carnegie Mus.* 32:281–290.

———. 1955. Notes on *Natrix erythrogaster* from the eastern and western extremes of its range. *Chicago Acad. Sci. Nat. Hist. Misc.* 147:1–3.

———. 1957. The eastern mud salamander, *Pseudotriton montanus montanus:* a new state record for New Jersey. *Copeia* 1957(2):152–153.

———. 1958a. *A Field Guide to Reptiles and Amphibians of the United States and Canada East of the 100th Meridian.* Boston: Houghton Mifflin.

———. 1958b. Notes on the herpetology of the Delmarva Peninsula. *Copeia* 1958(1):50–52.

———. 1975. *A Field Guide to Reptiles and Amphibians of Eastern and Central North America.* 2d ed. Boston: Houghton Mifflin.

———. 1981. Herpetofauna (reptiles and amphibians) of the Virginia Coast Reserve. *The Islands: Newsletter of the Virginia Coast Reserve.* The Nature Conservancy: 6–7.

———. 1993. The Delmarva Peninsula. *Md. Nat.* 37:7–21.

———. 1997. *A Field Guide to the Life and Times of Roger Conant.* Toledo, Ohio: Canyonlands Publishing Group, L.C.

Conant, R., and J. T. Collins. 1991. *A Field Guide to Reptiles and Amphibians, Eastern and Central North America.* 3d ed. Boston: Houghton Mifflin.

———. 1998. *A Field Guide to Reptiles and Amphibians, Eastern and Central North America.* 3d ed. expanded. New York: Houghton Mifflin.

Conant, R., J. C. Mitchell, and C. A. Pague. 1990. Herpetofauna of the Virginia barrier islands. *Va. J. Sci.* 41:364–380.

Cooper, J. E. 1949. Additional records for *Clemmys muhlenbergii* from Maryland. *Herpetologica* 5:75–76.

———. 1950. The scarlet snake *(Cemophora coccinea)* in Maryland. *Md. Nat.* 20(4):67–69.

———. 1956a. Aquatic hibernation of the red-backed salamander. *Herpetologica* 12(3):165–166.

———. 1956b. A Maryland hibernation site for herptiles. *Herpetologica* 12(3):238.

———. 1960a. Distributional survey V: Maryland and the District of Columbia. *Bull. Phila. Herp. Soc.* May-June: 18–24.

———. 1960b. The mating antic of the long-tailed salamander. *Md. Nat.* 30:17–18.

———. 1965. Distributional survey: Maryland and the District of Columbia. Reprinted from *Bull. Phila. Herp. Soc.* 8(3):18–24, and revised by H. S. Harris, Jr. (Nov. 1965). *Bull. Md. Herp. Soc.* 1(1): 3–14.

———. 1970. Book review of H. S. Harris 1969 distributional survey: Maryland and the District of Columbia. *Herp. Review* 2(2):6.

Cooper, J. E., L. R. Franz, F. Groves, J. D. Hardy, Jr., H. S. Harris, Jr., D. S. Lee, P. Wemple, and R. G. Tuck. 1973. Endangered amphibians and reptiles of Maryland. *Bull. Md. Herp. Soc.* 9(3):42–100.

Cooper, W. E., Jr., and L. J. Vitt. 1985. Blue tails and autotomy: enhancement of predation avoidance in juvenile skinks. *Z. Tierpsychol.* 70:265–276.

———. 1987. Intraspecific and interspecific aggression in lizards of the scincid genus *Eumeces:* chemical detection of conspecific sexual competitors. *Herpetologica* 43:7–14.

Cox, T. M. 1982. Milk snakes and related species in the U.S. *J. Northern Ohio Assoc. Herpetol.* 8(1):43–49.

Crother, B. I., J. Boundy, J. A. Campbell, K. de Queiroz, D. R. Frost, R. Highton, J. B. Iverson, P. A. Meylan, T. W. Reeder, M. E. Seidel, J. W. Sites, Jr., T. W. Taggart, S. G. Tilley, and D. B. Wake (Committee on Standard English and Scientific Names). 2000. *Scientific and Standard English Names of Amphibians and Reptiles of North America North of Mexico, With Comments Regarding Confidence in Our Understanding.* Herpetological Circular No. 29. St. Louis, Mo.: Society for the Study of Amphibians and Reptiles.

Czarnowsky, R. 1975. A new county record for *Gastrophryne carolinensis* in Maryland. *Bull. Md. Herp. Soc.* 11:185–186.

Delzell, D. E. 1958. Spatial movement and growth of *Hyla crucifer.* Ph.D. dissertation, University of Michigan.

DePari, J. A. 1996. Overwintering in the nest chamber by hatchling painted turtles, *Chrysemys picta,* in northern New Jersey. *Chelonian Conservation and Biology* 2(1):5–12.

Dickerson, M. C. 1931. *The Frog Book.* Garden City, N.Y.: Doubleday, Doran & Co.

Dodd, C. K., Jr. 2001. *North American Box Turtles: A Natural History.* Norman: University of Oklahoma Press.

Duellman, W. E., and L. B. Trueb. 1986. *Biology of Amphibians.* New York: McGraw Hill.

Dunn, E. R. 1918. A preliminary list of the reptiles and amphibians of Virginia. *Copeia* 1918 (53):16–27.

———. 1937. The status of *Hyla evittata* Miller. *Proc. Biol. Soc. Wash.* 50:9–10.

Dunson, W. A. 1985. Effect of water salinity and food salt content on growth and sodium efflux of hatchling diamondback terrapins *(Malaclemys). Physiol. Zool.* 58:736–747.

Eggers, J. M. 1989. Incidental capture of sea turtles at Salem Generating Station, Delaware Bay, New Jersey. In *Proceedings of* the 9th Annual Workshop on Sea Turtle Conservation Biology, Jekyll Island, Ga., comp. S. Eckert, K. Eckert, and J. Richardson, 221–223. Natl. Oceanic Atmos. Admin. Tech. Mem. NMFS-SEFC-232.

Eggers, J. M., M. W. Haberland, and J. C. Griffin. 1992. Growth of juvenile loggerhead sea turtles near PSE&G's Salem Generating Station, Delaware Bay, New Jersey. *Marine Turtle Newsletter* 59: 5–7.

Emlen, S. T. 1968. Territoriality in the bullfrog, *Rana catesbeiana. Copeia* 1968:240–243.

Ernst, C. H., and R. W. Barbour. 1989a. *Turtles of the World.* Washington, D.C.: Smithsonian Institution Press.

———. 1989b. *Snakes of Eastern North America.* Fairfax, Va.: George Mason University Press.

Ernst, C. H., J. E. Lovich, and R. W. Barbour. 1994. *Turtles of the United States and Canada.* Washington, D.C.: Smithsonian Institution Press.

Ernst, C. H., R. T. Zappalorti, and J. E. Lovich. 1989. Overwintering sites and thermal relations of hibernating bog turtles, *Clemmys muhlenbergii. Copeia* 1989(3):761–764.

Evans, J. J., A. W. Norden, F. Cresswell, K. Insley, and S. Knowles. 1997. Sea turtle strandings in Maryland 1991 through 1995. *Md. Nat.* 41(1–2):23–34.

Evans, L. T. 1953. The courtship pattern of the box turtle, *Terrapene c. carolina. Herpetologica* 9:189–192.

Ewing, H. E. 1943. Continued fertility in female box turtles following mating. *Copeia* 1943(2):112–114.

Fitch, H. S. 1954. Life history and ecology of the five-lined skink, *Eumeces fasciatus. Univ. Kansas Publ., Mus. Nat. Hist.* 8:1–156.

———. 1970. *Reproductive Cycles in Lizards and Snakes.* Lawrence: University of Kansas Printing Service.

Fitch, H. S., and R. R. Fleet. 1970. Natural history of the milk snake *(Lampropeltis triangulum)* in northeastern Kansas. *Herpetologica* 26:387–396.

Forester, D. C., and R. Czarnowsky. 1982. Sexual selection in the spring peeper, *Hyla crucifer:* role of the advertisement call. *Bull. Md. Herp. Soc.* 18:16–17.

Fowler, H. W. 1915. Some amphibians and reptiles of Cecil County, Maryland. *Copeia* 1915 (22):37–40.

———. 1925a. Records of amphibians and reptiles for Delaware, Maryland, and Virginia. Parts 1 and 2. *Copeia* 1925 (145):57–64.

———. 1925b. Records of amphibians and reptiles for Delaware, Maryland, and Virginia. Part 3, Virginia. *Copeia* 1925 (146):65–67.

Fowler, J. A. 1940. A note on the eggs of *Plethodon glutinosus. Copeia* 1940(2):133.

———. 1941. The occurrence of *Pseudotriton montanus montanus* in Maryland. *Copeia* 1941(3):181.

———. 1945. Notes on *Cemophora coccinea* (Blumenbach) in Maryland and the District of Columbia vicinity. *Proc. Biol. Soc. Wash.* 58:89–90.

———. 1946. The eggs of *Pseudotriton montanus montanus. Copeia* 1946:105.

———. 1947. The hellbender *(Cryptobranchus alleganiensis)* in Maryland. *Md. J. Nat. Hist.* 17(1):14–17.

Franz, L. R. 1972. Tiger salamander. *Bull. Md. Herp. Soc.* 8(4):100.

Frick, J. 1976. Orientation and behavior of hatchling green turtles *(Chelonia mydas)* in the sea. *Anim. Behav.* 24:849–857.

Funderburg, J. B., P. Hertl, and W. M. Kerfoot. 1974. A range extension for the carpenter frogs, *Rana virgatipes* Cope, in the Chesapeake Bay region. *Bull. Md. Herp. Soc.* 10(3):77–78.

Garber, S. 1988. Diamondback terrapin exploitation. *Plastron Papers* 17 (6):18–22. Cited in R. Wood, Diamondback terrapins *(Malaclemys terrapin)* (unpublished paper of the Wetlands Institute, Stone Harbor, N.J. [c. 1994]).

———. 1990. The ups and downs of the diamondback terrapin. *Conservationist*/NYSDEC, May-June 1990: 44–47.

Gergits, W. F., and R. G. Jaeger. 1990. Field observations of the behavior of the red-backed salamander *(Plethodon cinereus)*: courtship and agonistic interactions. *J. Herpetol.* 24:93–95.

Given, M. F. 1987. Vocalizations and acoustic interactions of the carpenter frog, *Rana virgatipes. Herpetologica* 43(4):467–481.

———. 1988a. Territoriality and aggressive interactions of male carpenter frogs, *Rana virgatipes. Copeia* 1988(2):411–421.

———. 1988b. Growth rate and cost of calling activity in male carpenter frogs, *Rana virgatipes. Behav. Ecol. Sociobiol.* 22:153–160.

———. 1993a. Male response to female vocalizations in the carpenter frog, *Rana virgatipes. Anim. Behav.* 46(6):1139–1149.

———. 1993b. Vocal interactions in *Bufo woodhousii fowleri. J. Herpetol.* 27(4):447–452.

———. 1999. Distribution records of *Rana virgatipes* and associated anuran species along Maryland's Eastern Shore. *Herp. Review* 30(3):144–147.

————. 2001. Department of Biology, Neumann College, Aston, Pa. Personal communication with the authors.

Gloyd, H. K., and R. Conant. 1990. *Snakes of the Agkistrodon Complex: A Monographic Review.* St. Louis, Mo.: Society for the Study of Amphibians and Reptiles.

Graham, S. 1973. The first record of *Caretta caretta caretta* nesting on a Maryland beach. *Bull. Md. Herp. Soc.* 9(2):24–26.

Green, N. B., and T. K. Pauley. 1987. *Amphibians and Reptiles in West Virginia.* Pittsburgh, Pa.: University of Pittsburgh Press.

Grobman, A. B. 1984. Scutellation variation in *Opheodrys aestivus. Bull. Florida State Mus. Biol. Sci.* 29(4):153–170.

Grogan, W. L., Jr. 1973. A northern pine snake, *Pituophis m. melanoleucus,* from Maryland. *Bull. Md. Herp. Soc.* 9(2):27–30.

————. 1974a. Effects of accidental envenomation from the saliva of the eastern hognose snake, *Heterodon platyrhinos. Herpetologica* 30:248–249.

————. 1974b. A new county record for the four-toed salamander, *Hemidactylium scutatum,* in Maryland. *Bull. Md. Herp. Soc.* 10(1):32–33.

————. 1974c. Notes on *Lampropeltis calligaster rhombomaculata* and *Rana virgatipes. Bull. Md. Herp. Soc.* 10(1):33–34.

————. 1975. A Maryland hibernaculum of northern brown snakes, *Storeria d. dekayi. Bull. Md. Herp. Soc.* 11(1):27.

————. 1981. Two new reptile county records for Maryland. *Bull. Md. Herp. Soc.* 17(3):110.

————. 1985. New distribution records for Maryland reptiles and amphibians. *Bull. Md. Herp. Soc.* 21:74–75.

————. 1994. New herpetological distribution records from Maryland's Eastern Shore. *Bull. Md. Herp. Soc.* 30(1):27–32.

————. 2001. Department of Biological Sciences, Salisbury University, Salisbury, Maryland. Personal communication with the authors.

Grogan, W. L., Jr., and P. G. Bystrak. 1973a. The amphibians and reptiles of Kent Island, Maryland. *Bull. Md. Herp. Soc.* 9(4):115–118.

————. 1973b. Early breeding activity of *Rana sphenocephala* and *Bufo woodhousei fowleri* in Maryland. *Bull. Md. Herp. Soc.* 9(4):106.

Grogan, W. L., Jr., and D. C. Forester. 1998. New records of the milk snake, *Lampropeltis triangulum,* from the coastal plain of the Delmarva peninsula, with comments on the status of *L. t. temporalis. Md. Nat.* 42(1–2):5–14.

Grogan, W. L., Jr., and C. M. Heckscher. 2001. Are northern pine snakes, *Pituophis m. melanoleucus,* indigenous to Delaware? *Md. Nat.* 44(1):20–36.

Groves, J. D., and H. S. Harris, Jr. 1967. *Pituophis:* description and notes on validity in Maryland. *Maryland Herpetofauna Leaflet* No. 11, June 17.

Groves, J. D., and A. W. Norden. 1995. Occurrence of the ground skink, *Scincella lateralis,* in Queen Anne's County, Maryland, and a comment on its reproductive cycle. *Bull. Md. Herp. Soc.* 31(3):143–146.

Groves, M. F. 1941. An unusual feeding record of the keeled green snake, *Opheodrys aestivus. Bull. Nat. Hist. Soc. Md.* 12(2):27.

Hardy, J. D., Jr. 1953. Notes on the distribution of *Mycrohyla carolinensis* in southern Maryland. *Herpetologica* 8:162–166.

———. 1969. Records of the leatherback turtle, *Dermochelys coriacea coriacea* (Linnaeus), from the Chesapeake Bay. *Bull. Md. Herp. Soc.* 5(3):92–96.

———. 1972. Reptiles of the Chesapeake Bay region. In: "Biota of the Chesapeake Bay." *Chesapeake Sci.* 13:S128–S134.

Harper, F. 1955. A new chorus frog *(Pseudacris)* from the Eastern United States. *Chicago Acad. Sci. Nat. Hist. Misc.* 150:1–6.

Harris, H. S., Jr. 1969. Distributional survey: Maryland and the District of Columbia. *Bull. Md. Herp. Soc.* 5(4):97–161.

———. 1975. Distributional survey (Amphibia/Reptilia): Maryland and the District of Columbia. *Bull. Md. Herp. Soc.* 11:73–167.

Heckscher, C. M. 1995. Distribution and habitat associations of the eastern mud salamander, *Pseudotriton montanus montanus,* on the Delmarva Peninsula. *Md. Nat.* 39(1–2):11–14.

———. 1999. *Delaware's Rare Animals of Conservation Concern.* Smyrna, Del.: Delaware Natural Heritage Program, Division of Fish and Wildlife, DNREC.

———. 2001. Delaware Natural Heritage Program. Personal communication with the authors.

Hulse, A. C., C. J. McCoy, and E. Censky. 2001. *Amphibians and Reptiles of Pennsylvania and the Northeast.* Ithaca, N.Y.: Cornell University Press.

Hunter, M. L., Jr., J. Albright, and J. Arbuckle, eds. 1992. *The Amphibians and Reptiles of Maine.* Maine Agricultural Experiment Station Bulletin 838. Orono: University of Maine.

Hurd, L. E., G. W. Smedes, and T. A. Dean. 1979. An ecological study of a natural population of diamondback terrapins *(Malaclemys t. terrapin)* in a Delaware salt marsh. *Estuaries* 2:28–33.

Johnson, C. 1966. Species recognition in the *Hyla versicolor* complex. *Tex. J. Sci.* 18(4):361–364.

Kaufmann, J. H. 1992a. Habitat use by wood turtles in central Pennsylvania. *J. Herpetol.* 26:315–321.

———. 1992b. The social behavior of wood turtles *(Clemmys insculpta),* in central Pennsylvania. *Herpetol. Monogr.* 6:1–25.

Keinath, J. A., D. E. Barnard, and J. A. Musick. 1991. *Status of Kemp's Ridley in Virginia and Adjacent Waters.* Report to U.S. Fish and Wildlife Service, Office of Endangered Species. Virginia Institute of Marine Science, Gloucester Point, Va.

Keinath, J. A., and J. A. Musick. 1990. Life history: *Dermochelys coriacea,* migration. *Herp. Review* 21:92.

———. 1991. Loggerhead sea turtle, *Caretta caretta* (Linnaeus). In *Virginia's Endangered Species,* coord. K. Terwilliger, 445–448. Blacksburg, Va.: McDonald and Woodward Publishing Co.

Keinath, J. A., J. A. Musick, and R. A. Byles. 1987. Aspects of the biology of Virginia's sea turtles: 1979–1986. *Va. J. Sci.* 38:329–336.

Kelly, H. A., A. W. Davis, and H. C. Robertson. 1936. *Snakes of Maryland.* Baltimore: Natural History Society of Maryland.

Klinger, R. C., and J. A. Musick. 1992. Annular growth layers in juvenile loggerhead turtles *(Caretta caretta). Bull. Mar. Sci.* 51:224–230.

Krenz, J. D., and D. E. Scott. 1994. Terrestrial courtship affects mating locations in *Ambystoma opacum. Herpetologica* 50:46–50.

Krzysik, A. J. 1980. Microhabitat selection and brooding phenology of *Desmognathus fuscus fuscus* in western Pennsylvania. *J. Herpetol.* 14:291–292.

Lee, D. S. 1968. Springs as hibernation sites for Maryland's herpetofauna. *Bull. Md. Herp. Soc.* 4(4):82–83.

———. 1972. List of the amphibians and reptiles of Assateague Island. *Bull. Md Herp. Soc.* 8(4):90–95

———. 1973a. Additional reptiles and amphibians from Assateague Island. *Bull. Md. Herp. Soc.* 9(4):110–111.

———. 1973b. An annotated list of amphibians, reptiles and mammals of Irish Grove Sanctuary, Somerset County, Maryland. *Md. Birdlife* 29(4):143–149.

———. 1973c. Seasonal breeding distributions for selected Maryland and Delaware amphibians. *Bull. Md. Herp. Soc.* 9(4):101–104.

———. 1993. Reflections on Roger Conant's contributions to regional herpetology. *Md. Nat.* 37(1–2):1–6.

Lee, D. S., and L. R. Franz. 1974. Comments on the feeding behavior of larval tiger salamanders, *Ambystoma tigrinum. Bull. Md. Herp. Soc.* 10(4):105–107.

Lee, D. S., and A. W. Norden. 1996. The distribution, ecology and conservation needs of bog turtles, with special emphasis on Maryland. *Md. Nat.* 40:7–46.

Leszczynski, Z., and R. T. Zappalorti. 1996. Observations on nesting behavior of the northern pine snake *(Pituophis melanoleucus melanoleucus)* in the New Jersey pine barrens. *Reptiles* May 1996:24–37.

Linzey, D. W., and M. J. Clifford. 1981. *Snakes of Virginia.* Charlottesville: University of Virginia Press.

Lutcavage, M., and J. A. Musick. 1985. Aspects of the biology of sea turtles in Virginia. *Copeia* 1985:449–456.

Mahmound, I. Y. 1967. Courtship behavior and sexual maturity in four species of kinosternid turtles. *Copeia* 1967:314–319.

Mansueti, R. 1940. The wood frog in Maryland, *Rana sylvatica sylvatica* (LeConte). *Bull. Nat. Hist. Soc. Md.* 10(10):88–96.

———. 1947a. The spadefoot toad in Maryland. *Md. J. Nat. Hist.* 17(1):7–14.

———. 1947b. The "water moccasin" myth in Maryland. *Md. J. Nat. Hist.* 17(3):54–58.

Martof, B. S., W. M. Palmer, J. R. Bailey, and J. R. Harrison III. 1980. *Amphibians and Reptiles of the Carolinas and Virginia.* Chapel Hill: University of North Carolina Press.

McCauley, R. H., Jr. 1941. A redescription of *Lampropeltis triangulum temporalis* (Cope). *Copeia* 1941(3):146–150.

———. 1945. *The Reptiles of Maryland and the District of Columbia.* Hagerstown, Md.: published by author.

McDiarmid, R. W., and R. Altig, eds. 1999. *Tadpoles: The Biology of Anuran Larvae.* Chicago: University of Chicago Press.

McLaughlin, J. M. 2001. Delaware Department of Agriculture. Personal communication with the authors.

McLeod, R. F., and J. E. Gates. 1998. Response of herpetofaunal communities to forest cutting and burning at Chesapeake Farms, Maryland. *Amer. Midl. Nat.* 139:164–177.

Meanley, B. 1951a. Carpenter frog, *Rana virgatipes,* on the coastal plain of Maryland. *Proc. Biol. Soc. Wash.* 64:59.

———. 1951b. *Eumeces laticeps* (Schneider) in the Alleghanian zone of Maryland. *Proc. Biol. Soc. Wash.* 64:59–60.

———. 1951c. *Natrix erythrogaster* in the Austroriparian zone of Maryland. *Proc. Biol. Soc. Wash.* 64:60.

Miller, R. W. 1979. Miscellaneous distributional records for Maryland amphibians and reptiles. *Bull. Md. Herp. Soc.* 15(2):56–58.

———. 1980. Distributional records for Maryland herpetofauna. *Bull. Md. Herp. Soc.* 16(3):99–105.

———. 1982. Distributional records for Maryland herpetofauna, II. *Bull. Md. Herp. Soc.* 18(3):161–164.

———. 1984a. Distributional records for Maryland herpetofauna. *Bull. Md. Herp. Soc.* 20(2):38–45.

———. 1984b. Notes on the distribution of *Eurycea longicauda* in Maryland. *Bull. Md. Herp. Soc.* 20(2):46–50.

Miller, R. W., and G. Grall. 1978. Reproductive data on *Lampropeltis triangulum temporalis* from Maryland. *Bull. Md. Herp. Soc.* 14(1):36–38.

Mitchell, J. C. 1985. Female reproductive cycle and life history attributes in a Virginia population of painted turtles, *Chrysemys picta. J. Herpetol.* 19:218–226.

———. 1988. Population ecology and life histories of the freshwater turtles *Chrysemys picta* and *Sternotherus odoratus* in an urban lake. *Herpetol. Monogr.* 2:40–61.

———. 1994. *The Reptiles of Virginia.* Washington, D.C.: Smithsonian Institution Press.

———. 2001. University of Richmond. Personal communication with the authors.

Mitchell, J. C., and J. M. Anderson. 1994. *Amphibians and Reptiles of Assateague and Chincoteague Islands.* Martinsville: Virginia Museum of Natural History.

Mitchell, J. C., and R. A. Beck. 1992. Free-ranging domestic cat predation on native vertebrates in rural and urban Virginia. *Va. J. Sci.* 43:197–207.

Mitchell, J. C., K. A. Buhlmann, and C. H. Ernst. 1991. Bog turtle, *Clemmys muhlenbergii.* In *Virginia's Endangered Species,* coord. K. Terwilliger, 457–459. Blacksburg, Va.: McDonald and Woodward Publishing Co.

Mitchell, J. C., and C. A. Pague. 1987. A review of reptiles of special concern in Virginia. *Va. J. Sci.* 38:320–328.

Mitchell, J. C., and K. K. Reay. 1999. *Atlas of Amphibians and Reptiles in Virginia.* Richmond: Virginia Department of Game and Inland Fish.

Mohr, C. E. 1935. Salamanders. *Natural History* 36(2):165–173.

———. 1943. The eggs of the long-tailed salamander, *Eurycea longicauda longicauda* (Green). *Proc. Pa. Acad. Sci.* 17:86.

———. 1944. A remarkable salamander migration. *Proc. Pa. Acad. Sci.* 18:51–54.

———. 1982. Notable but scarce or absent. *Del. Conserv.* 25(1):29.

Musick, J. A. 1972. *Herpetiles of the Maryland and Virginia Coastal Plain.* In: A checklist of the Biota of Lower Chesapeake Bay, M. L. Wass, compiler, Special Scientific Report No. 65. Gloucester Point, Va.: Virginia Institute of Marine Science.

———. 1988. *The Sea Turtles of Virginia with Notes on Identification and Natural History.* 2d ed. Gloucester Point, Va.: Virginia Institute of Marine Science.

Musick, J. A., R. Byles, R. Klinger, and S. Bellmund. 1984. *Mortality and Behavior of Sea Turtles in the Chesapeake Bay.* Summary Report for 1979–1983 to National Marine Fisheries Service, Northeast Region. Gloucester Point, Va.: Virginia Institute of Marine Science.

Nazdrowicz, N. H. 2001. Department of Entomology and Applied Ecology, University of Delaware. Personal communication with the authors.

Nemuras, K. T. 1966. Some records for *Clemmys muhlenbergii* in Cecil County, Maryland. *Bull. Md. Herp. Soc.* 2(2):1–2.

———. 1967a. Genus *Clemmys. Int. Turtle and Tortoise Soc. J.* 1:38–40.

———. 1967b. Notes on the natural history of *Clemmys muhlenbergii. Bull. Md. Herp. Soc.* 3(4):80–96.

Nemuras, K. T., T. Sparhawk, and H. S. Harris, Jr. 1966. New county records from Maryland's Eastern Shore. *Bull. Md. Herp. Soc.* 2(2):3–4.

Netting, M. G. 1929. Further distinctions between *Bufo americanus* Holbrook and *Bufo fowleri* Garman. *Papers of the Michigan Academy of Science, Arts and Letters* 11:437–443.

———. 1930. The occurrence of lizards in Pennsylvania. Reprinted from *Annals Carnegie Mus.* 19(3):169–174.

———. 1936. The chain snake, *Lampropeltis getulus getulus* (L.) in West Virginia and Pennsylvania. *Annals Carnegie Mus.* 25:77–82.

———. 1938. The occurrence of the eastern tiger salamander, *Ambystoma tigrinum tigrinum* (Green), in Pennsylvania and nearby states. *Annals Carnegie Mus.* 27:159–166.

Noble, G. K. 1929. The relation of courtship to the secondary sexual characters of the two-lined salamander, *Eurycea bislineta* (Green). *Amer. Mus. Novitates* 362:1–5.

Norden, A. W. 1994. Letter to the editor regarding wood turtles. *Herp. Review* 25(4):144–146.

———. 2001. Maryland Department of Natural Resources. Personal communication with the authors.

Norden, A. W., T. D. Schofield, and J. J. Evans. 1998. Sea turtle strandings from Maryland waters reported to the National Aquarium in Baltimore, 1990 through 1997. *Md. Nat.* 42(1–2):20–23.

Norden, A. W., and J. Zyla. 1989. The wood turtle, *Clemmys insculpta,* on the Maryland Coastal Plain. *Md. Nat.* 33(1–2):37–41.

Norman, W. 1939. Record of wood turtle from Eastern Shore, Maryland. *Bull. Jr. Div., Nat. Hist. Soc. Md.* 3(4):64.

Organ, J. A. 1960. The courtship and spermatophore of the salamander *Plethodon glutinosus. Copeia* 1960:34–40.

———. 1961. Studies of the local distribution, life history, and population dynamics of the salamander genus *Desmognathus* in Virginia. *Ecol. Monogr.* 31:189–220.

Organ, J. A., and D. J. Organ. 1968. Courtship behavior of the red salamander, *Pseudotriton ruber. Copeia* 1968:217–223.

Pearson, P. G. 1955. Population ecology of the spadefoot toad, *Scaphiopus h. holbrooki* (Harlan). *Ecol. Monogr.* 25:233–267.

Petranka, J. W. 1998. *Salamanders of the United States and Canada.* Washington, D.C.: Smithsonian Institution Press.

Phillips, P. J., and R. J. Shedlock. 1993. Hydrology and chemistry of groundwater and seasonal ponds in the Atlantic Coastal Plain in Delaware, USA. *J. Hydrology* 141:157–178.

Pluto, T. G., and E. D. Bellis. 1986. Habitat utilization by the turtle, *Graptemys geographica,* along a river. *J. Herpetol.* 20:22–31.

———. 1988. Seasonal and annual movements of riverine map turtles, *Graptemys geographica. J. Herpetol.* 22:152–158.

Pope, P. H. 1924. The life-history of the common water newt, *Notophthalmus viridescens,* together with observations on the sense of smell. *Annals Carnegie Mus.* 15:305–368.

———. 1928. The longevity of *Ambystoma maculatum* in captivity. *Copeia* 1928:99–100.

———. 1937. Notes on the longevity of an *Ambystoma* in captivity. *Copeia* 1937:140–141.

Pough, F. H., R. M. Andrews, J. E. Cadle, M. L. Crump, A. H. Savitzky, K. D. Wells. 2001. *Herpetology.* Upper Saddle River, N.J.: Prentice-Hall.

Pritchard, P. C. H. 1971. The leatherback or leathery luth, *Dermochelys coriacea.* IUCN Monogr. 1. Cited in Ernst et al. 1994.

———. 1980. *Dermochelys coriacea. Cat. Amer. Amphib. Rept.* 238:1–238.4.

Ralin, D. B. 1968. Ecological and reproductive differentiation in the cryptic species of the *Hyla versicolor* complex (Hylidae). *Southwestern Nat.* 13(3):283–300.

Reed, C. F. 1956a. Contributions to the herpetology of Maryland and Delmarva. No. 1: Distribution of the wood turtle, *Clemmys insculpta,* in Maryland. *Herpetologica* 12(1):80.

———1956b. Contributions to the herpetology of Maryland and Delmarva. No. 4: *Hyla cinerea* in Maryland, Delaware, and Virginia, with notes on the taxonomic status of *Hyla cinerea evittata. J. Wash. Acad. Sci.* 46(10):328–332.

———. 1956c. Contributions to the herpetology of Maryland and Delmarva. No. 5: Bibliography to the herpetology of Maryland, Delmarva, and the District of Columbia. Baltimore: published by the author.

———. 1956d. Contributions to the herpetology of Maryland and Delmarva. No. 6: An annotated checklist of the lizards of Maryland and Delmarva. Baltimore: published by the author.

———. 1956e. Contributions to the herpetology of Maryland and Delmarva. No. 11: An annotated herpetofauna of the Del-Mar-Va peninsula, including many new or additional localities. Baltimore: published by the author.

———. 1956f. The spadefoot toad in Maryland. *Herpetologica* 12:294–295.

———. 1957a. Contributions to the herpetology of Maryland and Delmarva. No. 15: The herpetofauna of Somerset County, Md. *J. Wash. Acad. Sci.* 47(4):127–128.

———. 1957b. Contributions to the herpetology of Virginia. No. 3: The herpetofauna of Accomack and Northampton counties, Va. *J. Wash. Acad. Sci.* 47(3):89–91.

———. 1957c. *Rana virgatipes* in southern Maryland, with notes upon its range from New Jersey to Georgia. *Herpetologica* 13:137–138.

———. 1958a. The carpenter frog in Worcester Co., Maryland. *Herpetologica* 13:276.

———. 1958b. Contributions to the herpetology of Maryland and Delmarva. No. 13: Piedmont herpetofauna on coastal Delmarva. *J. Wash. Acad. Sci.* 48(3):95–99.

———. 1958c. Contributions to the herpetology of Maryland and Delmarva. No. 17: Southeastern herptiles with northern limits on coastal Maryland, Delmarva and New Jersey. *J. Wash. Acad. Sci.* 48(1):28–32.

———. 1960. New records for *Hyla cinerea* in Maryland, Delaware, Virginia and North Carolina. *Herpetologica* 16:119–120.

Riemer, D. N. 1981. Multiple nesting by a female box turtle *(Terrapene c. carolina). Chelonologica* 2(2):53–56.

Roosenburg, W. M. 1994. Nesting habitat requirements of the diamondback terrapin: a geographic comparison. *Wetland J.* 1994, 6(2):8–11.

Root, R. W. 1949. Aquatic respiration in the musk turtle. *Physiol. Zool.* 22:172–178.

Rosen, M., and R. E. Lemon. 1974. The vocal behavior of spring peepers, *Hyla crucifer. Copeia* 1974:940–950.

Ross, J. P., S. Beavers, D. Mundell, and M. Airth-Kindree. 1989. *The Status of Kemp's Ridley.* Washington, D.C.: Center for Marine Conservation.

Roth, R. R. 2001. Department of Entomology and Applied Ecology, University of Delaware. Personal communication with the authors.

Rust, R. W., and Roth, R. R. 1981. Seed production and seedling establishment in the mayapple, *Podophyllum peltatum* L. *Amer. Midl. Nat.* 105(1):51–60.

Ryan, M. J. 1980. The reproductive behavior of the bullfrog *(Rana catesbeiana). Copeia* 1980:108–114.

Sayler, A. 1966. The reproductive ecology of the red-backed salamander, *Plethodon cinereus,* in Maryland. *Copeia* 1966:183–193.

Scarpulla, E. J. 1989. First records for the leatherback turtle *(Dermochelys coriacea)* along Maryland's Atlantic Coast. *Md. Nat.* 33(3–4):59–60.

Scott, D. 1986. Notes on the eastern hognose snake, *Heterodon platyrhinos* Latreille (Squamata: Colubridae), on a Virginia barrier island. *Brimleyana* 12:51–55.

Scott, J. 1991. *Between Ocean and Bay: a Natural History of Delmarva.* Centreville, Maryland: Tidewater Publishers.

Shaffer, Larry L. 1991. *Pennsylvania Amphibians and Reptiles.* Harrisburg: Pennsylvania Fish Commission Bureau of Education and Information.

Sipple, W. S. 1976. The carpenter frog *(Rana virgatipes)* in Caroline County, Maryland. *Bull. Md. Herp. Soc.* 12(4):129–130.

———. 1999. *Days Afield.* Baltimore, Md.: Gateway Press, Inc.

Smith, S. 2001. Maryland Natural Heritage Program. Personal communication with the authors.

Spotila, J. R., P. T. Plotkin, and J. A. Keinath. 1998. In water population survey of sea turtles of Delaware Bay. Unpublished report. Final Report to the NMFS Office of Protected Resources for work conducted under contract No. 43AANF600211 and NMFS Permit No. 1007.

Stetzar, E. 2001. Department of Biology, Delaware State University and Delaware Division of Fish and Wildlife. Personal communication with the authors.

Stickel, L. F. 1989. Home range behavior among box turtles *(Terrapene c. carolina)* of a bottomland forest in Maryland. *J. Herpetol.* 23:40–44.

Stickel, L. F., W. H. Stickel, and F. C. Schmid. 1980. Ecology of a Maryland population of black rat snakes *(Elaphe o. obsoleta). Amer. Midl. Nat.* 103(1):1–14.

Stine, C. J. 1953. Maryland salamanders of the genus *Ambystoma.* Part 1: Distribution. *Md. Nat.* 23 (1–2):75–78.

———. 1984. The life history and status of the eastern tiger salamander, *Ambystoma tigrinum tigrinum* (Green) in Maryland. *Bull. Md. Herp. Soc.* 20(3):65–108.

Stine, C. J., J. A. Fowler, and R. S. Simmons. 1954. Occurrence of the eastern tiger salamander, *Ambystoma tigrinum tigrinum* (Green) in Maryland, with notes on its life history. *Annals Carnegie Mus.* 33:145–148.

Stine, C. J., R. S. Simmons, and J. A. Fowler. 1956. New records for the eastern spadefoot toad in Maryland. *Herpetologica* 12(4):295–296.

Stone, W. 1906. Notes on reptiles and batrachians of Pennsylvania, New Jersey and Delaware. *Amer. Nat.* 40(471):159–170.

Tobey, F. J. 1985. *Virginia's Amphibians and Reptiles: A Distributional Survey.* Purcellville: Virginia Herpetological Society.

Truitt, B. 2001. Virginia Coast Reserve, The Nature Conservancy. Personal communication with the authors.

Tyning, T. F. 1990. *A Guide to Amphibians and Reptiles.* Boston: Little, Brown and Company.

Uzendoski, U. V., and P. A. Verrell. 1993. Sexual incompatibility and mate-recognition systems: a study of two species of sympatric salamanders (Plethodontidae). *Anim. Behav.* 46:267–278.

Verrell, P.A. 1982. The sexual behavior of the red-spotted newt, *Notophthalmus viridescens* (Amphibia: Urodela: Salamandridae). *Animal Behavior* 30:1224–1236.

Vitt, L. J., and W. E. Cooper, Jr. 1985. The evolution of sexual dimorphism in the skink *Eumeces laticeps:* an example of sexual selection. *Canad. J. Zool.* 63:995–1002.

———. 1986. Tail loss, tail color, and predator escape in *Eumeces* (Lacertilia: Scincidae): age-specific differences in costs and benefits. *Canad. J. Zool.* 64:583–592.

Walker, C. F. 1946. The amphibians of Ohio. Part 1: The frogs and toads. *Ohio State Mus. Sci. Bull.* 1:1–102.

White, J. F., Jr. 1987a. New frog species is discovered in Delaware. *Del. Nat. Educ. Soc. News* 23(4):3.

———. 1987b. Snakes . . . of the first state. *Del. Conserv.* 30(2):15–18.

———. 1988. Amphibians of Delaware. *Trans. Del. Acad. Sci.* 16:17–22.

———. 1989. Jeepers, creepers, where'd you find those peepers? *Del. Conserv.* 32(1):15–18.

Wilder, I. W. 1924a. The developmental history of *Eurycea bislineata* in western Massachusetts. *Copeia* 1924:77–80.

———. 1924b. The relation of growth to metamorphosis in *Eurycea bislineata* (Green). *J. Experiment. Zool.* 40 (1):1–112.

Williams, K. L. 1988. *Systematics and Natural History of the American Milk Snake, Lampropeltis triangulum.* 2d rev. ed. Milwaukee, Wis.: Milwaukee Public Museum.

Worthington, R. D. 1968. Observations on the relative sizes of three species of salamander larvae in a Maryland pond. *Herpetologica* 24(3):242–246.

Wright, A. H. 1914. *North American Anuran: Life Histories of the Anura of Ithaca, New York.* Washington, D.C.: Carnegie Institution of Washington.

———. 1932. *Life-Histories of the Frogs of Okefinokee Swamp, Georgia.* New York: Macmillan.

Wright, A. H., and A. A. Wright. 1949. *Handbook of Frogs and Toads.* Ithaca, N.Y.: Comstock Publishing Co.

———. 1957. *Handbook of Snakes of the United States and Canada.* 2 vols. Ithaca, N.Y.: Comstock Publishing Co.

Zappalorti, R. T. 1976. *The Amateur Zoologist's Guide to Turtles and Crocodilians.* Harrisburg, Pa.: Stackpole Books.

———. 1978. The bog turtle, smallest of North American turtles. *Bull. Chicago Herp. Soc.* 13:75–81.

Zappalorti, R. T., and J. Burger. 1985. On the importance of disturbed sites to habitat selection by pine snakes in the pine barrens of New Jersey. *Environ. Conserv.* 12:358–361.

Zappalorti, R. T., E. W. Johnson, and Z. Leszcynski. 1983. The ecology of the northern pine snake, *Pituophis melanoleucus melanoleucus* (Daudin) (Reptilia, Serpentes, Colubridae), in southern New Jersey, with special notes on habitat and nesting behavior. *Bull.Chicago Herp. Soc.* 18:57–72.

Zweifel, R. G. 1970. Distribution and mating call of the treefrog, *Hyla chrysoscelis,* at the northeastern edge of its range. *Chesapeake Sci.* 11(2): 94–97.

INDEX

Notes: All species are listed three times in the index: (1) by scientific name; (2) by English name by the "primary" part of the name, e.g., Eastern Cricket Frog is listed under "C" as Cricket Frog, Eastern; and (3) by English name under the appropriate order or suborder. For species accounts, only the first page of the account is listed, followed by the plate number(s) in bold. Page numbers in parentheses indicate the term is used in an illustration.

ABOUT THE DELAWARE NATURE SOCIETY

A nonprofit membership organization founded in 1964, the Delaware Nature Society fosters understanding, appreciation, and enjoyment of the natural world through education; preserves ecologically significant areas; and advocates stewardship and conservation of natural resources. The society maintains two nature centers—Ashland Nature Center near Hockessin, Delaware, and Abbott's Mill Nature Center near Milford, Delaware—and manages four preserves for biodiversity, research, and educational programs. The Delaware Nature Society is the state affiliate of the National Wildlife Federation.

The Delaware Nature Society publishes books on natural history topics to increase interest in the region's wealth of plants, animals, and living communities and the need for their conservation. *Amphibians and Reptiles of Delmarva* was undertaken to disseminate information about these fascinating animals and to encourage field exploration for the peninsula's intriguing but often misunderstood herpetofauna. Through this book the society seeks to heighten awareness of the value of all native species and the importance of protecting habitats and preserving natural areas.

The Delaware Nature Society annually offers programs on amphibians and reptiles for children, adults, and families. For more information about programs, publications, and services, please contact the society by mail, telephone, or e-mail, or visit the Web site:

Delaware Nature Society
P.O. Box 700
Hockessin, DE 19707
(302) 239-2334
webpage@dnsashland.org
www.delawarenaturesociety.org

ABOUT THE AUTHORS

James (Jim) F. White, Jr., a native Delawarean, graduated from the University of Delaware with a degree in entomology. He was one of the primary investigators for the five-year Delaware Herpetological Survey, which gathered distributional information throughout the state. Jim is a skilled nature photographer whose photographs have appeared in numerous publications. He has been involved with the Delmarva Ornithological Society for over twenty years, including serving as president. Jim is the associate director, land and biodiversity management, at the Delaware Nature Society, and also teaches a course in herpetology at the University of Delaware.

Amy Wendt White grew up in Wilmington, Delaware, and holds an undergraduate degree in geology and a graduate degree in environmental engineering. For a number of years, she worked as a project engineer with a consulting firm that investigated contaminated soil and groundwater. Working for the Delaware Nature Society, she coordinated the Delaware Stream Watch program, training school groups and other volunteers to monitor the state's waterways for pollution. She and Jim have also led excursions to national parks and wildlife refuges along the East Coast, as well as canoe trips on local waterways. Amy is a teacher-naturalist at the Delaware Nature Society.